THE COLLECTOR'S ENCYCLOPEDIA OF
GEISHA GIRL PORCELAIN

ELYCE LITTS

THE COLLECTOR'S ENCYCLOPEDIA OF
GEISHA GIRL PORCELAIN

ELYCE LITTS

COLLECTOR BOOKS
A Division of Schroeder Publishing Co., Inc.

The current values in this book should be used only as a guide. They are not intended to set prices, which vary from one section of the country to another. Auction prices as well as dealer prices vary greatly and are affected by condition as well as demand. Neither the Author nor the Publisher assumes responsibility for any losses that might be incurred as a result of consulting this guide.

Additional copies of this book may be ordered from:

Collector Books
P.O. Box 3009
Paducah, KY 42002-3009

or

Elyce Litts
P.O. Box 394
Morris Plains, NJ 07950

@$19.95 Add $1.00 for postage and handling.

Copyright: Elyce Litts, 1988

This book or any part thereof may not be reproduced without the written consent of the Author and Publisher.

Printed in Hong Kong by Everbest Printing Co. Ltd. for Four Colour Imports, Ltd., Louisville, Kentucky

Dedicated to
Frank and Jan
with Love and Thanks

Preface

Over ten years ago a colorful cocoa pot beckoned — "Take me home" — and so I did. In time it seemed a good idea to find matching cups and saucers. As it turned out, I found many examples of Geisha Girl Porcelain to catch my fancy and arouse my curiosity.

It took several months of inquiries and research after the first purchase to determine exactly what kind of porcelain I had acquired. Even to those who sold it, it remained a nameless curiosity. Nothing was in print concerning the wares, but somewhere, I felt, there had to be an answer.

Breaking the ice in a heretofore unexplored field is not easy. Hours of research often lead to dead ends. Fortunately, many efforts do bear glorious fruit. One discovery was that I was not alone in my love for these wares. Others were also quietly amassing collections.

In order to share the information I uncovered, I began writing articles for antique periodicals and in 1982 commenced publication of the *Geisha Girl Porcelain Newsletter*[1]. Such publications merely served to whet the appetite for knowledge of the increasing number of collectors and dealers in the wares. Writing a comprehensive volume on the topic seemed a proper and necessary next step.

Little did I know that the work had just begun. Years of research are not as difficult as putting all the information down into a concise format while filling the informational gaps in the process. It is, therefore, with deep gratitude that I thank the following friends and colleagues for their support:

Harry Rinker, noted antiques authority and editor, who generously gave of his own time and who tread where none had gone before by taking the reins over my writing and guiding me toward a more masterful product. I am deeply appreciative of the time and knowledge he shared with me.

Joan Van Patten and Joan Oates, of Nippon and Phoenix Bird fame, respectively, for sharing their catalog resources and offering new friendship and continued encouragement.

Librarians and local historians in remote areas who took the time to uncover some of the fascinating facts about local histories contained herein, including John Bardwell, Miriam Berezovske, David Boutros, Patricia Cronin, Anne Lodge, Marianne Tuba and Paul Waclawski.

Subscribers to the *Geisha Girl Porcelain Newsletter* who generously shared their collections and collecting experiences. Many of their pieces are illustrated in this volume. They include, in alphabetical order, Margery Buch, Peggie Cannon, Marcelle Cushman, Gertrude DeYoung, Shirley Williams Gleeson, Dora Guinn, Shirley Klein (a/k/a Mom), J. Lennon, Andrea MacDonald, Cathy Masamitsu, Linda Meyers, Nancy McKay, Barbara Peters, Gene Trolander, Adah Vosburgh, Murray and Sandy Zack. Heaven help me if I've forgotten anyone - my sincerest apologies in advance!

Jan, my dearest friend and antiquing partner for the past ten years, and her mom, Malva, who manages to find better Geisha Girl Porcelain buys at garage sales than I ever do.

And, lastly, but most of all, thanks to my husband, Frank, for his love, support and domestic skills. You'd recognize us if you saw us together . . . I'd be the one with the keyboard blisters, he'd be the one with the dishpan hands!

Elyce Dawn Litts

---

[1]The *Geisha Girl Porcelain Newsletter* is published bi-monthly. Annual subscription cost is $12.00. GGPN, P.O. Box 394, Morris Plains, NJ 07950.

Table of Contents

Introducing Geisha Girl Porcelain 8
The History of Geisha Girl Porcelain 10
On The Face Of It All 13
Methods of Design Applications 16
Czechoslovakia and Decaled Geisha Girl Porcelain 20
Distinguishing Among Japanese Wares 23
Form 26
Function 28
Child's World 37
From Eastern Shores To Western Stores 41
Marks 58
Japanese Marks 59
English Language Marks 65
Reproductions 72
Cataloging A Collection 75
Photo Album 77
Glossary 141
Just For Fun 143
Bibliography 144
Pattern Catalog and Price Guide 146
Index 173

Introducing Geisha Girl Porcelain

Geisha Girl Porcelain is a Japanese export ware whose production commenced the last quarter of the 19th century. Made in the form of the common dining and household utensils of the times, they featured lovely kimono clad ladies, sometimes with men and children, in scenes from pre-modern Japan.

Early catalogs described the wares as depicting Japanese figures, dancing girls, geisha dancers, etc., but for a long time, the wares had no formal name. Gradually, through the efforts of an active collecting community, they became widely known as **Geisha Girl Porcelain**.

The name is derived from the Western habit of calling any pretty lady in Japanese art a **geisha**, due to the notion that the geisha are the most lovely and intriguing of Japanese women. The Geisha traditionally wore the bright and colorful kimonos featured on the porcelain, while the rest of the mature Japanese female populace wore gray or brown (except on festive occasions). In fact, one early name for the porcelain, Kimono Lady wares, highlights this feature.

In truth, it must be stated that the ladies of Geisha Girl Porcelain are not necessarily geisha. **Geisha** is a Japanese word which translates to "art person". From the time they are young, geisha are taught the classical arts of singing, dancing and instrumental music. Their special training also includes etiquette, make-up and dress, language, conversation and poise—all in anticipation of a career in sophisticated entertainment. Burton Holmes aptly describes the geisha in his 1918 *Travelogues*[1]:

> "The art of being a geisha is the art of being perpetually and convincingly amiable . . . behind it all there are long hours of hard work at the samisen, with singing teachers, with the costumer and dancing-master . . . Geisha are, in fact, the most important part of a Japanese feast. Without geisha no entertainment in good society could possibly be given with success. They are not waitresses, however; they are artists, proficient in the art of entertaining and always clever, pretty and well-gowned. True they do serve both food and sake, but this they do artistically not as servants, but with the grace and graciousness of hostesses. A gentleman giving a dinner to his friends would never dream of permitting his wife to do the honors . . . The geisha are expected to liven conversation, amuse the guests with witty sayings and bright stories, delight them with pretty mannerisms, all this time keeping the sake cups well filled."

Whether one chooses to believe the women portrayed are the exotic geisha, or just lovely ladies of an earlier era, Geisha Girl Porcelain is admired by collectors for its highly scenic and colorful designs enhanced by temple buildings and pagodas, sampans gliding over the water's surface, cranes and butterflies in flight (Plate 1), ducks swimming in a pond sparkling with the reflections of gold carp maneuvering beneath its surface, and a multitude of Japanese flora and fauna. Bamboo, chrysanthemums, peonies, wisteria, irises, cherry and plum blossoms, pine and maple abound.

Over two hundred Geisha Girl scenes (called patterns) and variations thereof have been cataloged by the author. While all the major patterns have been accounted for, new variations periodically come to light. Some of the earliest documented patterns include the Butterfly, Carp, Circle Dance, Parasol, Child Reaching for Butterfly, Flute and Koto, and Flower Gathering. Produced some years later were the Doll's Tea Party and Bamboo Tree, etc. Although the bulk of Geisha ware production ceased during World War II, they have remained so popular that some of the patterns are still in production today.

A study of Geisha Girl Porcelain patterns affords a fascinating insight into many cultural and historical aspects of Japan — the mythical **shishi** (Plates 2-3), the tailless cat, prayer ribbons, carp banners, etc. These and more are detailed in the Pattern Catalog and Photo Album sections of this volume.

The architecture of the Japanese home is displayed in abundance. Traditional Japanese dwellings consist of a light wooden framework with thatched, shingled or tiled roof. While many of these buildings are displayed in their entirety in the Geisha Girl patterns, other scenes give us an intimate look at the details of these structures.

The pin tray (Plate 4) depicts a geisha placing a **kakemono**, a hanging artwork, in the **tokonoma** or alcove. This alcove is typically the extent of any interior architectural embellishment. It is this area to which the decorative ornaments of a Japanese household are generally confined. These would consist of a **kakemono**, an **ikebana**, and perhaps a small chest or porcelain treasure. To the left of the **tokonoma**, the wood grain is visible in the horizontal beam across the floor. The Japanese home was not painted or plastered over as was common in the West. To the side is an open **shoji**, a semi-transparent screen in a wood lattice framing. **Shoji** were used as sliding doors or room dividers.

An unusual kitchen, of a kind unfamiliar to Western eyes, is composed of a sunken brazier wherein a pot is placed for heating (Plate 5).

An interesting mixture of artistic styles is infused into the floral decor. In some instances, flowers are accurately portrayed as per the Western artistic tendency. For the most part, however, the flowers are stylized, alluding to the Japanese thinking that art is not a depiction of a particular item in nature, but a symbol of a whole group of such items. Thus, it is not the perfect peony out of the garden, but one indicative of a garden full of them.

Although never included in Geisha Girl scenery, hand-painted roses are sometimes used as a backdrop for a pattern (Plate 6). The asymetrical is often preferred to the symetrical in Japanese art.

The diversity of Geisha ware is a great attraction to collectors. Not only is there a variety of patterns, but border colors, shapes and sizes all present an array of possibilities. Collections can be comprised of examples of a single pattern or border color, or can be based upon a single form.

[1] B. Holmes, *Travelogues*. The Travelogue Bureau, 1918.

PLATE 1. Butterflies, flowers and birds in flight are exemplary of the lush flora and fauna and magnificent scenery found on Geisha Girl Porcelain items. Oftentimes shapes mimic the scenery as does this 6" chrysanthemum-shaped bon-bon dish in the Battledore pattern.

PLATE 2. Close-up of a playful *shishi*.

PLATE 3. After-dinner cup and saucer, Shishi pattern, from which close-up was derived.

PLATE 4. Pin Tray, Kakemono pattern.

PLATE 5. Saucer, Inside the Teahouse pattern.

PLATE 6. Plate, 8¼", Temple B pattern.

The History of Geisha Girl Porcelain

In the mid-19th century, Japan was in a state of radical political change. She had kept to herself, both politically and culturally, for many centuries, under a system of feudal rule[1]. Dealings and trade with the outside world had been kept to a minimum. Trading through the port of Imari was perhaps their most consistent endeavor. Because Japanese production failed to meet the outside world's demand for their wares, English potters actually began to profit from the manufacture of Japanese style wares.

Eventually, feudal rule gave way to a more centralized form of government which numbered among its priorities the establishment of Japan as an active, powerful member of the international community. The government believed that an important means of obtaining this status was to modernize Japan through the acquisition of Western science, technology, art, education and the establishment of broad international trade markets.

By 1890, Japan was embroiled in a rather large scale feud between Loyalists who emphasized maintenance of a distinctly Japanese culture in all arenas, and **Yoga**, Japanese who felt that Japan must emulate the West. The **Yoga** dominated. Emissaries were sent abroad to learn both Western technology and culture. In some circles, it even became preferable to wear Western style clothing in place of the traditional kimono. This included the court of the **Mikado**, the Japanese emperor, where, in the 1890's, it was mandated that all who presented themselves at state-functions must appear in modern European clothes.[2]

Meanwhile, the West became exceedingly curious about this country which had been more or less forbidden to them for so long. The desire for Japanese and other Oriental styles of artwork, furnishings and accessories increased.

Supply and demand . . . supplying those items demanded by the West provided Japan with a desirable foothold into the international marketplace. How did Japan meet this demand?

At the time, many of the great kilns that supplied the feudal lords with quality pottery and porcelain had substantially reduced their production due to the internal strife. Feudal lords had focused their money and attention on retaining their power, and had little need for the luxuries of life afforded by the kilns dedicated to fulfilling their ceramic desires. The new demand from the West, however, refueled the fires of the kilns. Once again they began to turn out quality wares, aimed this time for the foreign markets.

So extensive was the Western market that the limited production of these relatively few kilns could not meet the consumer demands. Additionally, those Westerners of the middle and lower income levels could not afford the exclusive wares. This provided the impetus for artisans, who were no longer solely supported within the dedicated kiln environment, and vassals, who no longer received feudal support for working the land, to establish many more kilns and decorating centers in an effort to obtain income through mass production of wares for the general foreign public.

It is said that, by the turn of the century, there were over 1,300 potters in Kaga province alone[3] employing some 2,700 people.[4] Many of these businesses were cottage industries or, more descriptively, family businesses. Mom, Dad, grandparents and children all participated in the creation of porcelain items for export, each contributing their share to the family income, motivated by duty, if not simply survival. "More interesting as the survivals of the old spirit and the old order under which all of the Japanese arts have grown and flourished were the little household potteries, each family group constituting a whole establishment, and all working together under patriarchal rule."[5] The men mixed the clays while the women filled the major molds. Children placed the clay in the molds for appendages and all would help decorate the wares.

As the desire for quantitative production increased, less time-consuming designs and production methods evolved from those previously employed. In her study of the Japanese porcelain industry of the late 1890's, E. Scidmore notes that "with modern trade competition, and . . . all art by the large wholesale orders destined for barbarian (horrors, she meant our forefathers, folks!) markets, the Chinese, or factory method is fast growing."[6] This meant that instead of a single individual shaping and decorating a singular item from start to finish, one person might shape the molds, another attach the handles, another enamel the flowers, another the hair, etc. The commercial development of the stencil method of design application also contributed greatly to the ability to mass produce the wares.

Nonetheless, a commentator noted: ". . . the Japanese, who were pre-eminent in the field of decoration, have now also come under the baleful influence of commercialism, but so instinctive is their feeling for beauty, that many of their modern productions, even those of minimum cost, still retain much of their old time charm."[7]

During the first two decades of the 20th century, production evolved even further. Large decorating centers opened in major cities such as Tokyo, Nagoya, Kobe and Yokohama (Illus. 2-1). The following was noted in the 1920 Commerce Reports by the attache of the American embassy in Tokyo[8]:

> "The great bulk of chinaware produced in Japan is made by the old methods of manufacture and to a very considerable degree is a household or community industry. For example, in the Seto district one family will be found making the models and molds. On the village streets one can see these molds being carried by hand on boards to another household where

---

[1]The feudal system revolved around a government by rich land owners who, for a fee of money, crops or services, allowed others to reside on their land.
[2]H. Munsterberger, *The Arts of Japan*, Charles Tuttle Co., 1957; B. Holmes, *Travelogues*. The Travelogue Bureau, 1918.
[3]S. Andacht, "East Meets West," *The Antique Trader Weekly*, July 2, 1980.
[4]H. Gorham, *Japanese and Oriental Ceramics*. Charles E. Tuttle Co., 1971.

[5]E.R. Scidmore, "The Porcelain Artists of Japan," *Harper's Weekly*, Jan. 22, 1898, p. 84.
[6]Op. Cit. 3, p. 86.
[7]H. Tachau, "Modern China for the Table," *House Beautiful*, January 1918, p. 98.
[8]"Japanese Pottery Industry," *Review of Reviews*, April 1920, p. 441.

they will be used for the forming of the ware. Cups and saucers are produced in large quantities in this district, one man being able to produce by casting 2,000 per day. The aggregate production of the numerous pottery villages in Japan amounts to a considerable figure, and much of it finds its way into the channels of foreign trade. Nevertheless, with the cost of living increasing in Japan by leaps and bounds and with labor costs rising in proportion, the day is not far distant when the highly organized and efficiently conducted modern pottery, with its labor-saving machinery and its ability to reduce costs by quantity production, will supersede the cottage and community system."

"The Japanese have not been slow in appreciating this tendency. In Nagoya, the center of the industry in Japan, a modern pottery has been built on the most up-to-date lines. Upon entering a modern plant, one is at first struck with the fact that labor is still by no means considered the first and greater factor in costs. Every ton of material is brought to the factory by man power. There is no railroad siding. All the materials, bulky as they are in the pottery industry, such as clay, feldspar, flint, wood and coal are carted in small one-horse wagons, each horse being led by a man. Such materials as come in bulk are piled on the wagon in shallow tray-like baskets, each containing an amount convenient for a man to carry. The second thing particularly noticeable is the large amount of hand labor employed in the breaking up and sorting of the raw materials, and also the exceedingly minute care taken in removing any foreign matter from the broken mass."

Yet another development involved the specialization of some of these centers who chose to purchase undecorated porcelain blanks from kilns and concentrate solely on the decoration side of the business. For instance, a 1914 Vantine catalog describes a teaset as "Seto ware decorated in Kobe" (Illus. 2-2). Other witnesses to such practice are those patterns, such as Temple A, which can be found with the marks of a variety of porcelain makers.

Thus, the Japanese pottery and porcelain industry was able to turn out large quantities of items for the West. In addition, they manufactured them in forms and designs that appealed to Western consumers, directed by their newly acquired education about their target market. In fact, the situation was rather ironic. While the West desired Oriental wares, they really were buying "Westernized" wares from the Orient. Truly Oriental wares still tended to be made solely for Japanese domestic use. The domestic trade was less flamboyant and deferred to more natural forms than the commercialized West.

Geisha Girl Porcelain, Phoenix Bird China, Satsuma-style export wares, etc. were created in response to Western demands. Balancing Japanese and Western design elements with Western utility, these items were widely acquired by appreciative Western consumers.

Geisha Girl Porcelain, in particular, was a circa 1890's offshoot of the Kutani kilns' red and gold wares which often portrayed Japanese people amid the lush gardens of Japan. Kutani, an area in what was formerly called Kaga province, is one of the oldest and most famous porcelain production centers in Japan. So popular did these wares become that their production became widespread. Over one hundred thirty-five producers have been noted, accounting in part for the wide diversity of the wares.

While various craftsmen continued the Kutani tradition of hand painting, the majority of Geisha Girl Porcelain producers, including some Kutani artisans, took advantage of the availability of the stencil method. In addition, many more colors were introduced into the design palette. The earliest documented borders are various shades of red including "terracotta," "Tokio" and "Japanese," as well as maroon, cobalt blue, "pale" and "nile" green. The late 1910's saw the introduction of pine green, blue-green and turquoise. These were joined in the late 1920's and 1930's by a pale cobalt blue, and in the Occupied Japan of the 1940's by black. Other border colors, whose commemcement dates are not so easily established, include yellow, tan, gold and brown.

As previously indicated, the bulk of Geisha Girl Porcelain was produced prior to World War II. Japan's involvement in the war brought her porcelain production to a virtual standstill and many of her kilns and decorating centers were destroyed. Nonetheless, production of her most popular wares did revive shortly thereafter.

Included among these was Geisha Girl Porcelain. During the Occupied Japan period (1945-1952), there was a resurgence of hand-painted Kutani-style Geisha ware. In particular, Rivers Edge patterned items with black or red borders have been noted. A letter to the author from a war veteran notes that he remembered seeing quite a bit of red bordered, stenciled Geisha ware in the stores catering to the armed forces after the war. Known examples of 1940's stenciled Geisha wares show it to often be of mediocre quality. Enameling was sparser and gold was rarely used. In all probability this resulted from the rush to market wares under a less than optimum production environment. It was about this time, too, that lithophaned Geisha Girl items appeared.

Japan's trade outlook did change direction after WWII. Her interests turned away from artistic production in order to focus on the industrial and scientific. In spite of this, Geisha ware continued to trickle from Japan, a testimony to its popularity. Modern productions include the Child Reaching for Butterfly, Parasol Modern, Fan A and Garden Bench patterns which can be found in import and department stores in the United States and Europe.

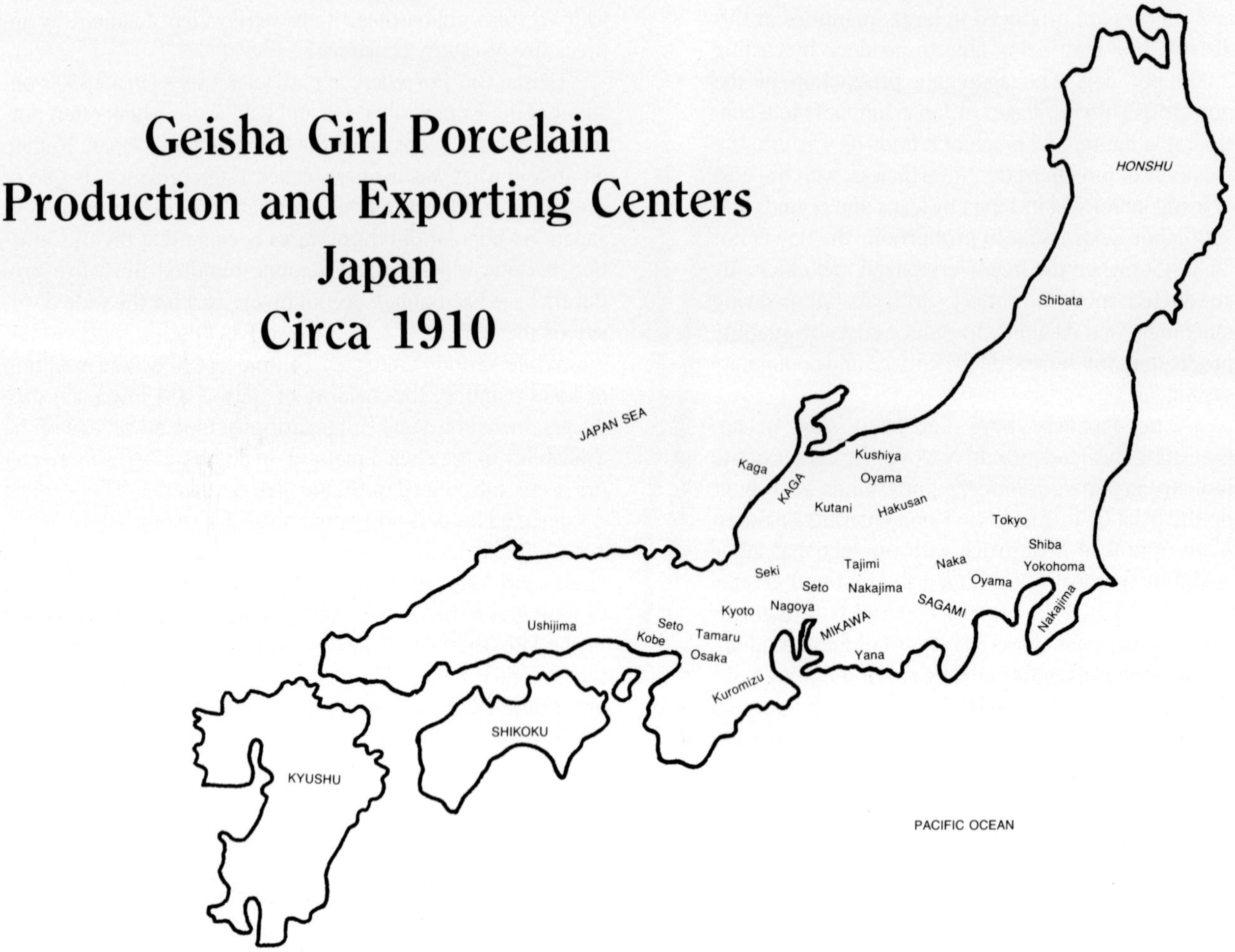

Geisha Girl Porcelain
Production and Exporting Centers
Japan
Circa 1910

ILLUS. 2-1. Map of Japan indicating some of the Geisha Girl Porcelain production and decorating centers.

ILLUS. 2-2. Ad in 1914 Vantine's catalog for a teaset produced in Seto and decorated in Kobe.

On The Face Of It All

The first step in identifying Geisha Girl ware is to determine which of the patterns and variations is portrayed. The identification procedure is not complicated, as illustrated by the sample below. Know where to look for the pattern and then determine the activity taking place therein. Identification by distinguishable characteristics becomes easier as more pieces are examined.

Placement of the Pattern

In the simplest manner, the pattern may encompass the entire porcelain form — covering the surface of a plate (Plate 7, for instance). It may be entirely wrapped around a form, such as a cocoa pot (Plate 8). It may also be placed on the front of a cylindrical form, such as a creamer (Plates 9-10), while additional scenery is placed on the reverse.

The alternative is that the pattern is enclosed within a reserve surrounded by flowers, butterflies, coins, diapers, etc. A reserve is an outline which may be geometric, fan or floral-shaped. There may be one or several of these on a single porcelain item, featuring various patterns or scenery. Often specific combinations of these reserves, such as the Parasol A and Lesson patterns (Plate 11), appear on numerous pieces as favorites of a particular producer.

Type of Pattern

Are the ladies proportionately larger than the scenery such that the eye is caught by their figures? This is the case with most Geisha Girl Porcelain. Sometimes, however, their size places them secondary to the rest of the scenery. These pieces are referred to as being in the "diminutive geisha" styling (Plate 12).

Pattern Names

The most important question remains: "What are the figures doing?" Geisha Girl Porcelain patterns were not formally named by their producers or vendors. Thus, pattern names have been assigned which collectors now use as a means of identifying and communicating about these wares. These names reflect either (a) the focal point of the scene, or (b) that portion of the pattern that distinguishes it from all others.

In the first instance, the Butterfly Dancers pattern (Plate 13) is so named because the featured ladies are wearing the elaborate butterfly costumes of a festival. No other cataloged pattern duplicates these figures. The sauce dish (Plate 14) depicts the Parasol pattern, the only activity shown being the ladies carrying parasols.

Condition (b) is illustrated by the mustard pot (Plate 15). While the lady pictured does carry a parasol, it is the magnificent rickshaw in which she rides that catches the viewer's eye. Since it is the rickshaw, rather than the parasol, that distinguishes this pattern, it is named accordingly the Lady in Rickshaw pattern.

It is important to note that sometimes the distinguishing factor is not a physically large portion of the scene. The Bird Cage pattern earned its name from the small cage being carried by one of two ladies in the scene (Plate 16).

Pattern Variations

Several of the patterns have variations on the same theme. Because the scenes portrayed Japanese life, and because there were many manufacturers of the wares, it is understandable that more than one company might have produced a version of the same pattern.

This versatility is most evident when considering the Parasol or Garden Bench pattern series. For instance, Parasol variant C features one or more ladies with yellow parasols. The Black Parasol features two women sharing a black parasol, while the Parasol D depicts a procession of strolling figures— the majority of whom carry parasols. The Garden Bench series has in common a single garden bench in each scene. The position of the bench, the number of ladies and children in the pattern, and the occupations of each differ from variant to variant.

Sometimes a single designer made adjustments to the pattern based upon the size and shape of the item being decorated. For instance, the master nut bowl (Plate 17) depicts five ladies in the Parasol D pattern. The matching, but smaller, individual nut cups show only three figures.

Another example of pattern variation comes as a result of the size constraints within a reserve. Fan Dance A features several ladies dancing to the accompaniment of a samisen player. Where this pattern is depicted in smaller reserves, only the instrumentalist and perhaps one dancer are included.

The alphabetical listing of pattern names in the Pattern Catalog will be helpful to you as you begin the identification procedure. The names have been kept simple and mostly in English to aid the collector in easily finding catalog entries for their items in the catalog. Full descriptions of each pattern include references to the appropriate Photo Album plates.

PLATE 7. Plate, 6¼", Battledore; pattern simply covers face of form.

PLATE 8. Cocoa Pot, 9½", Battledore; pattern is wrapped around form.

PLATE 9. Creamer, Basket B; pattern is placed on front of spherical form.

PLATE 10. Same Creamer showing scenic detail on reverse side.

PLATE 11. Cup/Saucer, Tea, Lesson and Parasol A, mark #19; patterns placed in reserves.

PLATE 12. Celery Set, Geisha in Sampan B, mark #14; "diminutive geisha" styling.

PLATE 13. Plate, 7", Butterfly Dancers; name reflects focal point of pattern.

PLATE 14. Sauce dish, Parasol C, #20; name reflects only activity in pattern.

PLATE 15. Mustard Jar with spoon, Lady in Rickshaw B; although figure carries a parasol, it is the rickshaw with flower-laden wheels which distinguishes this pattern from others.

PLATE 16. Roll Tray, Bird Cage, mark J#28; sometimes the uniqueness of a pattern is defined by only a small portion thereof, in this case—the cage.

PLATE 17. Nut Set, Parasol D, mark #19; the number of figures appearing in a pattern will vary depending upon the size of the item on which the pattern is depicted. There is no relation between the number of figures and the value of an item.

Methods of Design Application

Pattern Applications

Stenciling

Contributing to the many variations of Geisha Girl Porcelain are the differing methods of applying the design to the porcelain body. The most common of these methods is referred to as stenciling.

The word stencil, when used to describe Japanese wares, takes on a meaning different than the U.S. standard of "a sheet cut through with a design." The Japanese word for stencil gives us a clue to the meaning. The word is **kigata**, and its roots literally translate to "wooden pattern."

The Japanese had been famous since the 17th century for their skills at woodblock carving that resulted in the many famous and popular woodblock prints now cherished by collectors. When the demand for quantities of porcelain arose, this skill was integrated into the ceramic industry. Specifically, linear designs were carved into the wood blocks, which were then "inked" with special enamels. The enamel was wiped off the surface of the block and allowed to remain only in the grooves or cuts. Specially treated paper was then pressed onto the block. Upon removal of the paper, the enamel left the wood and clung to the sheet. The inked paper would then be placed upon a glazed porcelain surface, wetted and removed. The enamel would remain on the porcelain body which would then be fired to harden and assure permanence of the enamels. This stencil process, commonly called transfer in the U.S. and England, formed what is called the "underlying design" on stenciled Geisha Girl Porcelain. If one runs a finger over the surface of the porcelain, the distinct lines (Plate 18) of the underlying design can be felt. The vast majority of extant examples have a red-orange underlying design, although black or very dark brown are found. Grass-green, blue-green and bright blue underlyers are known, but rare.

The second step in the application process was the completion of the pattern with colored enamels, in most cases ones of a very bright hue. Thin washes were applied for grass, water and sky. Thicker enamels were used for flowers, leaves, kimonos, etc.

Because the remaining steps in the decorative process are the same for stenciled and hand-painted wares, the initial decoration of hand-painted wares will be discussed before proceeding to the rest of the process.

Hand-Painted Wares

Several producers of Geisha Girl Porcelain chose to continue the time honored tradition of wholly hand-painting wares (Plate 19). The overall design process differs because no overglaze stencil was used. Instead, the entire design was hand applied. Hand-painted items run the gamut from the finely detailed Spider Puppet pattern to the simply executed Mother and Son C variant.

Border Applications

Most border colors, except for cobalt blue which served to frame the patterns, were applied over the glaze. The variety of border designs were almost as varied as the patterns themselves. Butler Bros. catalogs from the early 1900's variously describe borders as "gold traced cobalt edges," "Tokio red bands and handles," "gold ornamented pale green edge," "floral wreath framing, gold ornamented Tokio red edge," "red and green Oriental border," etc.

Single color borders were applied in a one-eighth to one-half-inch width around the edges of body and lid. Some of the more exciting examples have a scalloped border often used to accentuate a fluted or scalloped edge porcelain body. On others, the border color was applied in a wave-like manner giving the piece a sense of motion.

Multi-color borders were produced in a myriad of styles. Bands of multiple colors such as cobalt blue and red-orange were used in the 1930's. **Nishikide** borders of red-orange, green, black and gold (Plate 20) and the colorful borders of Parasol D patterned items (Plate 21) are beautiful.

Color washes can be found overlying a stenciled floral band (Plates 22-23) or enamel flowers embellishing an enameled band (Plate 24). One can find circles segmenting the border (Plate 25) or colored geometrics forming the border (Plate 26).

Spouts, finials, handles and feet were similarly or complementarily decorated. All this required at least one or two more firings.

The Final Steps

Oftentimes design elements were highlighted in gold, or borders were embellished with gold lacing or flowers. The spout of the Rivers Edge Kutani teaset (Illus. 4-1) is lavishly decorated in a gold chrysanthemum and fern leaf design. The 1914 A.A. Vantine catalog in which it appeared states that "the gold in the decoration is the best that can be used, and is burnished by agate polishing."

Borders also may be embellished by gold lacing, netting, slashes or buds. Interestingly, gold seems to wear off cobalt blue bordered items more easily than the red bordered items, perhaps because it is adhered to a glaze rather than the enamel. Recall that the cobalt blue was placed under the glaze, while other enamels colors were placed over the glaze.

A change in the embellishment procedures took place circa 1910-1915. It revolved around the use of white and yellow enamels as a less expensive alternative to gold as a means of highlighting the accompanying decoration.

Because of the nature of gold enamel, it was necessary that it be fired at a lower temperature than the other enamels. If it were placed directly on the other colors and fired simultaneously with them, the gold would disappear into the enamel. In an effort to cut production time and costs by reducing the number of necessary firings, some factories began to use white enamel dots and slip to emphasize flowers and outline dwellings. Items with yellow or white dots, stars, lines and zigzags over the borders began to appear. Other factories simply changed the placement of the gold from atop the enamels to right next to them. It was a money-saving move by some, but does not apply to all producers. Thus, one can generally say that an example bearing such decor postdates 1910-1915, but can by no means claim with equal certainty that an example with gold atop the enamels pre-dates that period.

Moriage Geisha Ware

A.A. Vantine and Company is known to have produced Geisha Girl Porcelain with moriage decoration. This refers to raised decoration achieved by applying a liquefied clay slip to the porcelain surface. Bamboo or rubber tubing is filled with the slip which is allowed to trail over the porcelain body as the craftsman draws with the tube to create the design of choice.

Lustre Ware

Not to be excluded, there is even Geisha Girl Porcelain with a lustre background (Plate 27). Lustre is a coloring which imparts an iridescent or opalescent effect. Noted potter Bernard Leach[1] describes it as "obtained by the application of a thin skin of certain metals in liquid form to the surface of a glaze which is subsequently fired in a low reducing atmosphere." Reduction is defined as "a condition of burning gases in a kiln in which combustion is incomplete or smoky, the carbon present having the effect of reducing the oxides to their respective metal forms."

PLATE 18. The fine red lines are indicative of a stenciled underlying design. Each individual line can be felt by running a finger over the surface.

PLATE 19. Plate, 7½", Rivers Edge, mark J#11; note the difference in appearance between this hand painted example and the stenciled example in Plate 18.

PLATE 20. Hand painted *nishikide* border.

[1] B. Leach, *A Potter's Book*, Faber & Faber Ltd., 1944.

PLATE 21. Hand painted multi-color border of Parasol D pattern.

PLATE 22. Floral border of color wash over black stencil.

PLATE 23. Floral border of color wash over red-orange stencil.

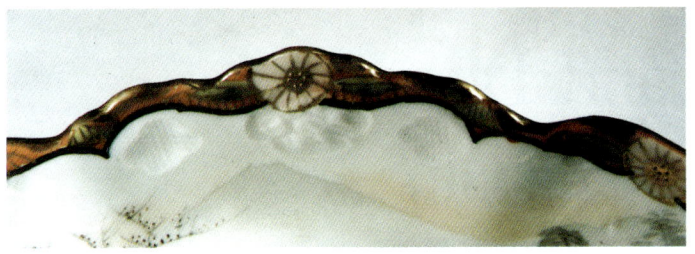

PLATE 24. Hand-painted floral border.

PLATE 25. Hand-painted border segmented by circles of different color.

PLATE 26. Hand-painted geometric border.

PLATE 27. Tea Cup/Saucer, Miscellaneous, mark J#68; lustre background.

ILLUS. 4-1. Kutani Rivers Edge Tea Set advertised in the 1914 *Oriental Store* catalog, A.A. Vantine and Company.

Czechoslovakia and Decaled Geisha Girl Porcelain

Decaled Wares

A decal is a screen printing of a design on specially treated paper. By saturating parts of fine mesh with special solutions, those parts are made impenetrable. Special inks or enamels are then forced through the unprotected parts of the mesh, creating a design on the treated paper laying below. Sometimes this is done several times with different mesh screens to achieve different colors, designs and consistencies. It is this mesh that gives decals their distinguishing feature — areas composed of dots of color.

The enamels are chemically fixed upon the paper which is then placed upon a glazed or unglazed ceramic body. The paper is wetted and removed, leaving the enamel decal adhered to the ceramic[1]. The process is called decalcomania, although in modern times it is sometimes also referred to as transferring.

Originally, it had been thought that all examples of decaled Geisha Girl Porcelain were made in Japan (Plates 28-29). However, this author's research findings indicate that many of these peculiar Geisha ware look-alikes are actually Czechoslovakian in origin. While this sounds absurd, a look at the history of the times and the status of the international market place explains the phenomenon.

Czechoslovakia was formed as a political entity in 1918, one result of the dissolution of the Austro-Hungarian empire. Within her boundaries were upwards of 90% of the potteries of the defunct empire. These firms, and the new state as a whole, were anxious to recover from the war years and regain their business status. By 1924, there was a financial reorganization of the Czech state, and the mark was stabilized, which coincided with a period of American investment in Europe.

Czechoslovakian industries began to enjoy what was to be a brief period of prosperity. They wished to extend their trade, as had the Japanese some sixty to seventy years earlier, beyond the local (European) countries, but here they faced several problems. The Japanese already had established a strong foothold on the Western markets. By 1920, two-thirds of the total imports of decorated china, parian, porcelain and bisque into the United States came from Japan[2].

In addition, a 1920 commentary by the American attache in Tokyo notes that "the decalcomania sheets, which were formerly (pre-1914) imported (by Japan) almost exclusively from Germany (the masthead of the Austro-Hungarian empire), are now coming principally from America. Some are being made in Japan, but it is likely that before long the domestic production will be displaced by the foreign article[2]."

This means that at the time of the formation of Czechoslovakia, a severing of business relations with Japan occured, and a competition began. Geisha Girl style wares, emulating the already popular Japanese article, appear to have been a direct result of this conflict.

Several styles of Czechoslovakian Geisha style wares have come to light. The first (Plate 30) is the most primitive in appearance. The decal, composed of unusually large terra-cotta red dots, is under the glaze. The kimonos bear yellow and blue over the glaze enameling. The accompanying mark (no. 64) is that of the Porcelain Factory of Victoria in Altrohlau. The Factory Victoria opened under the auspices of the Austro-Hungarian empire in 1904, and was one of those which ended up within Czechoslovakian borders. This plate was purchased for $7.00, and the author has seen a teaset consisting of pot, sugar bowl and four cups/saucers for $125.00.

A second style of Czechoslovakian decaled wares (Plates 31-32) is the closest in appearance to real Geisha ware. At first glance the scene with white ground, red-orange border and apparent black underlying design is deceptively similar to the Japanese article. Close inspection reveals the forgery. Not only is the pattern a decal, but the faces are very round and squat, more characteristic of European features than Japanese. In addition, the porcelain clay is much whiter than that from the Japanese kilns. The base of the teapot bears mark J#58. An identical hand-painted version of this also has been found. Another Czechslovakian pattern of this type has been noted featuring two ladies, one holding a tray with a teapot and accessories, with a third kneeling before them. It is accompanied by mark J#59.

Yet another style marks an obvious attempt at "fooling the public." The pattern is completely decaled and bears mark J#64. The author purchased a plate (Plate 33) for only $2.00, but has seen a twenty-three piece luncheon set noted as Oriental and selling for $175.00. Note the peculiar face behind the fence to the left of the plate.

A fourth type of Czechslovakian style Geisha ware is similar in decal to that in Plates 31-32, but it appears on a porcelain body shaded pale to pine green. Borders and appendages are usually black. Interestingly, this type, which is the most obviously un-Japanese in appearance, usually bears the name Czecho·slovakia encircled on the base.

Note, however, the pseudo-Oriental marks found on the other examples. This was a fairly common practice among Czechoslovakian firms. Some wares bear only the psuedo-mark which leads the unsuspecting public to believe the wares were made in Japan.

Without knowing Japanese, it is possible for the collector to distinguish these pseudo-marks from the real thing by comparing the overall size of the mark and the individual stroke characteristics. The Japanese marks are generally stenciled or hand painted. In the case of the former, the lines of the characters are pencil-point thin. As respects the latter, hand-signed marks are done with a pointed brush, pressed flat when a stroke is begun and lifted to its point by the end of the stroke. Thus, each stroke is wider at one end than the other. In either case, the Japanese mark is generally no more than one-half

---

[1] A. Kosloff, *Ceramic Screen Printing*, Routledge and Kegan Paul, 1972.
[2] "The Japanese Pottery Industry," *Review of Reviews*, April 1920, p. 44.

inch square. The Czechoslovakian strokes are very thick and even due to being **stamped** on the porcelain. They also are larger, generally about one inch square.

It appears that Czechoslovakia integrated her technological strengths (the creation of decals) with Japanese design and a bit of chicanery in an attempt to successfully compete with the Japanese in the Western markets. Unfortunately, the Czechs were not formidable enough opponents. By 1930 it is noted that:

> "In many foreign markets, (glass) is protected against the Japanese only by greater proximity to the dictators of European (not American) fashions . . . Potteries and porcelain-makers are just as vulnerable, and indeed the china industry, which had been exporting to the extent of 90%, seems the most hopeless of all."[3]

By 1933, the Great Depression landed a solid blow to Czechoslovakia. Her employment rate fell, porcelain production dipped sharply, and her largest porcelain producer lost a full two-thirds of its foreign market. Breakdown in the china trade was so severe that there was minimal recovery even by the end of the 1930's.

PLATE 28. Box, 5″ x 4″ x 2″, Samisen Practice and Mother and Daughter variant in reserves, mark #68.

PLATE 29. Close-up of patterns which were applied via decalcomania.

[3] E. Wiskemann, *Czechs and Germans: A Study of the Struggle in the Historic Provinces of Bohemia and Moravia*, Oxford University Press, 1938.

PLATE 30. Plate 6¼″, decaled pattern, Czechoslovakian mark #64.

PLATE 31. Czechoslovakian teaset, decaled pattern, Czechoslovakian mark J#58.

PLATE 32. Close-up of teapot in Plate 31.

PLATE 33. Plate, 7½″, J#64; yet another version of Czechoslovakian Geisha Girl type ware.

Distinguishing Among Japanese Wares

Geisha Girl Porcelain vs. Satsuma Wares

Of particular interest among Geisha Girl items are those that are sometimes mistaken for Satsuma, especially those in the Rendevous, Fan Dance B and Lantern A patterns. As previously noted, there were many porcelain producers in Japan, in both remote areas and major cities, all competing for a slice of the foreign trade. Thus, it is not surprising that the most popular patterns and styles were sometimes mixed and matched. Contributing to the confusion is the appearance of female figures and multi-color borders on both Geisha Girl and Satsuma-style wares. It falls to the lot of the collector to learn the differences between the two wares in order to make an accurate attribution. Certain characteristics aid in this determination.

A mark would be the easiest indication. For example, the author has seen floral covered (without a Geisha Girl pattern) pieces in the style of the Lantern A cup and saucer (Plate 34) listed as Satsuma-style in various books. However, the majority of pieces one finds in this pattern are marked Kutani.

The Rendevous pattern (Plate 35) is often mistaken for a Satsuma-style ware due to the background decor. Yet it, too, is often signed Kutani or marked with the names of other Geisha Girl Porcelain producers. The creamer (Plates 36-37) shows a similar background, but bears stenciled Geisha Girl Porcelain patterns. It, too, is marked Kutani.

The Fan Dance B patterned teaset (Plate 38) was sold to the author as Satsuma-style, yet it bears the mark of **Taniguchi**, a family firm known to have worked in Kaga province circa 1910.

Of course, we are not so fortunate to find all extant pieces with marks. Other indicators must be considered. True Satsuma wares are yellow to beige pottery, often bearing a crackle glaze. Some Satsuma-style wares made for export may be formed of porcelain. Kutani/Kaga/Seto wares are off-white to gray porcelain.

The style of painting, especially in the faces, is different. The Satsuma wares tend to have detailed faces with rounder features than the hand-painted Geisha Girl wares. Geisha Girl border coloring was bolder, and usually accompanied by gold or enamel lacing while a diapered, beaded border or interior frame is typical of Satsuma-style wares. Background decoration of maple leaves usually indicates Kutani/Kaga origins.

Another hint is to inventory the available examples of the particular pattern. Does a stenciled version exist? For example, amongst the Garden Bench series, there are stenciled and hand-painted variants.

Geisha Girl Porcelain and Satsuma

There sometimes are pieces that legitimately fall into two categories. The wholly hand-painted compote (Plates 39-40) may be considered both Geisha Girl Porcelain and Satsuma style. The pattern styling (Playing Catch) and the apple green borders are both indicative of Geisha ware. However, the diapered background is a uniquely Satsuma feature. A more Kutani-styled version of the pattern is depicted on the cup/saucer (Plate 41).

Geisha Girl Porcelain and Phoenix Bird China

The saucer (Plate 42)[1] falls into this "two styles" category. It is considered both Phoenix ware and Geisha Girl Porcelain because of the Phoenix backdrop for the Geisha Girl patterns.

PLATE 34. Tea Cup/Saucer, Lantern A; one of the patterns mistaken for Satsuma, but which often bears a Kutani mark.

PLATE 35. Sugar and Creamer, Rendevous, mark J#21; a hand painted pattern often mistaken for Satsuma because of the backdrop, but compare with Plates 36 and 37.

[1] Photo courtesy of Joan Oates, author of *Phoenix Bird China - Books One and Two.*

PLATE 36. Creamer, Mother and Son variant; note similarity between this backdrop and that in Plate 35. Patterns on this creamer are stenciled and creamer bears mark J#16, Kutani.

PLATE 37. Reverse of Creamer, Garden Bench G.

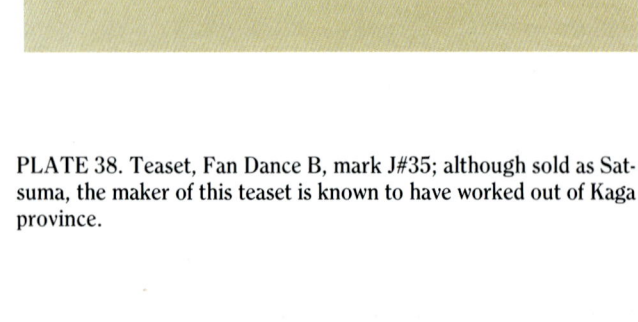

PLATE 38. Teaset, Fan Dance B, mark J#35; although sold as Satsuma, the maker of this teaset is known to have worked out of Kaga province.

PLATE 39. Compote, 4", Playing Catch, mark #56, interior view; an example of dual style descendancy (Kutani and Satsuma).

PLATE 40. Same compote, exterior view.

PLATE 41. After-Dinner Cup/Saucer, Playing Catch, J#52; this example bears a greater resemblance to Kutani style wares than its sister in Plates 39 and 40.

PLATE 42. Saucer, Mother and Son variant and Parasol E in reserves on Phoenix Bird backdrop, J#26b.

Form

Geisha ware is made from porcelain, a clay mixture of petuntse and kaolin. When fired in the heat of a kiln, it becomes a hard, translucent material. While porcelain weights vary from the thinnest "eggshell" to pottery look-alikes, all porcelain bodies have one thing in common — light can be seen through them. The thinner the porcelain, the more light shines through.

The older clays of the Kaga region were very gray and coarse. Having a high iron content, unglazed areas, such as lid extensions or bases, often bear an orange tint. The clays of the Seto area were somewhat less gray and much smoother by comparison. The distinction is helpful in determining the origin of a given piece and in distinguishing an older item from a new production.

Methods of porcelain construction are covered in many other sources[1], so only a few notes will be made herein as they specifically relate to Geisha Girl ware.

The earliest examples were made of several molded parts which were attached together when leather-hard, and then fired as a complete item. Specifically, handles, finials, feet and oftentimes spouts were made in molds separate from that of the body. Later examples often included these same parts in the body mold. This shows up as a hollow or depression inside the body at the joints involved.

Pinched, fluted or niched edges coupled with an uneven thickness of the porcelain body at these edges are indicative of hand formation and age. Such individual and time-consuming attention often was not devoted to wares during later periods of extensive mass production.

An examination of the base of an older item usually will turn up two distinctions: roughness and unglazed footrims or feet. These are manifestations of the way in which the items were fired. Resting flat on the kiln shelf, a stilt or stacked on other items, these surfaces were left unglazed.

The extensions of lids and the body surface with which they were in contact (interior surfaces) were left unglazed on old pieces. A rough edge and adjacent rough interior are good indicators that a piece now mistakenly labeled as a vase or brush pot is actually a low cracker jar or candy container with a lost lid. Illus. 7-1 diagrams the various lid types and what one would expect the accompanying body rim to look like.

Desirability of any porcelain item is often based on the creativity involved in the construction of the form. Scalloped, floriate-edged or unusually shaped items generally are preferred. Poorly fired and finished items—such as the eggcup (Plate 43) which is crooked, contains large bubbles inside the bowl, and has a visible joint between bowl and stem—are less desirable.

Relief molding enhances your piece of Geisha ware. By carving a decor into the mold, the resulting modeled body has decoration which stands out from the plane of the body. Relief decorations include flowers and vines (Plate 44).

Carving a mold so that the thickness of the porcelain wall varies results in varying amounts of light being able to pass through the porcelain body. Greater light passes through thinner walls. By carefully determining specific thicknesses, a scene can be imbedded in the porcelain. This is called a lithophane, most easily visible when the item is held up to the light. Geisha Girl Porcelain cups which have geisha face lithophanes in the bottom were produced after World War II.

---

[1] I. Stitt, *Japanese Ceramics of the Last 100 Years*, Crown Publishers, New York, 1974; J. Van Patten, *Collector's Encyclopedia of Nippon Porcelain, I*, Collector Books, Paducah, KY, 1979.

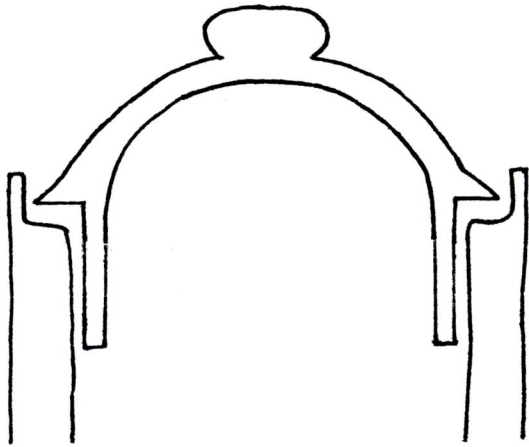
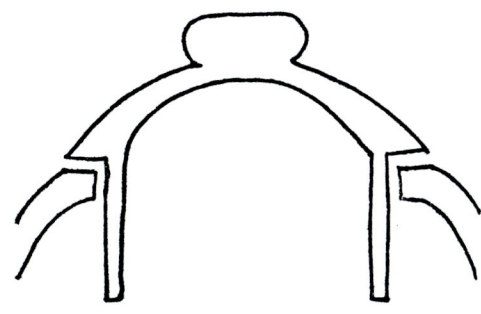

ILLUS. 7-1. Recognizing the distinctive appearances of adjoining sections enables the collector to detect those pieces that are missing or have the incorrect lid. Top Left: Flange lid often found on cocoa pots. Top Right: Flange lid on spherical body such as teapots, sugar bowls, etc. Middle: Inset lid most often found on biscuit jars and low cracker jars, also on some cocoa and teapots. Bottom: Cover used for tea caddies, ginger jars, etc.

PLATE 43. Eggcup, Cherry Blossom Ikebana; note the improper angle of the cup with respect to the stem and the visible seam line between the two.

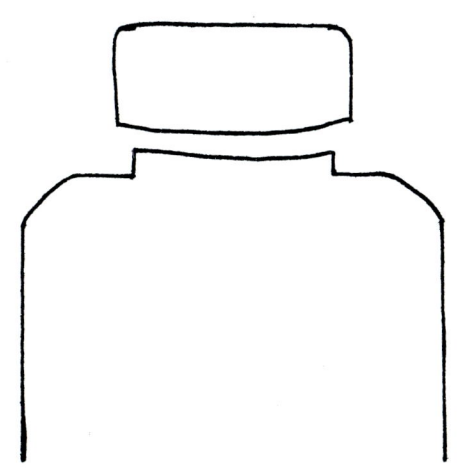

PLATE 44. Teapot, 6″, Battledore; molded-in-relief leaves begin at the base and extend into the center of the body.

Function

Those simple things in life which we take for granted, such as tea bags and pre-measured packages of hot cocoa mix, were not available to our ancestors at the turn of the century. Because dining needs were different than they are today, so were many of the utensils. Whereas we simply put the store-bought containers and packages on the table, our forebearers used a wide variety of service items both as a matter of convenience and etiquette. There was:

"a set of china for every course — beginning with the oysters and making way down through the fish, entrees, solid, salad, sweets and fruit, but even specialization has been specialized. Far be it . . . to eat tomato salad from the same plate as lobster salad[1]!"

Dining

Breakfast

On the breakfast table, one might have found an elegant pancake server — a large platter with a domed lid. Syrup would have been placed in a covered pitcher with an accompanying drip plate, serving to keep the tablecloth clean should a diner be less than graceful. And, of course, one would not have simply put the bottle of jam on the breakfast table. Jams, jellies, and condensed milk (no worry about the ice supply with the latter) had their own special serving containers. The cylindrical bodies of these containers had a hole in the bottom by which to push out the original container when finished; saved one from sticky fingers. Again, a drip plate accompanied these items.

Lunch

A luncheon get-together was a favorite function of the ladies. The table would be set with seven or eight inch lunch plates and two-handled bouillon cups with accompanying lids and drip plates. Diners removed thinly sliced pieces of bread or homemade rolls from the roll tray to six inch bread and butter plates. The hostess might have chosen to include two and three-quarter inch butter pats as part of the place settings. A complete luncheon set included a matching tea service.

Afternoon Tea

If the noon hour was not a good time for the gathering of friends, then afternoon tea was a must. Since the teabag was not invented until 1908, a tea caddy found a home in many kitchens. Its function was to store dry tea leaves and, to this end, it had two lids to keep out the moisture. The smaller lid sat snuggly in the mouth of the caddy while the outer lid sat on the body affording extra protection.

Whether loose or in those "new fangled" tea bags, etiquette dictated that the tea be prepared in the kitchen and brought to the table already in the pot. A matchholder or striker had a home nearby to store matches to light the stove. A sugar bowl, preferably containing blocks of sugar and accompanied by tongs, a pitcher of cream, and slices of lemon, mint leaves, and cloves on a six and one-quarter inch lemon plate were also provided by the proper hostess. The lemon plate had two small cut-out handles at either end to distinguish it as a serving piece. Note that all items in a teaset were of comparable size and similarly shaped.

The table would be appropriately laid out with bon bons, salted nuts, ices or fruit salads, sandwiches and cakes. Thus one might have seen a five and three-quarter to six and one-quarter inch master nut dish with three inch individual nut cups and a berry or ice cream set, sometimes referred to as a salad set, consisting of a seven or eight inch master bowl and four to five inch individual dishes. An eleven inch cake platter would have held tortes or finger sandwiches, and a nappy or bon-bon dish would have held the sweets. Cookies might have filled a six inch tall biscuit jar or a four and one-half inch tall low Cracker Jar.

Dinner

If your appetite wasn't completely satisfied by the end of the day, there was always dinner. Napkins were elegantly folded and placed in napkin rings. Relishes and celery were placed in the appropriate serving dishes. Salads were served on seven inch plates, to the chagrin of some reviewers of the then current etiquette.

"Doubtless from some one or the other of the arbitrary dictums, it is considered 'incorrect' by some to serve salad on other than a seven inch plate. Yet to manipulate lettuce, tomato and the several other ingredients of a salad so that all of them remain on a seven inch plate requires a greater knowledge of sleight of hand than most of us are gifted with."[2]

Salt granules were not as refined as they are today. During the Victorian period and extending into the first part of this century, salt dishes or cellars were used. These were shallow, two or three inch diameter bowls from which salt was spooned and then sprinkled over the food.

When shakers came into vogue, it was appropriate to put a salt and pepper at every other place on the dinner table. Thus we find some small individual salt and pepper shakers. Salt still was not highly refined and the salt shaker always had larger holes than the pepper. Complete condiment sets included a four by six inch tray supporting a shaker set and a small mustard jar with spoon.

Dinner plates ranged from eight and one-half to nine and one-half inches in diameter, but there seems to be a scarcity of them in Geisha ware. In addition to the breakage which befalls large items, Geisha Girl Porcelain dinner plates were simply not practical. Repeated use of a knife, for instance, would have caused considerable damage to the overglaze enamels and stenciling. Most of the plates were made for more delicate use, either smaller for sandwiches and salads, or larger, ten inches and more, for the serving of cakes and cookies.

The dining room sideboard might have been ornamented by urns or ewers, or the room made decorative by flowers placed in a wallpocket, a vase with a flat back made to hang on the wall.

---

[1] "New Glass and China," *Harper's Bazaar*, February 1904, p. 199.
[2] J. Belshaw, "China on our Tables," *Arts and Decoration*, January 1932, p. 58.

After Dinner

After dinner, coffee or cocoa was served. Demitasse or after dinner sets for coffee consisted of a cylindrical pot which widened toward the base and had a long spout, a creamer and sugar, and small cups and saucers. After dinner cups and saucers were also sold through open stock in a wide variety of shapes. The man of the house might have used a cup with a curved bar going across its diameter, called a mustache cup, to keep his upper lip from being saturated by the beverage.

A cocoa set was comprised of a pot with a short spout and matching cups and saucers. Cocoa pots ranged from seven to ten inches in height and came in a variety of shapes including cylindrical, fluted and widening at base, and ewer-shaped. Cocoa cups averaged three inches in height and were shaped to resemble the master pot. A sugar and creamer were **not** included in a cocoa set.

Japanese Accents In Dining

Several Japanese-style pieces were available to complement the Western style dinner wares. While Westerners used gravy boats, the Japanese used small sauce dishes. Rice being a staple of the Japanese diet, there were specific bowls in which to serve it. While Western tea wares included handled cups, the handleless tea cup is a Japanese-style utensil. Sake bottles and cups are also available.

The Bedroom

Just as things were different in the dining room, so we find differences in other areas of the home. Conveniences were not what they are today — there were no electric rollers, plastic wastebaskets, lightweight wall mirrors, etc. Instead there were lovely wooden vanities and beveled mirrors providing a place for the lady of the house to arrange herself.

Dresser and manicure sets were the accompanying utensils and provide today's collector with numerous jars and trays.

A rectangular tray, roughly eight by ten inches, served to hold a brush and comb or protect the wood from the drippings of a candle or perfume bottle.

Squat, round four and one-half inch diameter jars with holes centered in their lids were called hair receivers and were used to contain the hair removed from the brush or comb until it could be properly disposed of.

Face powder was loose so a powder jar, looking much like a hair receiver without the hole in its lid, was incorporated as part of the dresser set to hold the powder and a puff. A larger jar, six inches in diameter, was also available for jewelry or cosmetics. A smaller jar of similar shape was used as a puff or button box.

Hats were all the rage, but something was needed to hold those big hats onto those bouffant hairdos. That something was a hatpin and they too warranted their own holders, a four to four and one-half inch tall form with holes in the top. A two and one-half inch version of this holder was made for the stickpins used to adorn or hold in place blouse ties, collars, scarves, etc.

Yet another type of pin was used to hold the hair in place. These hairpins found a home on trays ranging from three and one-half to four inches by four and three-quarters inches.

Rings were safely hung from ring trees, porcelain hands or branches extending upward from a saucer-shaped base.

Complementary chambersticks to light the way from vanity to bed to bath were also available.

The dressing table or vanity could have been a rather crowded place. Manicure sets were also necessary for the ladies' proper preparation. They consisted of a seven inch round tray and several jars of varying sizes and shapes for holding creams, pumice, etc. The smallest is sometimes called a trinket box.

Of the wide variety of forms available to today's collector, the most common are tea and cocoa sets, small plates, hatpin holders, powder jars and hair receivers. The most difficult to find items include large vases, plates of nine inch diameter or more, large mugs, steins, chamber and candlesticks, perfume bottles, miniatures, urns, ewers, mustache cups and wallpockets.

Illus. 8-1 through 8-7, pages from a 1924 Thayer and Chandler catalog, provide a good overview of shapes as they relate to functionality.

Net Wholesale Prices

Cups and Saucers

THAYER & CHANDLER

AFTER DINNER COFFEE CUPS AND SAUCERS

| 71. Diam., 2½ in., 28c | 74. 2¼ in., 33c | 84. 2 in., 30c | 84½. 2 in., 30c | 75. Diam., 2 in. Each 30c | 47. 2½ in., 33c | 73. 2¾ in., 33c | 81. 2⅜ in. 38c |

AFTERNOON TEA CUPS AND SAUCERS

| 67. 2½ in., 30c | 63. 2¼ in., 28c | 72. 2¼ in., 37c | 13. 2¾ in., 45c | 21. 2⅞x2 in., 48c | 68. 3 in., 33c | 6. 2¾x2 in., 33c | Thomas 7. 3x1¾ in., 33c |

CHOCOLATE CUPS AND SAUCERS

| 53. 2⅞ in...45c | 14. 3 in......52c | 55. 3 in.....48c | 51. 3½ in....48c | 60. 2½ in....48c | 58. 3 in.....48c | 54. 3 in.....37c |

TEA CUPS AND SAUCERS

| Victoria, Thin J. & C. Special Selection. 18. 2⅞x2¼ in....53c | Ovide, Thin 33. 3⅝x1⅞ in...33c | Ovide 29. 3⅝x2¼ in....33c | Derby, Thin 20. 3⅜x2 in......38c | Boheme 23. 3¼x1⅞ in....45c | Charlotte, Thin 35. 3¼x1⅞ in....48c |

| 00. 3¾ in........65c | 01. 3½ in........58c | 61. 3½ in........45c | 45. 3¼ in........33c | 94. 3½ in........55c | Thomas 9. 2⅞x2⅛ in.....53c |

| Czecho 39. 3⅜x2⅛ in....38c | Thomas 10. 3⅞ in........45c | Bavarian 17. 3⅞x2 in......33c | Czecho 22. 3⅞ in........33c | Minerva 42. 3¼x1⅞ in....48c | Charlotte, Thin 36. 3¼x2¼ in....48c |

| Selesia 44. 3½x2¼ in....33c | Royal 34. 3½ inches....83c | Royal 93. 3½ inches....53c | 99. 3⅝ in........78c | 46. 3⅝ in........55c | 50. 2⅞ in........45c |

COFFEE CUPS AND SAUCERS

| 87. 3x2¾ in....39c | Derby 19. 4x2 inches....52c | 52. 2⅞ in......43c |

CREAM SOUP BOWLS

| 82. Diam. 5 in...75c | French 79. 5 inches....$1.10 | 80. Bowl 5 in...$1.48 |

BOUILLON CUPS AND SAUCERS

Thomas
78. 3¾x2 in......48c

Ovide
28. 3⅝x2¼ in......43c

J. & C. Thin
76. 3⅞x2 in......43c

12. 3⅝ in........65c

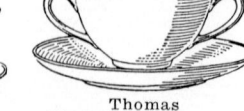
Thomas
85. Cream Soup.
4¼x2½ inches..48c

When article ordered is not in stock we will substitute a similar article as good unless you request us not to.

ILLUS. 8-1. 1924 Thayer and Chandler Catalog No. 56.

Net Wholesale Prices — # Cooky Trays, Cake Plates, Service Plates — THAYER & CHANDLER

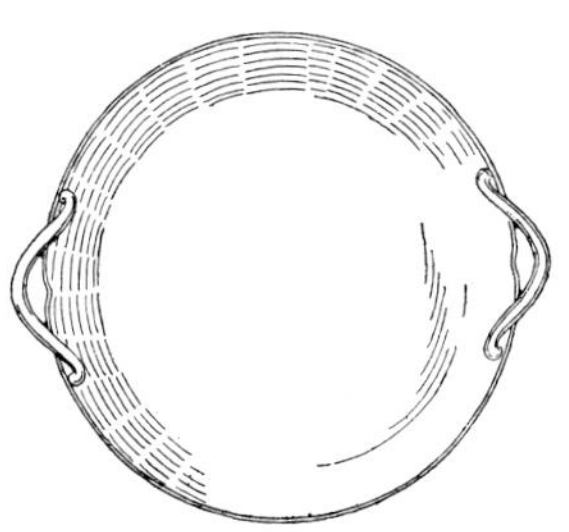

| 532. 7¼ inches..........65c | 549. 7¼ inches..........65c | 525. 6½ inches..........65c | 526. 7½ inches..........78c |

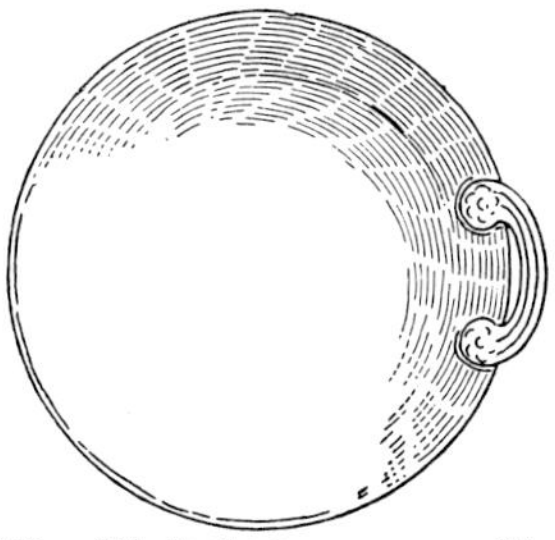

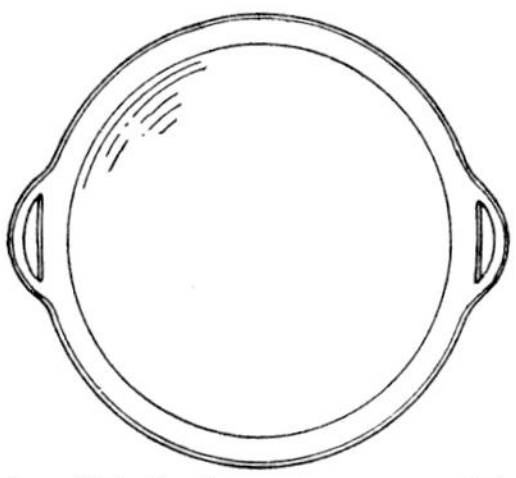

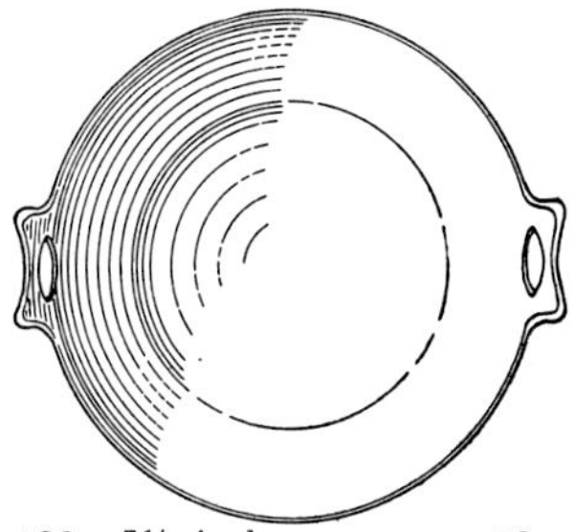

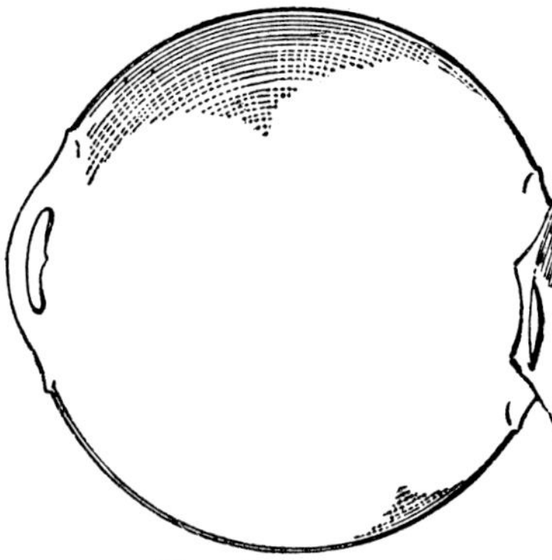

French
527. 10½ inches........$1.10

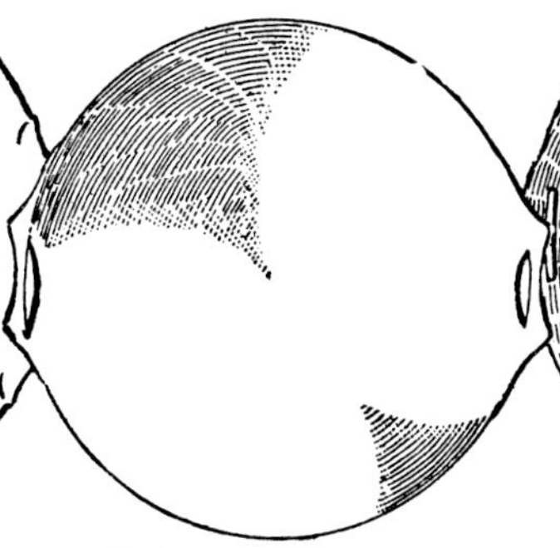

Hutschenreuther
543. 10½ inches........$0.89
544. 11   inches........ 1.00

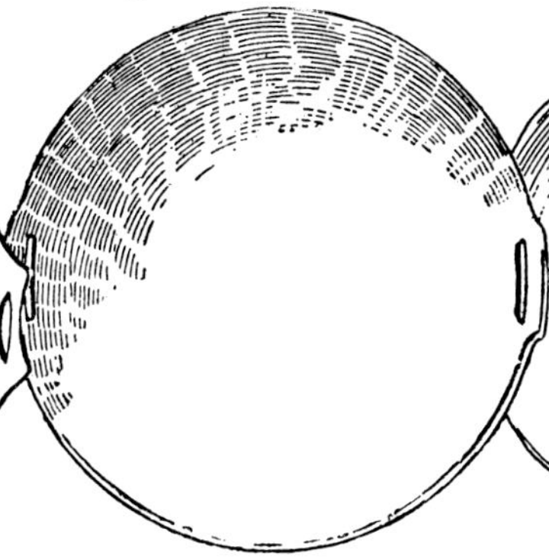

547. 10½ inches........$0.85
548. 11   inches........ 1.00

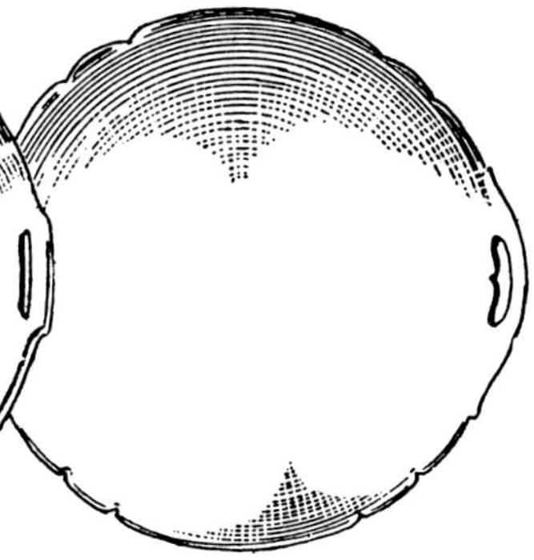

French
528. 10½ inches........$1.10

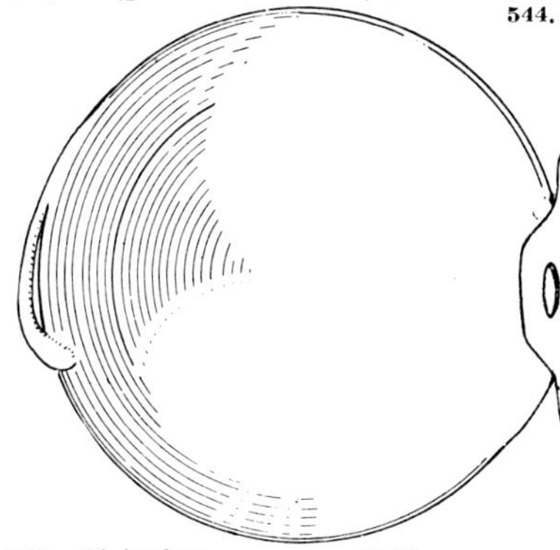

533. 11 inches..........$1.10

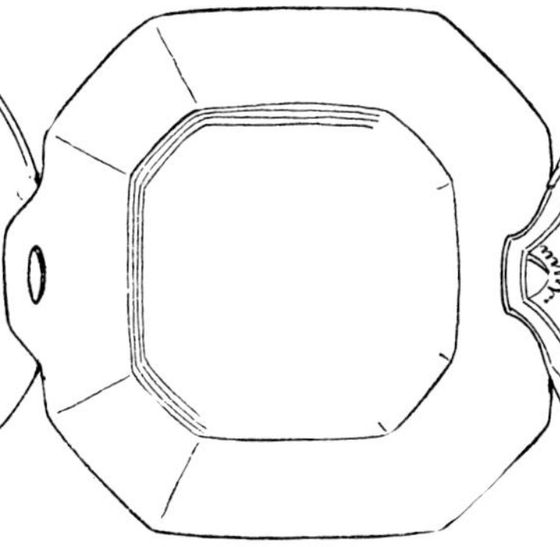

French
541. 11 inches..........$1.10

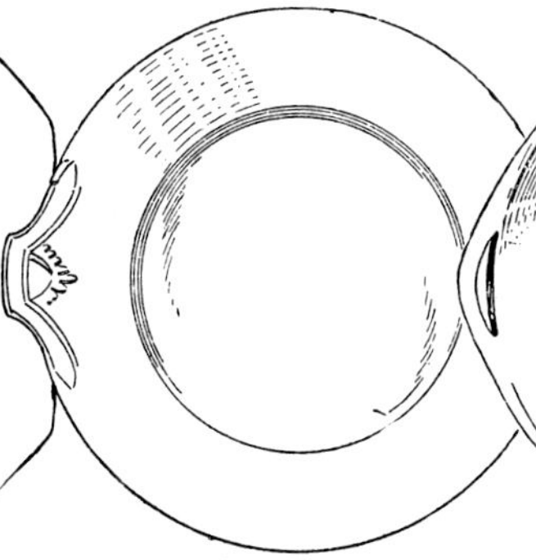

540. 10½ inches..........83c

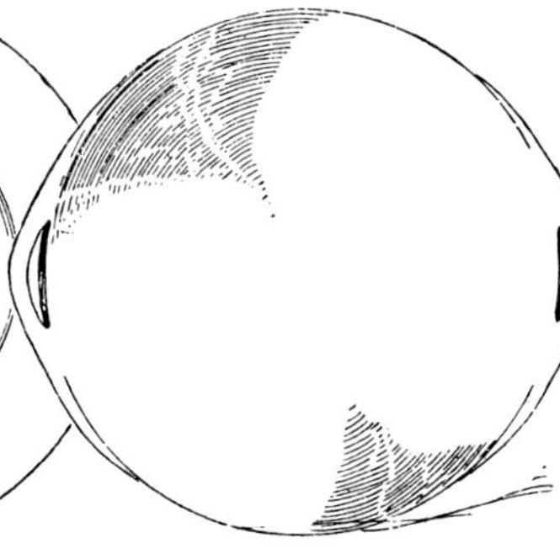

B. & Co.
531. 11 in., over handles..$1.55

Roll Tray, French
558. 14 inches.....................$1.10

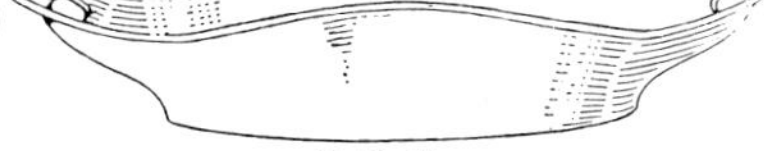

Roll Tray
555. 11x8½ inches..................98c

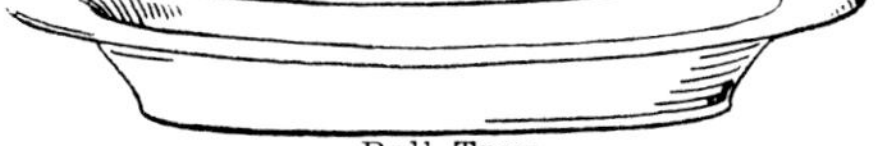

Roll Tray
556. 13x5½ inches..................95c

Service Plate Bargains

Few are the homes today where one finds no touch of individuality such as service plates supply. They play an important part in making the dinner a delightful event. In buying these plates you are going straight to the simple truths of **QUALITY, STYLE** and **VALUE.**

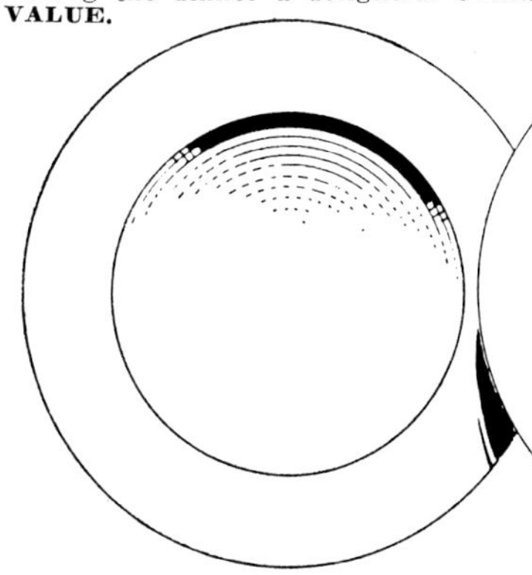

Hutschenreuther
135. 10½ inches..........95c

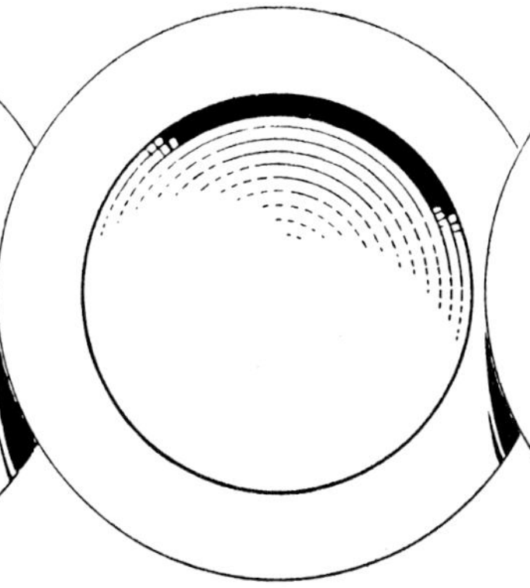

Boheme
125. 10½ in., 1¾-inch rim.68c

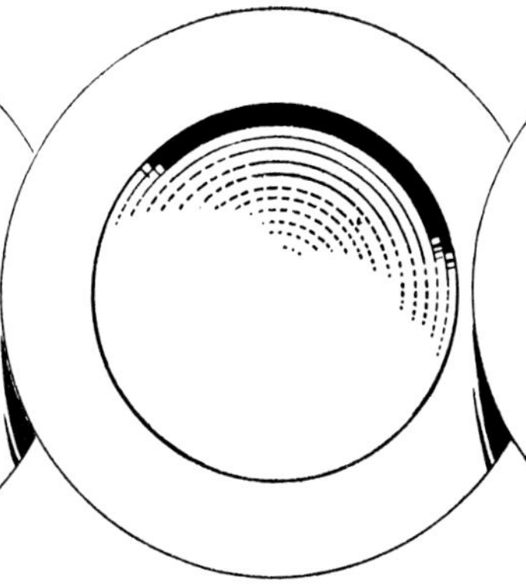

Thomas
165. 10¾ in., 1¾-inch rim.95c

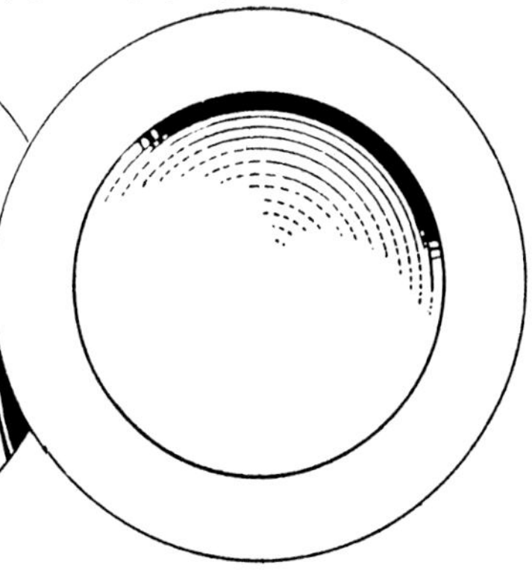

Rosenthal
170. 10¼ in., 1½-in. rim.$0.98
171. 11 in., 1⅝-in. rim. 1.35

ILLUS. 8-2. 1924 Thayer and Chandler Catalog No. 56.

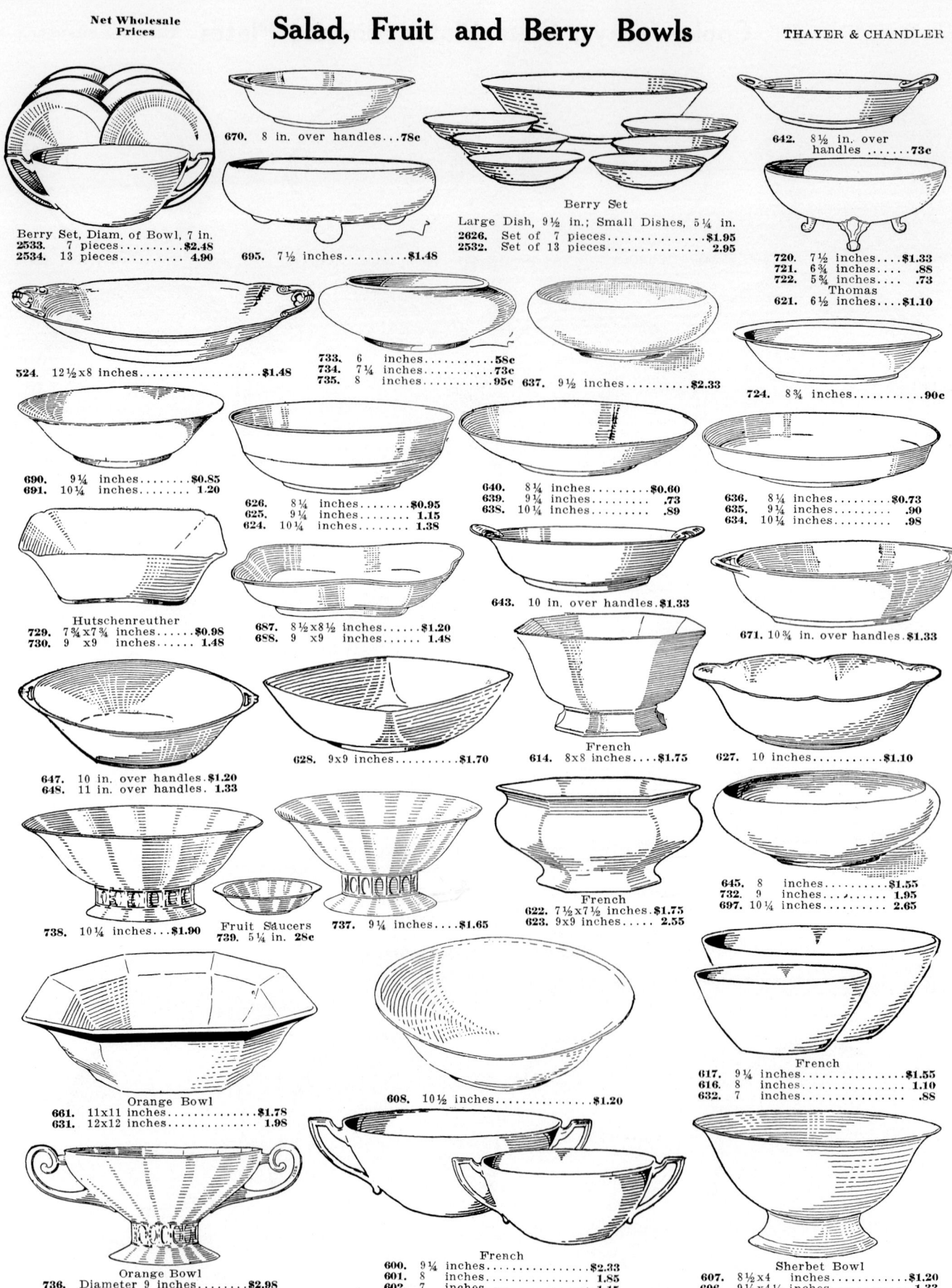

ILLUS. 8-3. 1924 Thayer and Chandler Catalog No. 56.

ILLUS. 8-4. 1924 Thayer and Chandler Catalog No. 56.

ILLUS. 8-5. 1924 Thayer and Chandler Catalog No. 56.

CHICAGO **Bon-Bon Dishes, Boxes, Etc.** Net Wholesale Prices

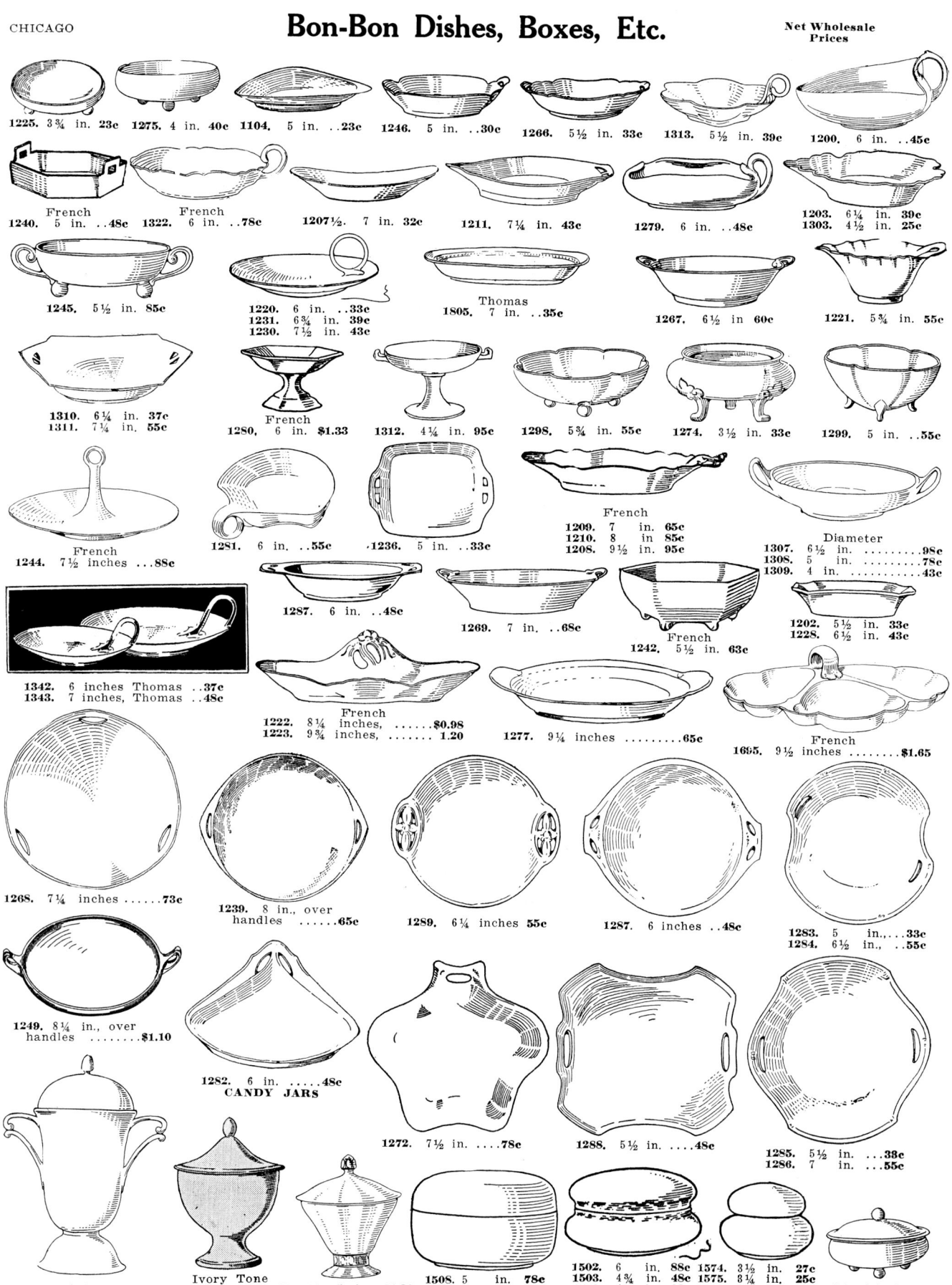

ILLUS. 8-6. 1924 Thayer and Chandler Catalog No. 56.

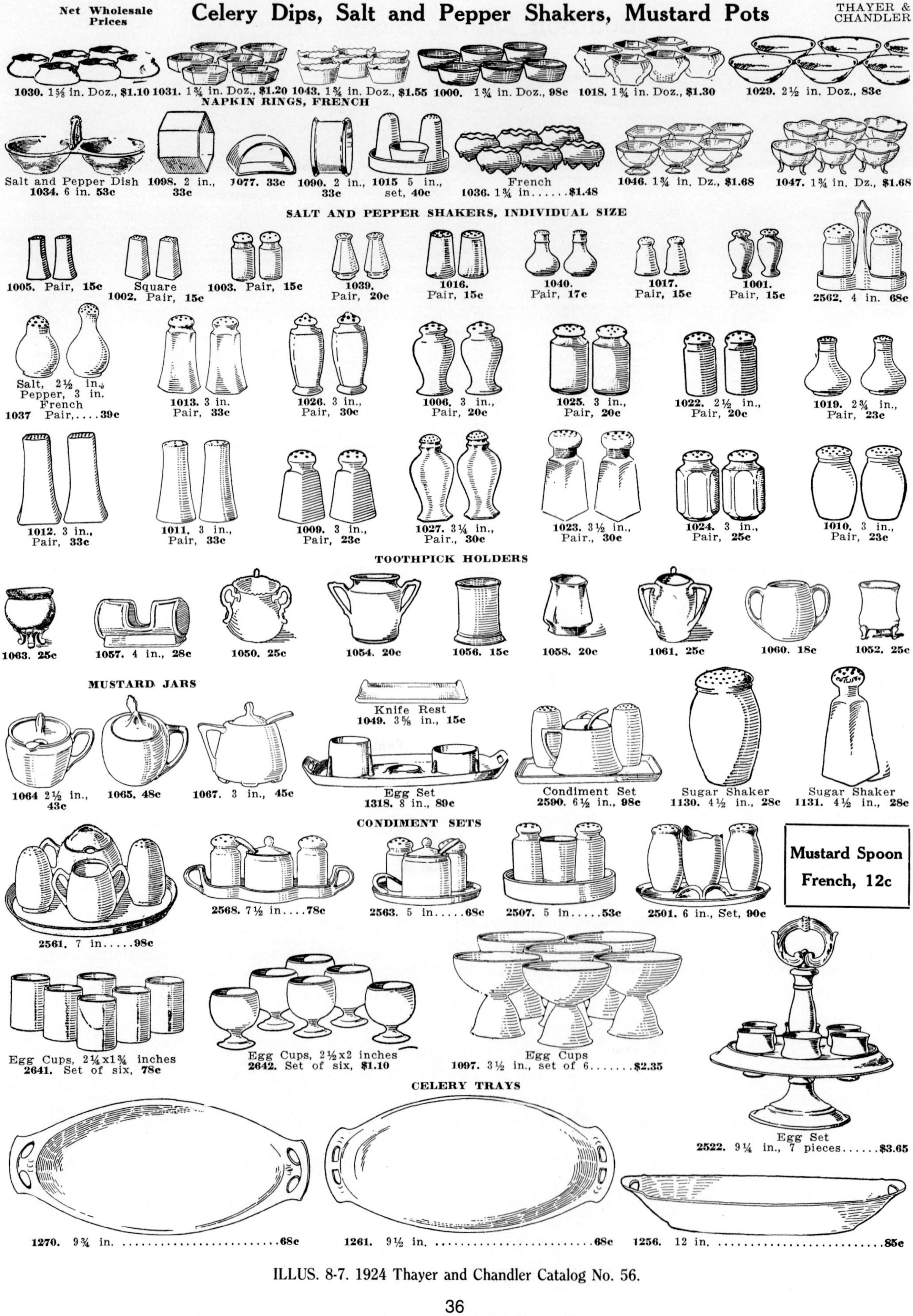

Net Wholesale Prices — **Celery Dips, Salt and Pepper Shakers, Mustard Pots** — THAYER & CHANDLER

1030. 1⅝ in. Doz., $1.10   1031. 1¾ in. Doz., $1.20   1043. 1¾ in. Doz., $1.55   1000. 1¾ in. Doz., 98c   1018. 1¾ in. Doz., $1.30   1029. 2½ in. Doz., 83c

NAPKIN RINGS, FRENCH

Salt and Pepper Dish 1034. 6 in. 53c   1098. 2 in. 33c   1077. 33c   1090. 2 in. 33c   1015 5 in., set, 40c   French 1036. 1¾ in. ...... $1.48   1046. 1¾ in. Dz., $1.68   1047. 1¾ in. Dz., $1.68

SALT AND PEPPER SHAKERS, INDIVIDUAL SIZE

1005. Pair, 15c   Square 1002. Pair, 15c   1003. Pair, 15c   1039. Pair, 20c   1016. Pair, 15c   1040. Pair, 17c   1017. Pair, 15c   1001. Pair, 15c   2562. 4 in. 68c

Salt, 2½ in. Pepper, 3 in. French 1037 Pair, ... 39c   1013. 3 in. Pair, 33c   1026. 3 in., Pair, 30c   1006. 3 in., Pair, 20c   1025. 3 in., Pair, 20c   1022. 2½ in., Pair, 20c   1019. 2¾ in., Pair, 23c

1012. 3 in., Pair, 33c   1011. 3 in., Pair, 33c   1009. 3 in., Pair, 23c   1027. 3¼ in., Pair, 30c   1023. 3½ in., Pair, 30c   1024. 3 in., Pair, 25c   1010. 3 in., Pair, 23c

TOOTHPICK HOLDERS

1063. 25c   1057. 4 in., 28c   1050. 25c   1054. 20c   1056. 15c   1058. 20c   1061. 25c   1060. 18c   1052. 25c

MUSTARD JARS

1064. 2½ in., 43c   1065. 48c   1067. 3 in., 45c   Knife Rest 1049. 3⅝ in., 15c   Egg Set 1318. 8 in., 89c   Condiment Set 2590. 6½ in., 98c   Sugar Shaker 1130. 4½ in., 28c   Sugar Shaker 1131. 4½ in., 28c

CONDIMENT SETS

2561. 7 in. ..... 98c   2568. 7½ in. .... 78c   2563. 5 in. .... 68c   2507. 5 in. .... 53c   2501. 6 in., Set, 90c

Mustard Spoon French, 12c

Egg Cups, 2¼x1¾ inches 2641. Set of six, 78c   Egg Cups, 2½x2 inches 2642. Set of six, $1.10   Egg Cups 1097. 3½ in., set of 6 ...... $2.35

Egg Set 2522. 9¼ in., 7 pieces $3.65

CELERY TRAYS

1270. 9¾ in. .... 68c   1261. 9½ in. .... 68c   1256. 12 in. 85c

ILLUS. 8-7. 1924 Thayer and Chandler Catalog No. 56.

A Child's World

Much of what was made for mother was duplicated for daughter. Teapots averaging three and one-half inches in height and matching creamer, sugar bowl and cups and saucers (Plates 45-48) were available for a tea party. There were also after dinner cups and saucers (Plates 49-52), four and one-quarter inch to five and one-half inch table plates (Plates 53-55) and small pitchers (Plates 56-57).

Additionally, children could play with mugs (Plates 58-59), tiny bowls (Plate 60), small jars (Plate 61) and diminutive steins. For that special child, there was even a rare celery set (Plate 62).

Of course, proper manners must be followed even during play. A miniature wash pitcher and bowl (Plate 63) helped drive home that point.

Playtime was further enhanced by miniature pieces so the doll house could be similarly outfitted. Coffee and tea pieces no larger than two inches in height (Plate 64) were a delight.

PLATE 45. Toy Teaset, Fishing B.

PLATE 46. Toy Teapot, Paper Carp, mark J#16.

PLATE 47. Toy Teapot, Pointing H.

PLATE 48. Toy Creamer and Sugar, Parasol C, mark #20.

PLATE 49. Toy After-Dinner Cup, Boy With Doll in reserve.

PLATE 50. Reverse of Plate 49, scenic reserve.

PLATE 51. Toy After-Dinner Cup/Saucer, Torii, #20.

PLATE 52. Toy After-Dinner Cup, Mother and Son A.

PLATE 53. Toy Plate, 4⅜" Long Stemmed Peony, mark J#9.

PLATE 54. Toy Plate, 5⅜", Bird Cage.

PLATE 55. Toy Plate, 4¼", Fan Dance A and Fan C in reserves, mark #19.

PLATE 56. Toy Pitcher, 3⅝", Parasol B, mark #19.

PLATE 57. Toy Pitcher, 5¾" x 2", Meeting A.

PLATE 58. Child's Mug, 3½", Geisha in Sampan B, mark #19.

PLATE 59. Reverse of Mug in Plate 58.

PLATE 60. Toy Bowl, 2¼" x 1", Flower Gathering C, mark #20.

PLATE 61. Toy Jar, 2¼", Pointing A.

PLATE 62. Toy Celery Set, 6½" master, Flower Gathering A, mark #20.

PLATE 63. Toy Pitcher 2⅞" and Waste Bowl, Pointing A.

PLATE 64. Miniatures, all under 1¾": center - Demitasse Pot, Court Lady, others - Sugar, Creamer, Tea Cups/Saucers, Processional.

From Eastern Shores To Western Stores

Geisha Girl Porcelain was distributed through many outlets. It found its way into fine Oriental shops, department stores, novelty shops, the Five and Dime store, and specialty boutiques. It was wholesaled, retailed, used with advertising and given away as premiums or promotions.

Butler Bros.

Butler Bros., a St. Louis based firm, was perhaps one of the best known wholesalers of the wares. Through the pages of their catalogs, retailers could purchase one dozen seven and one-quarter inch table plates in the Parasol pattern for one dollar and seventy-five cents or a thirteen piece chocolate set in the Flower Gathering pattern for two dollars. Parasol patterned teacups and saucers were offered at one dollar and ninety cents for two dozen!

Butler Bros. marketing approach allowed retailers to sell Geisha Girl Porcelain in sets or as open stock (Illus. 10-1 through 10-4). This is important!

A "set" handed down from Grandma actually may be a compilation of open stock items. All items of an original set will bear the same pattern, executed via the same application method, and be of like or complementary size.

While an unmatched cocoa or tea "set" may be as beautiful and as cherished as a matched set, it is important that the prospective buyer be able to tell the difference. The latter has a greater monetary and investment value than the former.

Another wholesaler of "novelty items" advertised a seventeen piece teaset for one dollar and sixty-five cents. The minimum order was a case consisting of twenty-four sets. A "wooden (display) box, satin lined, assorted colors" was available for an additional one dollar and thirty-five cents, almost as much as the teaset!

R.H. Macy and Co.

Retailers, too, included the wares in their porcelain line. R.H. Macy and Company of New York advertised several salad bowls in their Fall/Winter 1906-1907 catalog. At that time, a nine-lobed fruit or salad bowl in the Garden Bench A pattern with a red border sold for $.49. A Bamboo Trellis set of master and six individual bowls in red cost $2.49.

A.A. Vantine and Company

At least one retailer chose to control the actual manufacture of the wares they carried in their stores. A.A. Vantine and Company has a success story dating back to 1865, when the business was begun in Yokohama, Japan, for the purpose of manufacture and exportation of goods to the West. By 1870, their first retail store was opened at 814 Broadway, New York City.

Vantine's business expanded rapidly as buyers were sent throughout the Far East to import everything from rugs and fabrics to jewelry and porcelain. By the 1890's they had moved to larger quarters at 877-879 Broadway (Illus. 10-5 and 10-6). By 1914, other stores were located at Fifth Avenue and 39th St., New York and in Boston and Philadelphia. Mail order business was also active.

The firm actually dropped from the hands of the original owner during this growth period. Around 1870, a young farm boy named James Irving Raymond came to New York City and offered his labors free to Vantine's for the opportunity to learn the business. At the end of that year, he did manage, however, to purchase a small interest in the company. By 1875, Mr. Raymond had become a full-fledged partner in the business, and in 1887 he purchased the outstanding interests, becoming full owner but retaining the famous Vantine name[1]. The store was passed on to his son in 1905 and apparently remained in business until 1951.

Four trademarks are known to have been used by A.A. Vantine and Company. As of 1910, there were two Japanese marks (J#69 and J#70). By 1914 the crossed flags (mark #41) and by 1921 the name (mark #70) were in use. A fifth mark in the likeness of an enameled postage stamp (#42) was also used, but the respective time period is unknown.

The merchandise for Vantine's Oriental Store was furnished by the Vantine owned factories in Yokohama and Nagoya, Japan. There, among other fine items produced, were expensive examples of Geisha Girl Porcelain. Their teasets ranged from the simply detailed Seto/Kobe wares to the ornately gilded Kutani wares to the rare moriage Geisha ware. A teaset of the Seto variety in the Meeting pattern was advertised for seven dollars and fifty cents in a 1914 Vantine catalog. A Kutani teaset in the Rivers Edge pattern was offered for ten dollars the same year (Illus. 2-2 and 4-1).

The celery tray and upright spooner (Plates 65-66) display a powder blue border unique to Vantines. On their bases is Vantine's postage stamp style mark #42. The puff box (Plate 67) bears Vantine's mark #70.

Vantine's also took the opportunity to use their merchandise for advertising purposes. A lovely toilet cream jar (Plates 68-69) bears the Vantine name and trademark on its lid. Sachet jars which contained dried herbs and petals noted the contents on the jars (Plates 70-73), along with the bright gold words, "A.A. Vantine Co." On the sides below the handles, as well as on the base, appears the Vantine trademark — the Japanese and what is assumed to be the Vantine flags crossed with a moon and star above and the word "trademark" below (mark #41). Since the jar would sit on a shelf to emit its aroma, and was pretty enough to be reused, it served to prolong the exposure of the company's name.

Advertising Premiums and Give-aways

Other companies also were taken in by the utility of these wares for advertising purposes, just as they were by Nippon porcelain and depression and carnival glass. Salt and pepper shakers and mustard jars were the most widely offered, probably because they were something almost everybody was sure to use on a daily basis. Tiddy's Home Furnishing Company was an up-and-coming business around 1919 and sold teas and coffees as well as household furnishings. Their promotional

[1]*National Cyclopedia of American Biography.* 1910: Vol. 14.

shakers read "Everything to Make Home Comfortable at Tiddy's Home Furnishing Co., 224-226 S. Oak Street, Mt. Carmel, PA" (Plate 74). C.D. Kenney, a well-known Baltimore department store, gave away shakers that read "Drink and Enjoy Kenny's Teas and Coffees, C.D. Kenney Co."

Hoover Furniture Company of Harrisburg, PA, gave away mustard pots bearing their company and town names (Plate 75) as did Horner's in Hagerstown, MD (Plate 76). Horner added the word "good" to qualify his furniture and apparently it was an apt description. In 1903, he opened the business in his home at 200 W. Jonathan St., Hagerstown. By 1908, it had been moved to 20 W. Franklin St. and expanded into 22 W. Franklin by 1915. The store was relocated to large quarters at 36-38 W. Franklin St. by 1919, by which time Mr. Horner had moved to 717 Oak Hill Ave.

Pat Cronin, reference librarian at the Washington County Free Library, provided an interesting observation about the various Horner locations. She noted that "Jonathan St. homes are small, with front steps right on the sidewalk; the Franklin St. address is a larger building, closer to the 'downtown' area; Oak Hill Avenue has very large, elegant, Victorian homes, with expansive front and back yards, so I would guess that the business was successful."

It is interesting to note that all of these advertising items bear a version of the Parasol pattern.

Montgomery Ward and Co.

Another retailer was a long-time fan of Geisha Girl Porcelain. From 1908 through the 1920's, Montgomery Ward and Company's *Pure Food Groceries* catalogs (Illus. 10-7 through 10-12) offered Geisha Girl Porcelain as a premium with the purchase of every five pounds of tea. The 1908 catalog offered "A Japanese Cup and Saucer of quaint design" in the following ad:

"Accept with our compliments the beautiful Japanese Tea Cup and Saucer contained in this package. They are of genuine Japanese manufacture and imported direct from Japan for our customers. Every canister of Gold Medal Tea contains one Japanese Tea Cup and Saucer suitable for use as ornament at home and very desirable for gifts to friends."

Doll's Tea Party

Catching the eye and winning the hearts of children was always a good way to drum up business, and at least a few stores carried "Doll's Tea Party" sets with the store name included as a part of the decoration. After all, what child wouldn't remind Mommy and Daddy to take her back to that great store where they got that terrific toy teaset! Hahne's set (Plate 77) is bottomstamped "NIPPON", reads "Hahne and Co., Doll's Tea Party" and depicts their former falling star logo. Unfortunately, the company has no records remaining regarding the issuance of this set.

The single cup (Plate 78) reads "Emery, Birel, Thayer Company, Kansas City, Doll's Tea Party, 1916". Bullene, Moore, Emery and Co. opened in 1892 and, according to old papers, purchased at least some of their wares from A.A. Vantine in New York, which they in turn sold at discount prices. At some point, the name was changed to Emery, Birel, Thayer, who gave a Doll's Tea Party every year between 1915 and 1953.

[2]*Kansas City Times*, November 26, 1938.

Girls aged twelve and under brought their favorite dolls to the store's special tea room where they were judged for uniqueness, costume, most distant origin, etc. All participants received a teacup as a rememberance of the event[2]. Though there is no specific evidence remaining from company records, it is plausible that the cup shown is exemplary of the ones used as prizes since it does carry a year mark.

Souvenir Items

Souvenir shops also found a use for Geisha Girl Porcelain. The gold-rimmed candy dish (Plate 79) has its heritage emblazoned across its middle. The Tuscarora Mountains span a wide range in Pennsylvania, cutting across four or five counties. The Lincoln Highway, renamed Route 30 in 1928, runs along the borders of two of these counties, Franklin and Fulton. Along this highway, four miles east of McConnellsburg and the same distance west of Fort Louden, is the Tuscarora Summit. There, in 1917, a man named Leslie Wallace Seylar opened a lunch room and novelty stand. Mr. Seylar was affectionately know as "Doc" because he also owned the town pharmacy.

The history of the piece is somehow made more special by knowing the history of its vendor. "Doc" Seylar's life is best explained in the eulogy that appeared November 11, 1937 in the *Fulton Democrat* of McConnellsburg, PA, as follows:

". . . Mr. Seylar was one of Fulton County's best known citizens and successful business men. He enjoyed a wide circle of friends and acquaintants, not only in his home community but throughout this and other states.

Leslie Wallace Seylar was born at Cove Gap in Franklin County, August 7, 1872 . . . As a young man he became steward in a hotel in Pittsburgh, Pa. He later entered the newspaper profession and was a reporter for papers in St. Louis, Mo., Dayton, Ohio and Chicago, Ill. While thus engaged he gained a wide experience and visited many parts of this country. Later he returned to his native home community and conducted the general store at Cove Gap. After several years he went to Atlantic City, N.J. where he engaged in the hotel business.

In 1901 he was united in marriage with Miss Rhetta Fisher of West Virginia who died in 1904. To this union there was one daughter . . .

On May 23, 1908 he was married to Estelle Logue, daughter of B.W. and Maria Daniels Logue and having bought the Dickson Drug Store in McConnellsburg, resided here ever since. He later erected the new building on the Lincoln Way where he conducted the Rexall Store. In 1917 he opened his lunch room and novelty stand on the top of the Tuscarora Mountain, being one of the first to open such a place of business along the Lincoln Highway. This latter place of business, especially during the summer months is no doubt one of the largest patronized places of its kind in this part of the country. Here Mr. Seylar was a congenial host to the thousands of tourists from all parts of the United States and here he had the opportunity to meet and entertain many prominent people. His stories and reminiscences and his gifted keen memory and ability to quote poetry made him a winsome personality.

In 1925 at the beginning of the first administration of Governor Gifford Pinchot, Mr. Seylar was appointed a member of the State Board of Commissioners and he served until his resignation in 1935. In his telegram to Mrs. Seylar, Mr. Pinchot on learning of Mr. Seylar's death, said, 'His service to Pennsylvania will long be remembered.' . . .

He is survived by Mrs. Seylar and son Joseph B. at home and his daughter . . . and an unusually large circle of friends, for one of his strongest characteristics was his winsome personality.

His funeral service . . . was one of the largest attended in recent years and the crowded church and the unusually large offerings of beautiful floral tributes bore testimony to the esteem in which he was held."

The postcards (Illus. 10-13, 10-14) depict "Doc" Seylar's Rest House; note the large word "Souvenirs" in the window above the Cola sign.

Young's Hotel in York Beach, ME, (circa 1899-1960's) and Boone Island in neighboring York chose a Geisha Girl Chinese Coin motif (Plate 80) into which they integrated some publicity. York Beach was a rural area in Maine which slowly grew into a summer resort after the Civil War. As early as the 1870's, rooming houses and later hotels were built along the beach area. York Beach and the lighthouse on Boone Island, ten miles off shore, served as a vacation spot through the 1920's and 1930's. Unfortunately, the area succumbed to the Depression and never recovered. It was largely taken over by the military during World War II because of its position on the shore. The hotel sat vacant for many years and was razed in the 1960's. The peak period for this area was between the turn of the century and the 1920's which coincides with the 1910's dating for the use of the Chinese Coin motif pattern.

A most amusing anecdote belongs to a little teapot (Plates 81-83) whose base is stamped "Cafe Martin, New York." The cafe was opened in New York City in 1899. Its owner was known as an innovator in his time for introducing Art Nouveau styling to the cafe and for allowing women entrance into a drinking establishment! Nothing like gaining publicity by being different. These tiny teapots were offered as a cute little bit of bric-a-brac to attract the female clientele. The author also has seen French tins of licorice drops from this cafe. After all, only a "naughty" woman would get caught with liquor on her breath. The Cafe Martin was closed down during Prohibition.

Geisha Girl Porcelain items used for advertising are scarce. As such, they are considered a valuable addition to any collection.

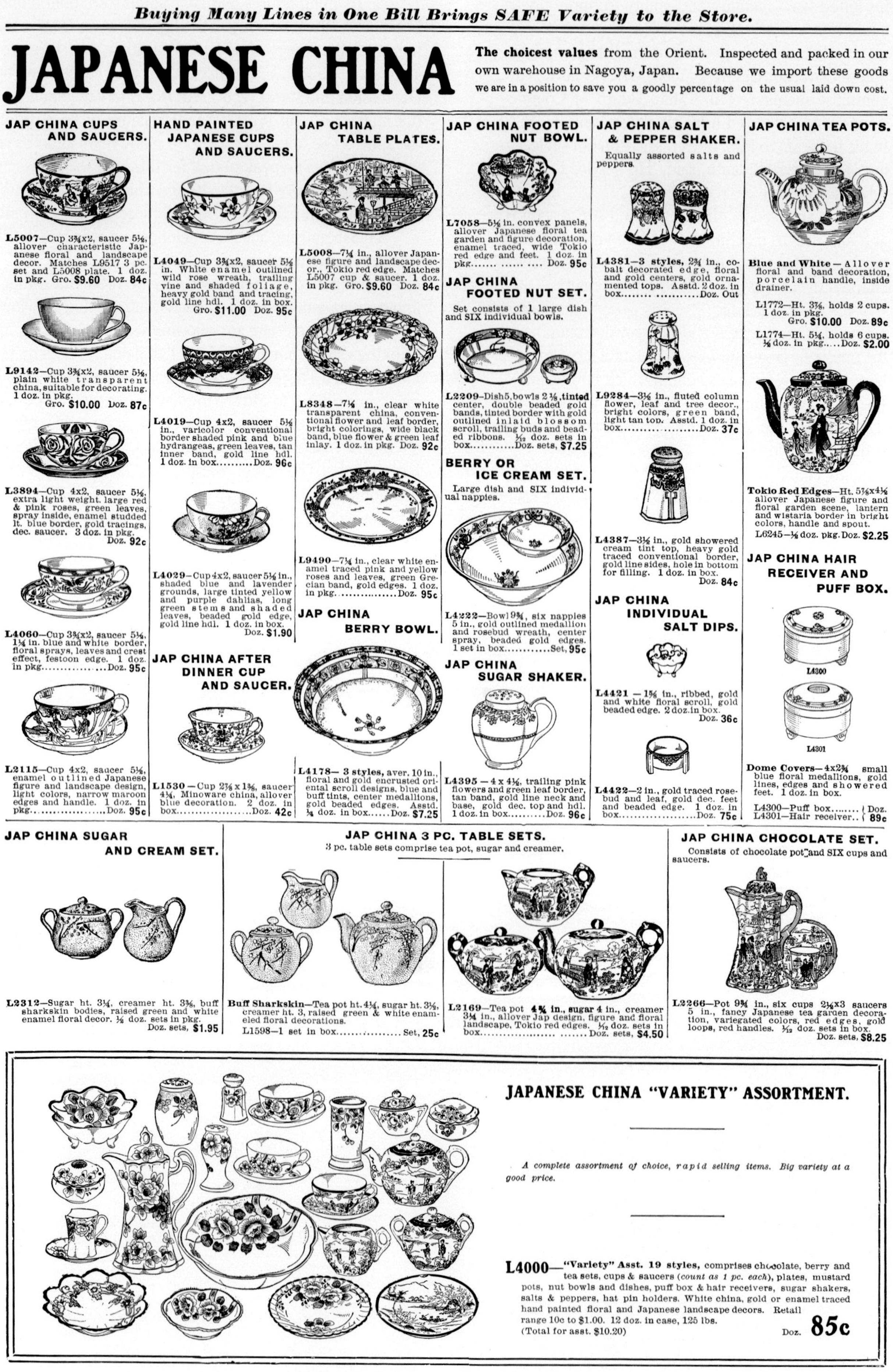

Buying Many Lines in One Bill Brings SAFE Variety to the Store.

JAPANESE CHINA

The choicest values from the Orient. Inspected and packed in our own warehouse in Nagoya, Japan. Because we import these goods we are in a position to save you a goodly percentage on the usual laid down cost.

JAP CHINA CUPS AND SAUCERS.

L5007—Cup 3¾x2, saucer 5½, allover characteristic Japanese floral and landscape decor. Matches L9517 3 pc. set and L5008 plate. 1 doz. in pkg. Gro. **$9.60** Doz. **84c**

L9142—Cup 3¾x2, saucer 5½, plain white transparent china, suitable for decorating. 1 doz. in pkg. Gro. **$10.00** Doz. **87c**

L3894—Cup 4x2, saucer 5½, extra light weight. large red & pink roses, green leaves, spray inside, enamel studded lt. blue border, gold tracings, dec. saucer. 3 doz. in pkg. Doz. **92c**

L4060—Cup 3¾x2, saucer 5½, 1¼ in. blue and white border, floral sprays, leaves and crest effect, festoon edge. 1 doz. in pkg.................Doz. **95c**

L2115—Cup 4x2, saucer 5½, enamel outlined Japanese figure and landscape design, light colors, narrow maroon edges and handle. 1 doz. in pkg...................Doz. **95c**

HAND PAINTED JAPANESE CUPS AND SAUCERS.

L4049—Cup 3¾x2, saucer 5½ in. White enamel outlined wild rose wreath, trailing vine and shaded foliage, heavy gold band and tracing, gold line hdl. 1 doz. in box. Gro. **$11.00** Doz. **95c**

L4019—Cup 4x2, saucer 5½ in., varicolor conventional border shaded pink and blue hydrangeas, green leaves, tan inner band, gold line hdl. 1 doz. in box..........Doz. **96c**

L4029—Cup 4x2, saucer 5½ in., shaded blue and lavender grounds, large tinted yellow and purple dahlias, long green stems and shaded leaves, beaded gold edge, gold line hdl. 1 doz. in box. Doz. **$1.90**

JAP CHINA AFTER DINNER CUP AND SAUCER.

L1530—Cup 2⅞x1⅜, saucer 4¼, Minoware china, allover blue decoration. 2 doz. in box....................Doz. **42c**

JAP CHINA TABLE PLATES.

L5008—7¼ in., allover Japanese figure and landscape decor., Tokio red edge. Matches L5007 cup & saucer. 1 doz. in pkg. Gro. **$9.60** Doz. **84c**

L8348—7¼ in., clear white transparent china, conventional flower and leaf border, bright colorings, wide black band, blue flower & green leaf inlay. 1 doz. in pkg. Doz. **92c**

L9490—7¼ in., clear white enamel traced pink and yellow roses and leaves, green Grecian band, gold edges. 1 doz. in pkg.................Doz. **95c**

JAP CHINA BERRY BOWL.

L4178— 3 styles, aver. 10 in., floral and gold encrusted oriental scroll designs, blue and buff tints, center medallions, gold beaded edges. Asstd. ¼ doz. in box......Doz. **$7.25**

JAP CHINA FOOTED NUT BOWL.

L7058—5½ in. convex panels, allover Japanese floral tea garden and figure decoration, enamel traced, wide Tokio red edge and feet. 1 doz. in pkg....... .... Doz. **95c**

JAP CHINA FOOTED NUT SET.

Set consists of 1 large dish and SIX individual bowls.

L2209—Dish 5, bowls 2⅛, **tinted** center, double beaded gold bands, tinted border with gold outlined inlaid blossom scroll, trailing buds and beaded ribbons. 1/12 doz. sets in box............Doz. sets, **$7.25**

BERRY OR ICE CREAM SET.

Large dish and SIX individual nappies.

L4222—Bowl 9¾, six nappies 5 in., gold outlined medallion and rosebud wreath, center spray, beaded gold edges. 1 set in box............Set, **95c**

JAP CHINA SUGAR SHAKER.

L4395—4 x 4½, trailing pink flowers and green leaf border, tan band, gold line neck and base, gold dec. top and hdl. 1 doz. in box..........Doz. **96c**

JAP CHINA SALT & PEPPER SHAKER.

Equally assorted salts and peppers.

L4381—3 styles, 2¾ in., cobalt decorated edge, floral and gold centers, gold ornamented tops. Asstd. 2 doz. in box........ ....Doz. Out

L9284—3½ in., fluted column flower, leaf and tree decor., bright colors, green band, light tan top. Asstd. 1 doz. in box...................Doz. **37c**

L4387—3½ in., gold showered cream tint top, heavy gold traced conventional border, gold line sides, hole in bottom for filling. 1 doz. in box. Doz. **84c**

JAP CHINA INDIVIDUAL SALT DIPS.

L4421 — 1⅝ in., ribbed, gold and white floral scroll, gold beaded edge. 2 doz. in box. Doz. **36c**

L4422—2 in., gold traced rosebud and leaf, gold dec. feet and beaded edge. 1 doz. in box...................Doz. **75c**

JAP CHINA TEA POTS.

Blue and White—Allover floral and band decoration, porcelain handle, inside drainer.

L1772—Ht. 3⅞, holds 2 cups. 1 doz. in pkg. Gro. **$10.00** Doz. **89c**

L1774—Ht. 5¼, holds 6 cups. ½ doz. in pkg.....Doz. **$2.00**

Tokio Red Edges—Ht. 5⅞x4½ allover Japanese figure and floral garden scene, lantern and wistaria border in bright colors, handle and spout.

L6245—½ doz. pkg. Doz. **$2.25**

JAP CHINA HAIR RECEIVER AND PUFF BOX.

L4300

L4301

Dome Covers—4x2¾ small blue floral medallions, gold lines, edges and showered feet. 1 doz. in box.

L4300—Puff box........ } Doz.
L4301—Hair receiver.. } **89c**

JAP CHINA SUGAR AND CREAM SET.

L2312—Sugar ht. 3¼, creamer ht. 3⅜, buff sharkskin bodies, raised green and white enamel floral decor. ½ doz. sets in pkg. Doz. sets, **$1.95**

JAP CHINA 3 PC. TABLE SETS.

3 pc. table sets comprise tea pot, sugar and creamer.

Buff Sharkskin—Tea pot ht. 4¼, sugar ht. 3½, creamer ht. 3, raised green & white enameled floral decorations.

L1598—1 set in box.................Set, **25c**

L2169—Tea pot **4¾ in., sugar 4** in., creamer 3¼ in., allover Jap design, figure and floral landscape, Tokio red edges. 1/12 doz. sets in box.................. ....Doz. sets, **$4.50**

JAP CHINA CHOCOLATE SET.

Consists of chocolate pot and SIX cups and saucers.

L2266—Pot 9¾ in., six cups 2⅛x3 saucers 5 in., fancy Japanese tea garden decoration, variegated colors, red edges, gold loops, red handles. 1/12 doz. sets in box. Doz. sets, **$8.25**

JAPANESE CHINA "VARIETY" ASSORTMENT.

A complete assortment of choice, rapid selling items. Big variety at a good price.

L4000—**"Variety" Asst. 19 styles,** comprises chocolate, berry and tea sets, cups & saucers (*count as 1 pc. each*), plates, mustard pots, nut bowls and dishes, puff box & hair receivers, sugar shakers, salts & peppers, hat pin holders. White china, gold or enamel traced hand painted floral and Japanese landscape decors. Retail range 10c to $1.00. 12 doz. in case, 125 lbs. (Total for asst. $10.20) Doz. **85c**

ILLUS. 10-1. Page from 1916 Butler Bros. catalog.

AFTER DINNER CUPS AND SAUCERS —Continued.

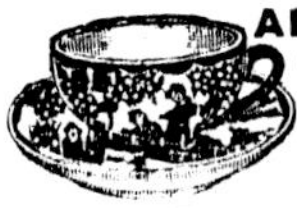

L1535—2⅞x1⅝, saucer 4⅝ allover flowers and figures, red band edges. 1 doz. in pkg. Doz. 84c

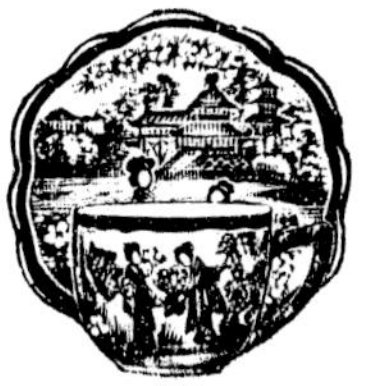

L5004—2¾x2⅛, saucer 4⅞, transparent china, allover Japanese floral and scenic decorations in natural colors. Tokio red band edge and handle. doz. in pkg. Doz. 95c

BREAD AND BUTTER PLATES.

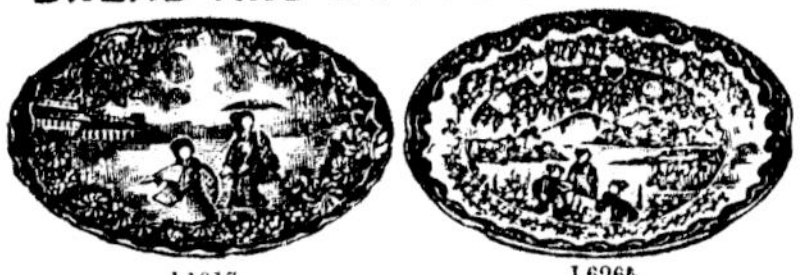

L1617 L6265

L1617—6 in. fluted flange, Japanese girls and landscapes, colored floral borders, Tokio red edge. 1 doz. in pkg .... Doz. 79c

L6265—6 in., china, cobalt and gold edge, Japanese figure and landscape. 1 doz. in pkg. Doz. 96c

TABLE PLATES.

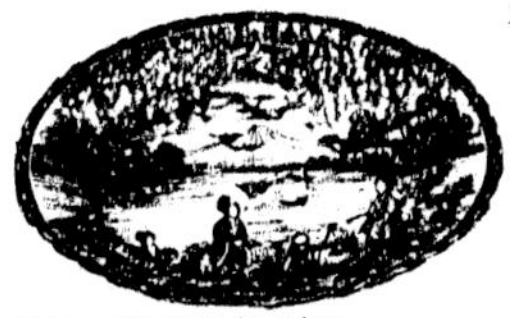

L6276—8⅛ in., transparent china, twist flut ed flange, color ed Japanese landscape and mountain view with half framing of flowers, gold ornament ed Tokio red edge. ½ doz. in pkg. ....Doz. $2.15

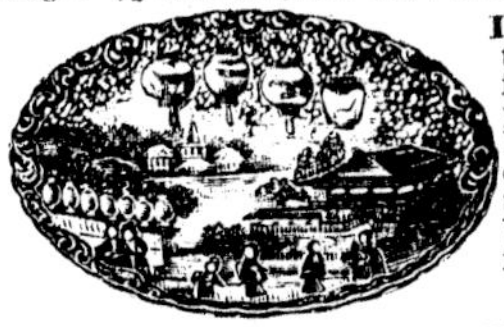

L6277—8⅛ in., thin china, gold illuminated temple, pagoda and landscape scenery, gold scroll traced cobalt blue edge. ½ doz. in pkg. Doz. $2.25

CAKE PLATE.

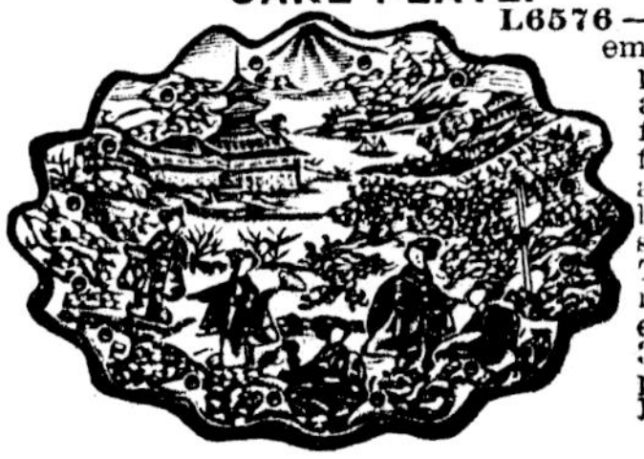

L6576—11 in. embossed perforated flange, flowers and landscape, Tokio red edge. 3 in pkg. Each, 36c

MUSTARD POT.

Each with spoon.

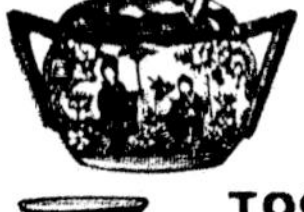

L6190—3x3, ribbed Japanese decoration, Tokio red edge and handles. 1 doz. in pkg............ .Doz. 85c

TOOTH PICK HOLDER.

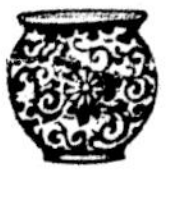

L1737—Ht. 2¼, vase shape, allover blue and white Japanese decoration. 1 doz. in pkg....Doz. 25c

EGG CUPS.

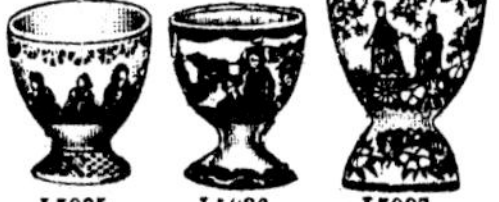

L5035 L5036 L5037

L5035—2 x 2⅛ in., blue Japanese figures. Doz. 25c

L5036—1⅞x2⅛, in., allover figures and landscape, red edge. 1 doz. in pkg. Doz. 32c

L5037—2¾x3⅛, footed, allover picture decoration, Tokio red and gold edge ......Doz. 75c

HAIR RECEIVER.

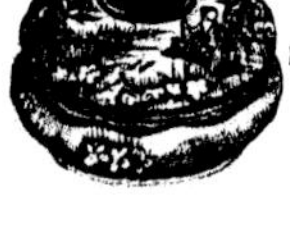

L6211—3⅜x2¾, gold relieved landscape and lantern decorations, gold traced Tokio red edges. Doz. $1.75

AFTER DINNER CUPS AND SAUCERS.

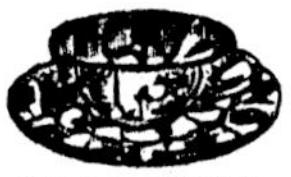

L1529—3x1⅛, saucer 4¼, Mino china, allover pale green Japanese decorations. 1 doz. in pkg........Doz. Out

A LEADER.

Direct importation at special price.

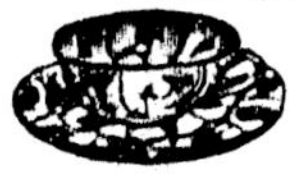

L1530 Cup 3x1¾, saucer 4¾ in., Mino ware, all over blue decoration. 1 doz. in pkg. Doz. 39c

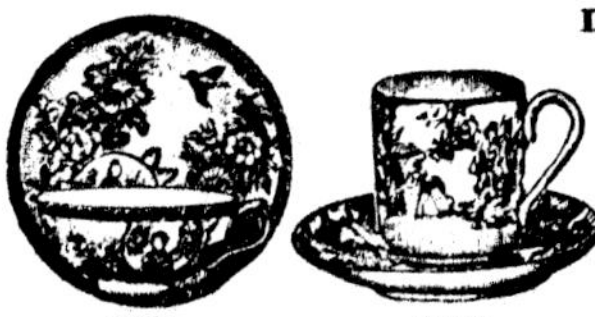

L1531 L1534

L1531—3x1¾, saucer 4¼, Japanese scenes and figures, asstd. colors, Tokio red border and handle. 1 doz. in pkg.................................Doz. 65c

L1534—Cup 2⅞x2¼, Tokio red edges, allover colored Japanese decoration, gold lined handle. 1 doz. in pkg............. Doz. 79c

CONDENSED MILK JARS.

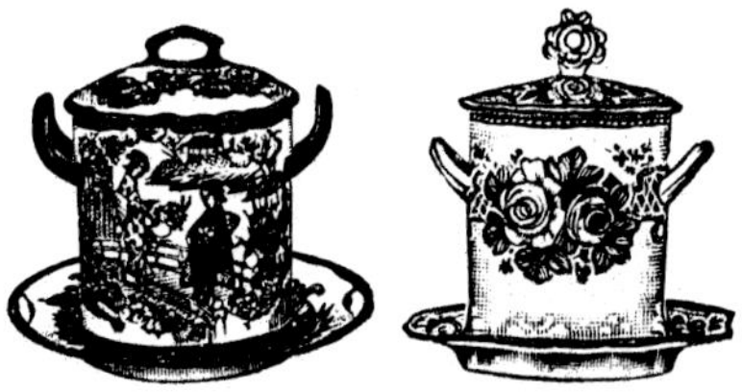

L6477 L6478

L6477—3⅜x5, saucer 6¼, Japanese picture decorated, Tokio red edges, handles and knob. 3 in pkg......................Each, 33c

L6478—Ht. 5½ in., saucer 6 in., blue tinted surface, rose clusters sides and cover, gold beaded edges and ornamented handles and cover. 3 in pkg......................Each, 39c

SUGAR AND CREAM SET.

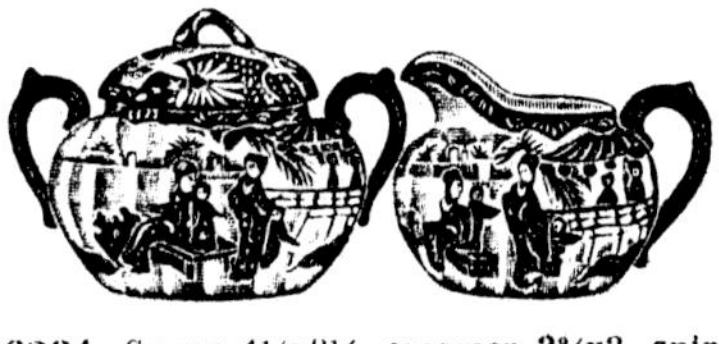

L6234—Sugar 4¼x3¼, creamer 3¾x3, spiral ribbed, gold ornamented Kitani tea garden decoration, gold and maroon edges, handles and knobs. 3 sets in pkg............Set, 50c

CHOCOLATE SETS.

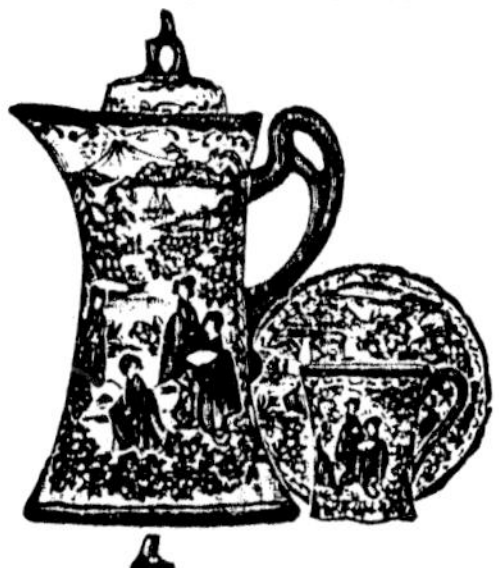

Consists of chocolate pot and SIX cups and saucers. 1 set in pkg.

L6290—9½ in. pot, cups 2½x2⅞, saucers 4¾, ribbed panel, allover Japanese scene in colors, Tokio red edges, inner gold scrolls. 1 set in pkg. Set, $1.25

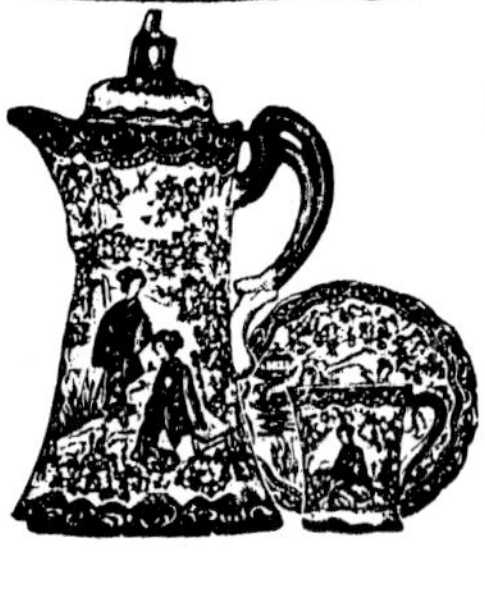

L6291—9¾ in. pot, cups 2⅛x2¾, saucers 4¾, paneled, Geisha, landscape and cherry blossoms gold traced, cobalt edges, beaded enamel band, cobalt handle and knob. Set, $1.50

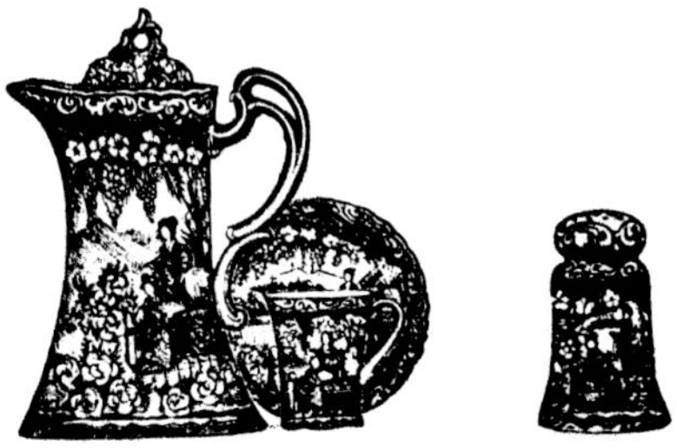

L6348 L6349

L6348, Chocolate Set—9¼ in. tapering column pot, six 2⅛x3 cups and saucers. 1 set in pkg.............................Set, $1.75

L6349, Salt and Pepper—3⅛ in. ribbed, column shape, with corks. 1 doz. in box, asstd. Doz. 65c

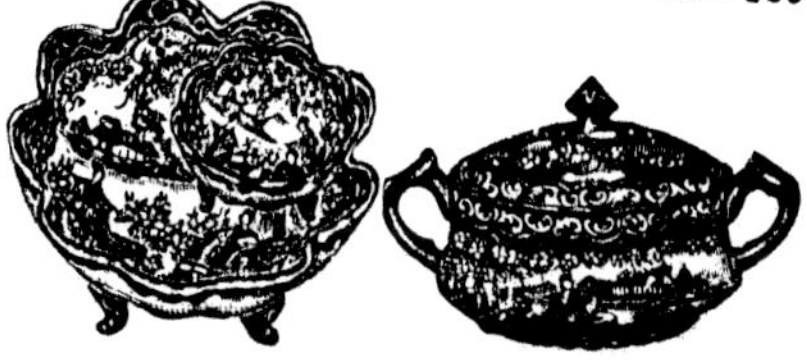

L6350 L6351

L6350, Footed Nut Set—5¾ in. bowl, 6 three in. serving dishes. 1 set in pkg....Set, 65c

L6351, Cracker Jar—6x4, low shape fancy handles. 2 in pkg.... ....Each, 50c

ILLUS. 10-2. 1906 Butler Bros. offerings include examples of Flower Gathering, Garden Bench, Geisha Face, Battledore and Long Stemmed Peony patterns.

CUPS AND SAUCERS.

Transparent China.

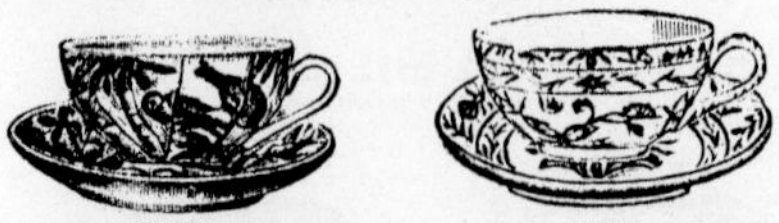

L1550 L1549

L1550 — Large size, cup 3¾x2, saucer 5⅛, transparent, rich allover blue print decorations. 1 doz. in pkg. .... Doz. **$1.15**

L1549—3¾x2, saucer 5⅛ selected allover blue decoration. 1 doz. in pkg....... Doz. **$1.25**

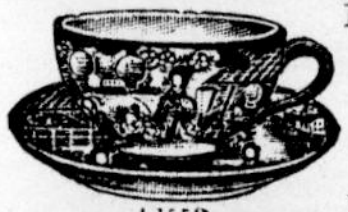

L1553

L1553—3¾x2, saucer 5⅛, selected, allover girls and tea garden, gold and Tokio red edge. **Matches L1628 plate.** 1 doz. in pkg......... Doz. **$1.32**

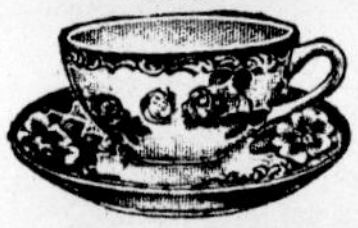

L6128 — 3¾x2, saucer 5⅛, 3 elaborate floral and foliage decorations with outlining ornamental colored scroll, dark green and maroon band edges, gold line handles. 1 doz. in pkg. asstd.......... Doz. **$1.35**

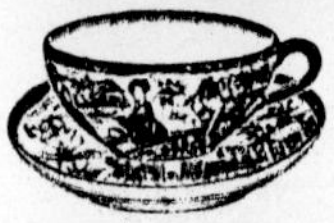

L6129—4⅜x2, saucer 5⅛, characteristic allover Japanese figure and landscape enamel and gold traced Tokio red edges and handle. 1 doz. in pkg........... Doz. **$1.75**

L5015—Cup 3¾x2, saucer 5⅛, fluted inside decoration in colors and gold, gold traced Tokio red edges and handles, outer sprays. Matches 6566 plate..... .... Doz. **$1.95**

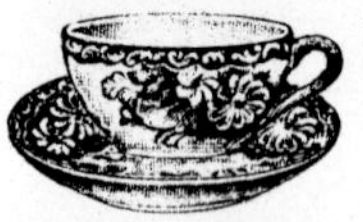

L6136 — 3¾x2, saucer 5⅛, selected transparent china, 2 tone chrysanthemums with gold and green foliage in triple spray design all around, gold scroll ornamented cobalt blue edges and handle. 1 doz. in pkg ..... Doz. **$1.75**

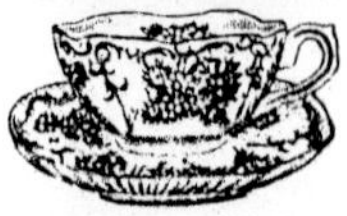

L6567 — 3¾x2¼, saucer 5⅛, fluted, pink and green bouquets, gold sprays and scroll border, gold striped edges, base and handle. 1 doz. in pkg. ..... Doz. **$1.80**

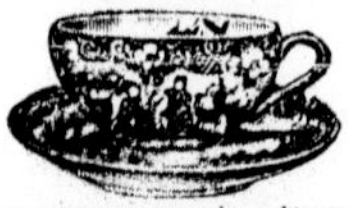

L6131 — 3¾x2, saucer 5⅛, selected transparent china, island, lake and mountain scene Japanese figures in the foreground, attractive colorings, gold striped maroon panels alternating with floral bouquets in border designs, gold decorated nile green edges. 1 doz. in pkg........... Doz. **$1.87**

L6132 — 3⅞x2, saucer 5⅛, transparent china, tripe floral clusters with leaves alternating with gold vines and flowers, gold ornamented cobalt blue edges and handle, spray inside. 1 doz. in pkg......... Doz. **$1.95**

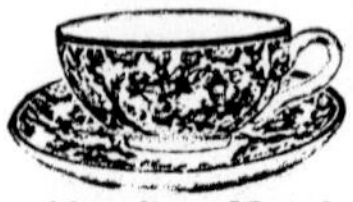

L6138—3¾x2, saucer 5⅛, twin tinted floral and foliage medallions with gold sprays, embossed gold half circle divisions, ornamental green border, gold band edges and handle. **Matches L6273 plate.** 1 doz. in pkg.......................... Doz. **$2.20**

AFTER DINNER CUPS AND SAUCERS.

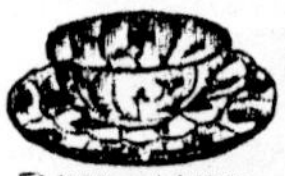

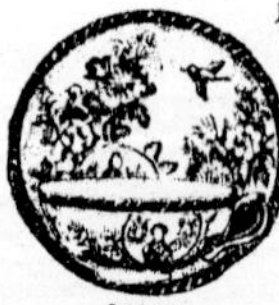

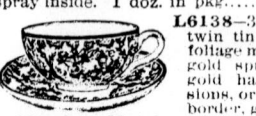

L1529 and L1530 L1531

L1529—3x1⅛, saucer 4¼, Mino china, allover pale green Japanese decorations. 1 doz. in pkg. Doz. **39c**

L1530—3x1⅜, saucer 4¼ in., Mino ware, allover blue decoration. 1 doz. in pkg............. Doz. **42c**

L1531—3x1⅜, saucer 4¼, Japanese scenes, and figures, asstd. colors, Tokio red border and handle. 1 doz. in pkg. .... Doz. **65c**

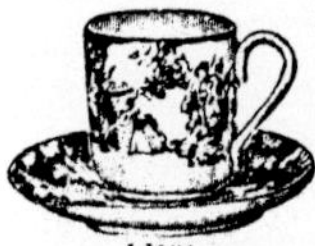

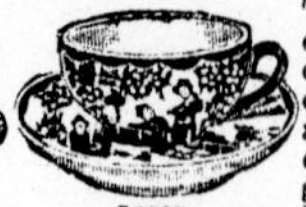

L1534 L1535

L1534—2⅞x2¼, saucer 4¾, Tokio red edges, allover colored Japanese decoration, gold lined handle. 1 doz. in pkg............................ Doz. **84c**

L1535—2⅞x1⅝, saucer 4⅜, allover flowers and figures, red band edges. 1 doz. in pkg. Doz. **87c**

JAPANESE CHINA CHOCOLATE POT.

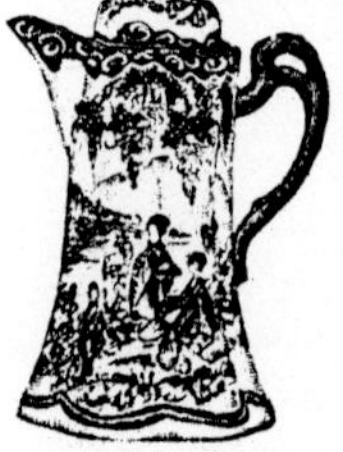

L5110—Ht. 9⅛, convex paneled, gold decorated Tokio red edges, handles and spout, Japanese figure and landscape decoration gold illuminated. 1 in pkg. Each, **50c**

SALAD OR BERRY BOWLS.

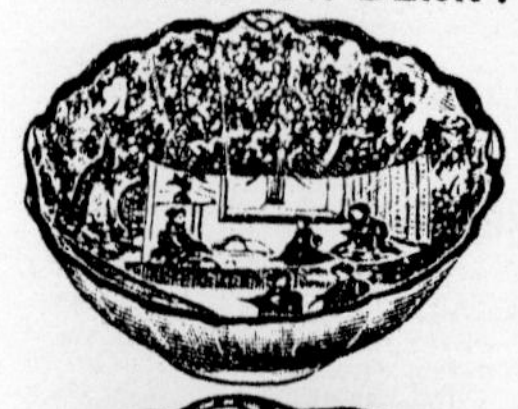

L6152—8¾ in., deep fluted, Geisha dancers, garlanded with flowers, gold ornamented pale green edge. 3 in pkg. Doz. **$4.00**

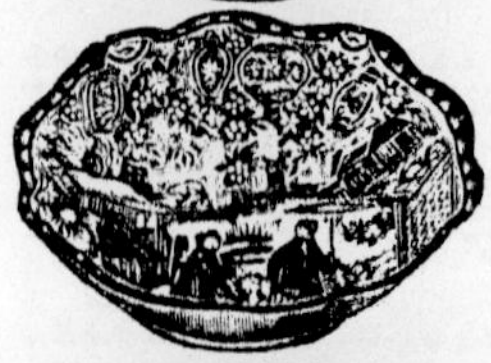

L7102—8¾in., scalloppanels, floral landscape and figures in tints, enamel traced, Tokio red edge. ¼ doz. in pkg. Each, **33c**

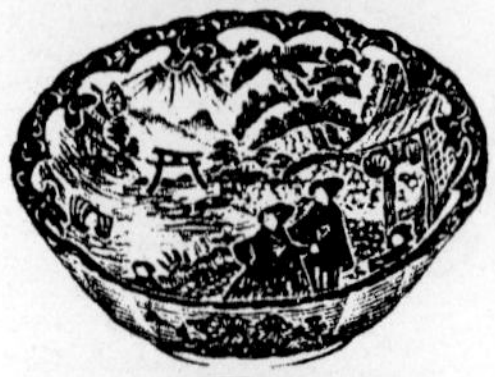

L7103—8¾ in., garden and landscape, life colors, gold ornamented cobalt edge, colored floral sprays. 3 in pkg. Each, **39c**

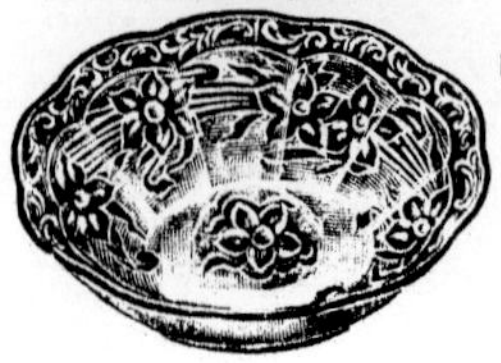

L7104 — 8½ in., embossed scallop panels, lt. blue ground, flower and leaf wreath, spray on tan center, **gold wreath** on cobalt edge. 1 in pkg. Each, **39c**

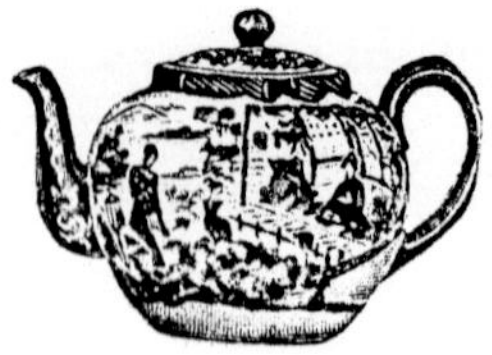

L7294 — 5½ in., allover bold illuminated **bright Japanese figure and floral landscape**, gold ornamented Tokio red edged handle and spout. Doz. **$4.25**

"SANSUI" DECORATED JAPANESE CHINA.

Transparent white china, attractive Japanese garden, on land and water scene background, floral wreath framing, cobalt blue edges decorated in gold.

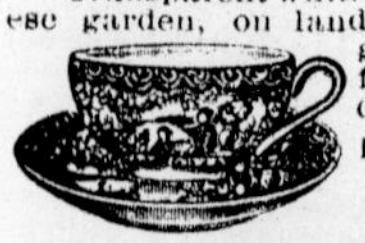

L6340, Cup and Saucer —Tea size, 3⅞x2, saucer 5⅛. ½ doz. in pkg. Doz. **$1.95**

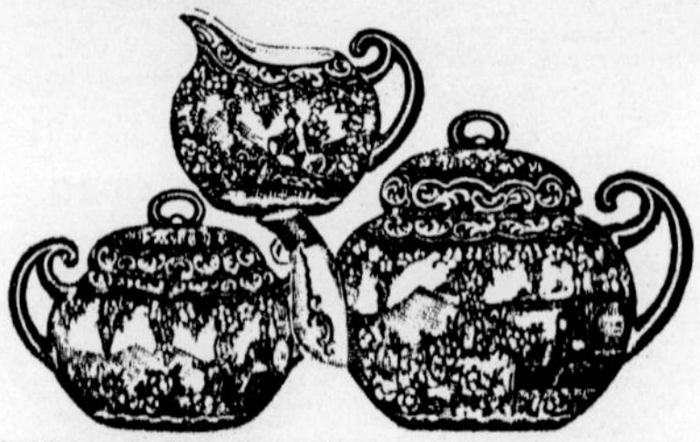

L6341, 3 Pc. Set—Teapot 5x5⅛, covered sugar 3¾x4¾, creamer 3¾x3¼, ribbed, melon shaped. 1 set in pkg... .... Set, **85c**

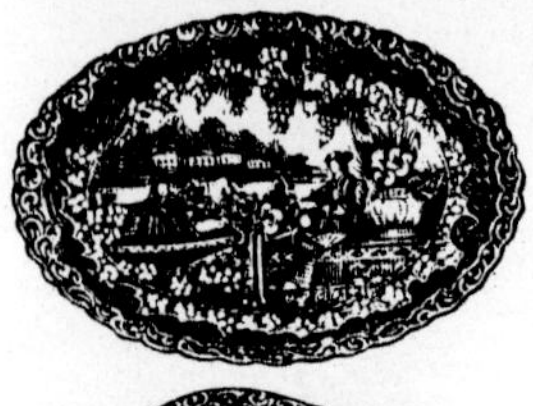

L6343, Table Plate—7⅛ in. fluted flange. ½ doz. in pkg. Doz. **$1.85**

L6342, Table Plate—8⅛ in. fluted edge. ½ doz. in pkg. Doz. **$2.25**

L6344, Spoon Tray—7¾x5¼, fancy shape, open handle, 3 in pkg. Each, **25c**

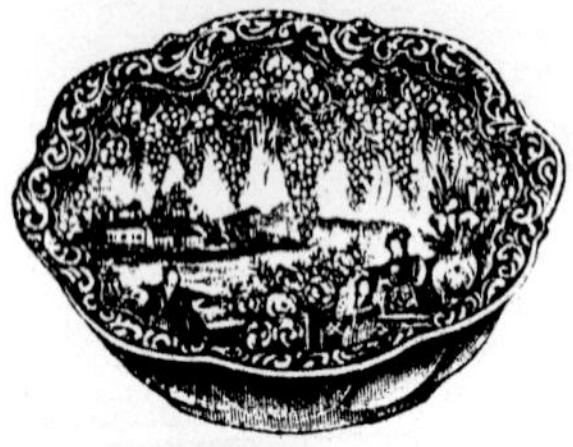

L6345, Footed Salad Bowl 10 in. 2 in pkg. Each, **69c**

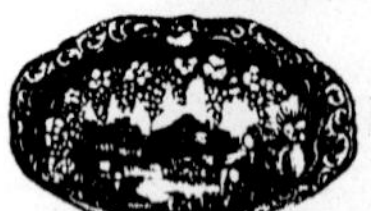

L6346, Sauce Dish—5⅛ in. ½ doz. in pkg. Doz. **$1.35**

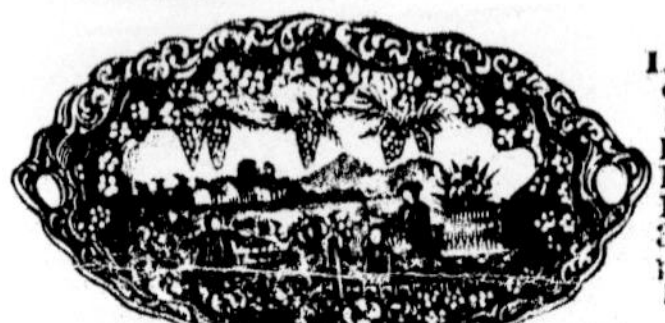

L6347, Open HandleCake Plate—10⅛ in. 3 in pkg. Ea. **65c**

ILLUS. 10-3. Left Column: Geisha Face and Garden Bench samples from a 1910 Butler Bros. catalog. Remainder is from 1911 catalog, including: Middle: Inside Teahouse, Torii, Flute and Koto patterned items. Right: *Sansui* translates to "hills and streams, landscape, scenery", certainly appropriate to the ornately decorated Geisha Girl Porcelain items depicted. Bottom: Entire lunch set in Servant with Sack pattern.

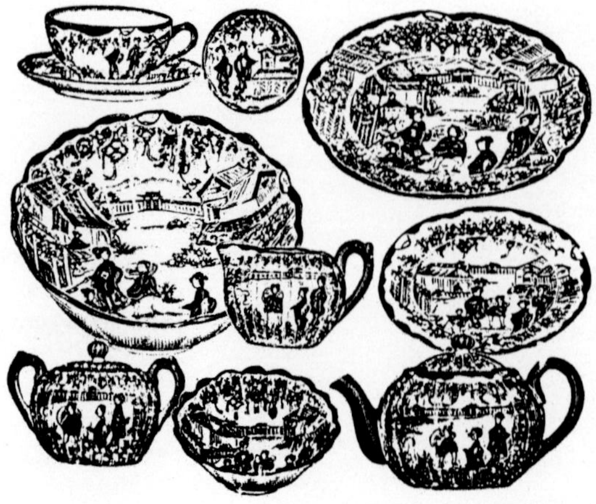

JAPANESE CHINA TEA OR LUNCH SET.

L101 Transparent white china, allover Japanese figure and landscape decoration, floral and lantern wreath framing, gold ornamented Tokio red edges and handles. Set consists:

1 only teapot 5x4½
1 " sugar 4x3⅝
1 " creamer 3⅞x3.
1 " 9 in. berry bowl.
6 " cups and saucers, 3¾x2 in. cups, 5 in. saucers
6 " 4⅜ in. sauce dishes
6 " 3¾ in. ind. butter plates
6 " 6¼ in. bread and butter plates
6 " 8⅛ in. table plates
Total 34 pcs. in case. Set, **$4.25**

SALT AND PEPPER SHAKERS.

Each with cork. 1 dz. box, 6 salts, 6 peppers.

L7032—3 in., 2 styles Japanese scene, floral border, Tokio red top and base.......Doz. **32c**

L6181—3¼x2⅝, allover Japanese decoration cobalt top & base, gold ornamented.
....................Doz. **42c**

L7743—2 styles, 3⅝ in., ribbed, lt. green tints, current and grape decors., shaded green foliage, gold ornamented cobalt band, gold decorated top...........Doz. **45c**

L7165—3⅜ in., paneled, pastel tints, cherry trees, gold line neck and base...........Doz. **69c**

L8185—3 in., hexagon, clear white china, gold outlined pink roses and leaves, beaded gold scrolls, gold decorated top and line base.
....................Doz. **85c**

JAP TEA POT.

L6245—Ht. 5⅝, allover Japanese figure and floral garden scene, lantern and wistaria border in bright colors. Tokio red edges, hdl. and spout, glazed inside. ⅙ doz. pkg. Doz. **$2.25**

19 STYLES JAP CHINA ASSORTMENT.

Made up in Japan from merchandise especially selected for the purpose, all fresh, attractive merchandise, no odds and ends in these lots. You get a big variety of class goods with very moderate investment and you avoid the trouble of selecting.

L1000—Variety Asst. 19 styles, comprises chocolate, berry and tea sets, cups and saucers, plates, mustard pot, nut bowls, sugar shakers, hair receivers, puff boxes, salts and peppers and hat pin holders. Allover Japanese landscape decorations, Tokio red edges, hand painted floral designs, gold ornamented, cups and saucers count as 1 pc. Retails from 10 to 50c each. 1/12 doz. case...........Complete. **$10.68** Doz. **89c**

ILLUS. 10-4. Top Left: From 1913 Butler Bros. catalog. Top Right: 1914 Butler Bros. catalog offerings included Geisha in Sampan, Child Reaching for Butterfly. Bottom: 1915 Butler Bros. catalog offered a Parasol C Tea Service in their "variety pack," a Child Reaching for Butterfly plate and a Parasol mustard jar.

"VARIETY" ASSORTMENT.

L3000—"Variety" Asst. 19 styles, comprises chocolate, berry and tea sets, cups and saucers, plates, mustard pots, nut bowls and dishes, bonbon boxes and hair receivers, sugar shakers, salts and peppers and hatpin holders. White china, gold or enamel traced hand painted floral and Japanese landscape decors. Cup and saucer count as 1 pc. Retail range 10c to $1.00. (Total for asst. **$9.00**) 1/12 doz. in case, 125 lbs. Doz. **75c**

TABLE PLATE

L5008—7¼ in., allover Japanese figure and landscape decor. Tokio red edge. Matches L007 cup & saucer and L9517, 3 pc. set. 1 doz. in pkg......Doz. **89c**
Gro. **$10.00**

MUSTARD POTS.

L2602—3¾ in., white enamel traced Japanese landscape decoration, maroon edges, handles and knob. 1 doz. in pkg. with spoons......Doz. **75c**

47

ILLUS. 10-6. 1907 postcard depicting Vantine's New York Main Floor — View from Balcony Tea Room.

ILLUS. 10-5. 1910 postcard depicting Vantine's Oriental Store Curio Room.

PLATE 65. Celery Dish, Vantine's Blue, mark #42.

PLATE 66. Upright Spooner, Vantine's Blue, mark #42.

PLATE 67. Puff Box, Flower Gathering C, mark #70.

PLATE 68. Vantine's Toilet Cream Jar, Cloud B.

PLATE 69. Vantine's Toilet Cream Jar, reverse, Cloud B; note crossed flags trademark on lid.

PLATE 70. Red Vantine's Sachet Jar, front, note company emblazoned on front of jar.

PLATE 71. Vantine's Sachet Jar, Fan C and scenic reserves on reverse.

PLATE 72. Blue Vantine's Sachet Jar, front.

PLATE 73. Vantine's Sachet Jar, reverse with Checkboard pattern.

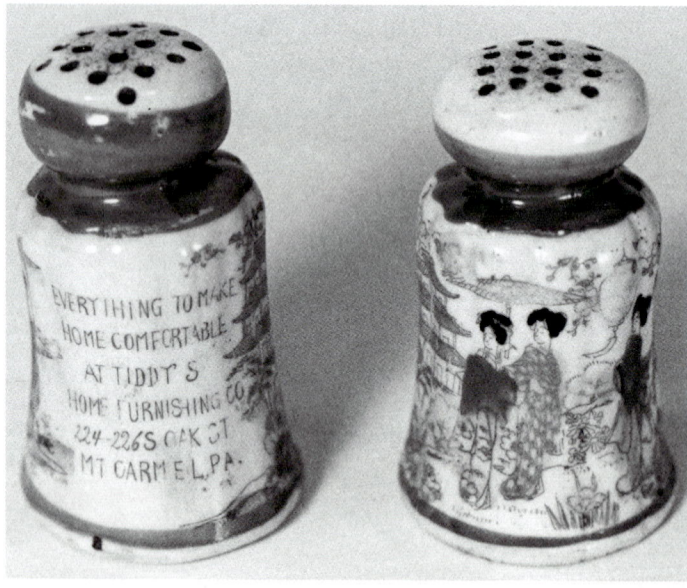

PLATE 74. Salt and Pepper Shakers, Parasol E, from Tiddy's Home Furnishing Co., Mt. Carmel, PA.

PLATE 75. Mustard Jar, Parasol L, from Hoover Furniture Co., Harrisburg, PA.

PLATE 76. Mustard Jar with spoon, Parasol L, from Horner's Good Furniture, Hagerstown, MD.

FINE TEAS

Our Very Finest—
TriangleClub Teas

Lower Prices
Still further price reductions will be found in this issue on all our teas. In buying our teas direct from the best tea-growing countries or from the leading importers and selling direct to you, we can always save you money and give you better, more fragrant teas than usually offered. Order the five pound boxes containing the chinaware.

India and Ceylon (Black)
The perfume of the Orient is released when you brew a cup of this delicious tea. Whether it is made heavy or light the exceptional flavor is still there.
A7750—1 pound	$	.74
A7752—3 pounds		2.19
4A11452—5 pounds		3.63

Pan-Fired Japan (Green)
A very high-grade short tender leaf tea, the finest leaves picked from the top of the bush. Draws light and clear.
A7710—1 pound	$	.84
A7712—3 pounds		2.49
4A11448—5 pounds		4.12

Basket-Fired Japan
Specially selected grade of very first crop Basket-fired Uncolored Japan Tea. Draws a clear, pale liquor.
A7714—1 pound	$	.84
A7716—3 pounds		2.49
4A11449—5 pounds		4.12

Formosa Oolong (Dark Brown)
A tippy toasty brown leaf. Fragrant and delicious. A selection from the most famous crop of Oolong from the Island of Formosa.
A7761—1 pound	$	.74
A7773—3 pounds		2.19
4A11451—5 pounds		3.63

Moyune Gunpowder (Green)
The finest grade of Gunpowder tea that grows. Draws fragrant and mild.
A7791—1 pound	$	.74
A7785—3 pounds		2.19
4A11454—5 pounds		3.63

Oolong and Gunpowder
A superfine mixture of very fancy Formosa Oolong and Moyune Gunpowder.
A70—1 pound	$	.74
A72—3 pounds		2.19
4A11457—5 pounds		3.63

English Breakfast (Black)
Genuine Russian Caravan Tea, from the Keemun district. This tea will appeal to lovers of black teas. A rich amber colored brew.
A7720—1 pound	$	.74
A7722—3 pounds		2.19
4A11478—5 pounds		3.63

This 7-inch Japanese hand-painted plate packed in 5-lb. cartons of Triangle Club Brand Tea.

Oriental Brand Teas
3 pounds, $1.62

Pan-Fired Japan (Green)
Generally known as Sun-dried Japan. Short, fine leaf. Draws light liquor. Mild, delicate flavor.
A710—1 pound	$	.55
A712—3 pounds		1.62
4A11432—5 pounds		2.68

Basket-Fired Japan (Green)
Oriental Basket-Fired Japan tea continues to be one of our biggest sellers. You will find it to be distinctly better than other Basket-fired teas offered at a higher price.
A720—1 pound	$	.55
A722—3 pounds		1.62
4A11433—5 pounds		2.68

Formosa Oolong
Brown, curly leaf. Very fragrant, light amber liquor. If you are accustomed to this variety you will enjoy a cup of this tea.
A730—1 pound	$	.55
A732—3 pounds		1.62
4A11436—5 pounds		2.68

Orange Pekoe Ceylon (Black)
A Short, Black, Curly Leaf. Draws a light amber liquor—most delicious flavor. A much finer tea than the price indicates.
A740—1 pound	$	.55
A742—3 pounds		1.62
4A11439—5 pounds		2.68

Gunpowder (Green)
Hoochow Gunpowder. Uniform leaf. Excellent quality, light liquor.
A750—1 pound	$	.55
A752—3 pounds		1.62
4A11435—5 pounds		2.68

English Breakfast (Black)
Small, curly leaf. Draws amber liquor. Fine, rich flavor.
A760—1 pound	$	.55
A762—3 pounds		1.62
4A11437—5 pounds		2.68

This Japanese hand-painted cup and saucer packed in 5-lb. boxes of Oriental and Arcadia Brand Teas.

Arcadia Brand Teas
3 pounds, $1.32

Basket-Fired Japan (Green)
Long Green Leaf. Draws light liquor. Very mild.
A780—1 pound	$	.45
A782—3 pounds		1.32
4A11441—5 pounds		2.17

Formosa Oolong
Curly Brown Leaf. Draws a light amber liquor. Sweet flavor.
A790—1 pound	$	.45
A792—3 pounds		1.32
4A11445—5 pounds		2.17

Gunpowder (Green)
Round Green Leaf. Draws pale liquor. Mild and sweet.
A5571—1 lb.	$	.45
A5573—3 lbs.		1.32
4A11444—5 lbs.		2.17

Pan-Fired Japan (Green)
Formerly known as Sun-Dried. Short green leaf. Looks and tastes like a tea above the average quality.
A770—1 pound	$	.45
A772—3 pounds		1.32
4A11440—5 pounds		2.17

English Breakfast (Black)
Short, Curly Black Leaf draws deep, amber liquor. Strong, rich flavor.
A5561—1 pound	$	.45
A5563—3 pounds		1.32
4A11442—5 pounds		2.17

Shipping Weight on Teas
3 pounds............4 pounds
5 pounds............7 pounds

Lipton's Ceylon Teas
1 pound, 76c

(Yellow Label) Blend A
A5591—1 pound tin	$	.76
A5593—Five 1-pound tins		3.75

(Red Label) Blend B
A5581—1 pound tin	$	.66
A5583—Five 1-pound tins		3.25

Japan Tea Siftings
2 packages, 37c

Japan Tea Siftings are the small broken leaves, sifted from the Early Spring Teas. Makes a fine cup of amber liquor. First pickings of the early leaves.

One-Pound Packages
A74— 2 packages	$	.37
A74— 5 packages		.90
A74—10 packages		1.75

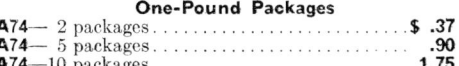

You can lower your food bills by serving Rice more often. — Montgomery Ward & Co. Saint Paul

ILLUS. 10-7. June, 1921 Montgomery Ward and Co. *Pure Food and Groceries* catalog.

FINE TEAS

74c and 82c a pound

Our Very Finest—Triangle Club Teas

OUR direct manner of buying teas means that we can always offer you better, fresher, more fragrant teas than are usually offered and save you money, too. Our Triangle Club Brand Teas are absolutely the finest obtainable and we know they will more than please you.

Japanese Hand Painted Plate
Packed in 5-Pound Cartons

This 7-inch Japanese hand-painted plate packed in 5-lb. cartons of Triangle Club Brand Tea.

India and Ceylon (Black)

The perfume of the Orient is released when you brew a cup of this delicious tea. Whether it is made heavy or light the exceptional flavor is still there.

A7750—1 pound.......... $ .74
A7752—3 pounds......... 2.19
4A11452—5 pounds....... 3.63

Pan-Fired Japan (Green)

A very high-grade short tender leaf tea, the finest leaves picked from the top of the bush. Draws light and clear.

A7710—1 pound.......... $ .82
A7712—3 pounds......... 2.43
4A11448—5 pounds....... 4.02

Formosa Oolong

A tippy toasty brown leaf. Fragrant and delicious. A selection from the most famous crop of Oolong from the Island of Formosa.

A7761—1 pound.......... $ .74
A7773—3 pounds......... 2.19
4A11451—5 pounds....... 3.63

Oolong and Gunpowder

A superfine mixture of very fancy Formosa Oolong and Moyune Gunpowder.

A70—1 pound........... $ .74
A72—3 pounds.......... 2.19
4A11457—5 pounds...... 3.63

Basket-Fired Japan

Specially selected grade of very first crop Basket-fired Uncolored Japan Tea. Draws a clear, pale liquor.

A7714—1 pound.......... $ .82
A7716—3 pounds......... 2.43
4A11449—5 pounds....... 4.02

English Breakfast (Black)

Genuine Russian Caravan Tea, from the Keemun district. This tea will appeal to lovers of black teas. A rich amber colored brew.

A7720—1 pound.......... $ .74
A7722—3 pounds......... 2.19
4A11478—5 pounds....... 3.63

Moyune Gunpowder (Green)

The finest grade of Gunpowder tea that grows. Draws fragrant and mild.

A7791—1 pound.......... $ .74
A7785—3 pounds......... 2.19
4A11454—5 pounds....... 3.63

Oriental Brand Teas   Arcadia Brand Teas

Basket-Fired Japan (Green)

Oriental Basket-Fired Japan tea continues to be one of our biggest sellers. You will find it to be distinctly better than other Basket-fired tea offered at a higher price.

A720—1 pound........... $ .55
A722—3 pounds.......... 1.62
4A11433—5 pounds....... 2.68

Orange Pekoe Ceylon

A Short, Black, Curly Leaf. Draws a light amber liquor—most delicious flavor.

A740—1 pound........... $ .55
A742—3 pounds.......... 1.62
4A11439—5 pounds....... 2.68

Formosa Oolong

Brown, curly leaf. Very fragrant, light amber liquor.

A730—1 pound........... $ .55
A732—3 pounds.......... 1.62
4A11436—5 pounds....... 2.68

Gunpowder (Green)

Hoochow Gunpowder. Uniform leaf. Excellent quality, light liquor.

A750—1 pound........... $ .55
A752—3 pounds.......... 1.62
4A11435—5 pounds....... 2.68

Special Introductory Offer!
Japan Tea

To acquaint you with the special values we offer in teas, we have reduced the price on this popular Japan tea. To order once means that you will always buy your teas from us. This tea would be good value at 70 cents a pound.

A710—1 pound.......... $ .51
A712—3 pounds......... 1.50
4A11432—5 pounds...... 2.53

English Breakfast (Black)

Small, curly leaf. Draws amber liquor. Fine, rich flavor.

A760—1 pound.......... $ .55
A762—3 pounds......... 1.62
4A11437—5 pounds...... 2.68

English Breakfast (Black)

Short, Curly Black Leaf draws deep, amber liquor. Strong, rich flavor.

A5561—1 pound......... $ .45
A5563—3 pounds........ 1.32
4A11442—5 pounds...... 2.17

Japanese Cup and Saucer
In 5-Pound Cartons of Tea
This beautiful Japanese hand-painted Cup and Saucer is packed in all five-pound boxes of the Oriental and the Arcadia Brand Teas. It will make a fine addition to your china closet.

Pan-Fired Japan (Green)

Formerly known as Sun-Dried. Short, green leaf. Looks and tastes like a tea above the average quality.

A770—1 pound.......... $ .45
A772—3 pounds......... 1.32
4A11440—5 pounds...... 2.17

Basket-Fired Japan (Green)

Long Green Leaf. Draws light liquor. Very mild.

A780—1 pound.......... $ .45
A782—3 pounds......... 1.32
4A11441—5 pounds...... 2.17

Formosa Oolong

Curly Brown Leaf. Draws a light amber liquor. Sweet flavor.

A790—1 pound.......... $ .45
A792—3 pounds......... 1.32
4A11445—5 pounds...... 2.17

Gunpowder (Green)

Round Green Leaf. Draws pale liquor. Mild and sweet.

A5571—1 pound......... $ .45
A5573—3 pounds........ 1.32
4A11444—5 pounds...... 2.17

Lipton's Ceylon Teas

(Yellow Label) Blend A
A5591—1 pound tin............. $ .76
A5593—Five 1-pound tins....... 3.75
(Red Label) Blend B
A5581—1-pound tin............. $ .66
A5583—Five 1-pound tins....... 3.25

Japan Tea Siftings
2 packages, 36c

Japan Tea Siftings are the small broken leaves, sifted from the Early Spring Teas. Makes a fine cup of amber liquor. First pickings of the early leaves. 1-pound packages.

A74— 2 packages........... $ .36
A74— 5 packages............ .87
A74—10 packages........... 1.70

Cookies for Summer

DAINTY little cookies, just the thing for serving with tea or dessert, will be found on pages 31 and 32 of this catalog. We pride ourselves particularly on the freshness of all our bakery products. See our special assortment of Fancy Cookies in 6-pound boxes.

Montgomery Ward & Co. Saint Paul

Order from the catalog until August 31, 1921.

ILLUS. 10-8. August, 1921 Montgomery Ward and Co. *Pure Food and Groceries* catalog.

TEA
Choicest Selections – Extra Low Prices

Triangle Club Brand Tea
74¢ A Pound

Our Triangle Club Brand of Tea represents the highest tea quality. Fresh New 1923 Crop Teas. Only choicest selections of the finest products of the famous tea growing countries are sold under this label—itself a guarantee of superior quality. Triangle Club Brand Tea is supremely fragrant and rich in flavor. The average store considers 80 cents a pound a bargain price for this grade of tea.

Pan Fired Japan
A very high grade short, tender green leaf tea. New season's crop.
3 A 7710 —1-lb. Package ..... $ .74
3 A 7710 —Three 1-lb.pkgs. ... 2.19
1 A 3329 —5 pounds 3.55

India and Ceylon (Black)
Finest quality Ceylon mixed with highest grade Dargheeling. Very flavory.
3 A 7750 —1-lb. Package ..... $ .74
3 A 7750 —Three 1-lb. pkgs. .. 2.19
1 A 3333 —5 pounds 3.55

Moyune Gunpowder (Green)
The finest grade of Gunpowder Tea. Draws light, flavory liquor.
3 A 7791 —1-lb. Package ..... $ .74
3 A 7791 —Three 1-lb. pkgs. .. 2.19
1 A 3335 —5 pounds 3.55

English Breakfast (Black)
Genuine Russian Caravan Tea.
3 A 7720 —1-lb. Package ..... $ .74
3 A 7720 —Three 1-lb.pkgs. .. 2.19
1 A 3345 —5 pounds 3.55

Moyune Young Hyson
Very fancy, curly green leaf. Makes a light, sweet, mild tea.
3 A 716 —1-lb. Package ..... $ .74
3 A 716 —Three 1-lb. pkgs .. 2.19
1 A 3326 —5 pounds 3.55

Oolong and Gunpowder
A mixture of very fancy Formosa Oolong and Moyune Gunpowder.
3 A 70 —1-lb. Package ..... $ .74
3 A 70 —Three 1-lb.pkgs .. 2.19
1 A 3338 —5 pounds 3.55

Basket Fired Japan
Specially selected first crop Basket Fired Uncolored Japan Tea. Olive green leaf. New season's crop.
3 A 7714 —1-lb. Package ..... $ .74
3 A 7714 —Three 1-lb.pkgs .. 2.19
1 A 3330 —5 pounds 3.55

Formosa Oolong
A light amber liquor. Fragrant and soothing.
3 A 7761 —1-lb. Package ..... $ .74
3 A 7761 —Three 1-lb. pkgs .. 2.19
1 A 3332 —5 pounds 3.55

Japan Tea Siftings
5 Packages 84¢

Japan Tea Siftings are made from small broken leaves sifted from the Early Spring Teas. This is by far the greatest tea value we can offer you. Though the price is very low, you will be more than pleased with the quality. If you want to enjoy a good cup of tea at a very low price we recommend these Tea Siftings.
1-pound Packages
3 A 74 —2 packages .... 34¢
3 A 74 —5 packages .... 84¢

Arcadia Brand Tea
45¢ A Pound

Combines Good Quality and Low Price
The different varieties of tea packed under this brand are selected and graded for their excellent cup quality. All Fresh New 1923 Teas. Thousands of our customers have made this their favorite brand. This grade combines good quality and low price. You would have to pay about 60 cents a pound for this grade of tea in most stores. Make a fair comparison and you will at once appreciate the big value this brand offers. Remember too, that every pound of tea you buy from Ward's, no matter what grade you may select, is sure to be fresh and fragrant. You get no shelf dried stock when you order from us.

Gunpowder
Round green leaf. Draws pale liquor. Mild and sweet.
3 A 5571 —1-lb. package ..... $ .45
3 A 5571 —Three 1-lb. pkgs ... 1.32
1 A 3327 —5 pounds 2.05

English Breakfast (Black)
Short, curly, black leaf. Draws deep amber liquor. Strong, rich flavor.
3 A 5561 —1-lb. package ..... $ .45
3 A 5561 —Three 1-lb. pkgs ... 1.32
1 A 3325 —5 pounds 2.05

Basket Fired Japan
Long green leaf. Draws light liquor. Very mild. New season's crop.
3 A 780 —1-lb. package ..... $ .45
3 A 780 —Three 1-lb. pkgs ... 1.32
1 A 3324 —5 pounds 2.05

Oolong
Curly brown leaf. Draws a light amber liquor. Fine flavor.
3 A 790 —1-lb. package ..... $ .45
3 A 790 —Three 1-lb. pkgs ... 1.32
1 A 3328 —5 pounds 2.05

Young Hyson (Green)
Short, curly green leaf. A medium light liquor. Mild.
3 A 713 —1-lb. package ..... $ .45
3 A 713 —Three 1-lb. pkgs ... 1.32
1 A 3368 —5 pounds 2.05

Pan Fired Japan
New Season's Crop
Short green leaf. Looks and tastes like a tea above the average quality.
3 A 770 —1-lb. package ..... $ .45
3 A 770 —Three 1-lb. pkgs. .. 1.32
1 A 3322 —5 pounds 2.05

Included in 5-Pound Cartons of Tea
A Japanese hand painted Plate, 7 inches in diameter is packed in every 5-pound carton of **Triangle Club Brand Tea**. With each 5-pound carton of our **Oriental and Arcadia Brand Teas**, we pack a beautiful Japanese hand painted Cup and Saucer. It doesn't take long to get a complete set of this handsome chinaware if you buy your tea in 5-pound cartons.

Old-Fashioned Tea
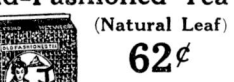
(Natural Leaf) 62¢ A Pound

Old fashioned Natural Leaf Japan is a high quality tea, having a pale liquor that is delightfully fragrant. The flavor is very delicate. This variety of tea is very popular with our customers. If you try a package, you will be delighted, we assure you.
3 A 736 —1 pound .... $ .62
3 A 736 —3 pounds 1.83
1 A 3311 —5 pounds 2.95

Ward's Black Ceylon Tea

77¢ A Pound

We want you to try our own brand of Ceylon Tea. Fresh, new season's crop flavory Ceylon tea, packed by experts on the plantation in Ceylon in 1-pound lead packets. **Equal to advertised brands sold at much higher prices.**
3 A 77 —1-pound Package ... $ .77
3 A 77 —3 Packages 2.28
3 A 77 —5 Packages 3.75

Oriental Brand Tea
55¢ A Pound

Under this brand we list the New 1923 Crop Teas of extra fancy quality at prices unusually low for teas of this grade. Tea packed under this label is most popular with Ward's customers because it gives unusual value for the price. If you want a really fancy grade of tea and do not care to pay a fancy price we recommend Oriental Brand. Most stores ask not less than 70 cents a pound for this fancy grade.

Gunpowder
Hoochow Gunpowder. Uniform leaf. Excellent quality, light fluid.
3 A 750 —1-lb. package ..... $ .55
3 A 750 —Three 1-lb. pkgs. .. 1.62
1 A 3317 —5 pounds 2.55

Orange Pekoe
A short black, curly leaf. Draws a light amber liquor—very good flavor.
3 A 740 —1-lb. package ..... $ .55
3 A 740 —Three 1-lb. pkgs. .. 1.62
1 A 3321 —5 pounds 2.55

Mixed
Basket Fired Japan and Oolong. Mixed in proper proportions.
3 A 768 —1-lb. package ..... $ .55
3 A 768 —Three 1-lb. pkgs .. 1.62
1 A 3331 —5 pounds 2.55

Basket Fired Japan
Oriental Basket Fired Green Japan Tea. New season's crop.
3 A 720 —1-lb. package ..... $ .55
3 A 720 —Three 1-lb. pkgs .. 1.62
1 A 3316 —5 pounds 2.55

Oolong
Very fragrant, light amber liquor.
3 A 730 —1-lb. package ..... $ .55
3 A 730 —Three 1-lb. pkgs .. 1.62
1 A 3318 —5 pounds 2.55

Young Hyson (Green)
Curly green leaf. Makes a liquor very much like Gunpowder tea.
3 A 725 —1-lb. package ..... $ .55
3 A 725 —Three 1-lb. pkgs .. 1.62
1 A 3314 —5 pounds 2.55

English Breakfast (Black)
Small curly leaf. Draws amber liquor. Fine, rich flavor.
3 A 760 —1 lb. package ..... $ .55
3 A 760 —Three 1-lb. pkgs .. 1.62
1 A 3319 —5 pounds 2.55

Pan Fired Japan
Generally known as Sun Dried Japan. Short, fine leaf. Draws light fluid. Mild, delicate flavor. New season's crop.
3 A 710 —1-lb. package ..... $ .55
3 A 710 —Three 1-lb. pkgs. .. 1.62
1 A 3315 —5 pounds 2.55

Lipton's Black Ceylon Tea
Blend A (Yellow Label)
A well known advertised brand.
3 A 5591 —1-pound Tin ...... 85¢

All these Teas are fragrant, fresh New 1923 Crop   — Montgomery Ward & Co. Saint Paul

ILLUS. 10-9. Nov.-Dec., 1922 Montgomery Ward and Co. *Pure Food and Groceries* catalog.

FINE TEA
Triangle Club Brand Tea
Choicest Selection of the Finest Teas

Our Triangle Club Brand Tea represents the highest attainment in tea quality. Only the choicest selection of the finest tea from the famous tea growing countries of the world are sold under this label—itself a guarantee of superior quality. Triangle Club Brand Tea is delightfully fragrant and rich in flavor.

Order Your Tea by Parcel Post
Parcel Post Rates
For 1st and 2nd zones (within 150 miles of St. Paul).
Add 6c for 1-pound package.
Add 8c for 3-pound package.
Add 11c for 5-pound package.
For 3rd zone (within 300 miles of St. Paul).
Add 8c for 1-pound package.
Add 12c for 3-pound package.
Add 18c for 5-pound package.

Pan Fired Japan
A very high grade short, tender green leaf tea.
A 7710 —1 pound........ $ .74
A 7712 —3 pounds....... 2.19
4 A 11448—5 pounds...... 3.63

Basket Fired Japan
Specially selected first crop Basket Fired Uncolored Japan Tea. Olive green leaf.
A 7714 —1 pound........ $ .74
A 7716 —3 pounds....... 2.19
4 A 11449—5 pounds...... 3.63

India and Ceylon
(Black)
The perfume of the Orient is released when you brew a cup of this delicate tea.
A 7750 —1 pound........ $ .71
A 7752 —3 pounds....... 2.10
4 A 11452—5 pounds...... 3.48

Moyune Gunpowder
(Green)
The finest grade of Gunpowder Tea that grows. Draws light, flavory liquor.
A 7791 —1 pound........ $ .71
A 7785 —3 pounds....... 2.10
4 A 11454—5 pounds...... 3.48

English Breakfast
(Black)
Genuine Russian Caravan Tea
A 7720 —1 pound........ $ .71
A 7722 —3 pounds....... 2.10
4 A 11478—5 pounds...... 3.48

Oolong and Gunpowder
A mixture of very fancy Formosa Oolong and Moyune Gunpowder.
A 70 —1 pound........ $ .71
A 72 —3 pounds....... 2.10
4 A 11457—5 pounds...... 3.48

Formosa Oolong
A light amber liquor. Fragrant and soothing.
A 7761 —1 pound........ $ .71
A 7773 —3 pounds....... 2.10
4 A 11451—5 pounds...... 3.48

Arcadia Brand Tea — Extra Low Prices — Oriental Brand Tea

The different varieties of tea packed under this brand are selected and graded for their excellent cup quality. This grade combines good quality and low price.

Under this brand we list teas of extra fancy quality at prices unusually low for teas of this grade. First crop pickings, fresh and fragrant.

Gunpowder
Round green leaf. Draws pale liquor. Mild and sweet.
A 5571 —1 pound........ $ .39
A 5573 —3 pounds....... 1.14
4 A 11444—5 pounds...... 1.87

Oolong
Curly brown leaf. Draws a light amber liquor. Fine flavor.
A 790 —1 pound........ $ .39
A 792 —3 pounds....... 1.14
4 A 11445—5 pounds...... 1.87

Gunpowder
Hoochow Gunpowder. Uniform leaf. Excellent quality, light fluid.
A 750 —1 pound........ $ .50
A 752 —3 pounds....... 1.47
4 A 11435—5 pounds...... 2.42

Pan Fired Japan
Generally known as Sun Dried Japan. Short, fine leaf. Draws light fluid. Mild, delicate flavor.
A 710 —1 pound........ $ .56
A 712 —3 pounds....... 1.65
4 A 11432—5 pounds...... 2.72

English Breakfast (Black)
Short, curly black leaf. Draws deep amber liquor. Strong, rich flavor.
A 5561 —1 pound........ $ .39
A 5563 —3 pounds....... 1.14
4 A 11442—5 pounds...... 1.87

Basket Fired Japan
Long green leaf. Draws light liquor. Very mild.
A 780 —1 pound........ $ .50
A 782 —3 pounds....... 1.47
4 A 11441—5 pounds...... 2.42

Orange Pekoe Ceylon
A short, black, curly leaf. Draws a light amber liquor — very good flavor.
A 740 —1 pound........ $ .50
A 742 —3 pounds....... 1.47
4 A 11439—5 pounds...... 2.42

Basket Fired Japan
Oriental Basket Fired Green Japan Tea.
A 720 —1 pound........ $ .56
A 722 —3 pounds....... 1.65
4 A 11433—5 pounds...... 2.72

Pan Fired Japan
Formerly known as Sun Dried. Short green leaf. Looks and tastes like a tea above the average quality.
A 770 —1 pound........ $ .50
A 772 —3 pounds....... 1.47
4 A 11440—5 pounds...... 2.42

English Breakfast (Black)
Small curly leaf. Draws amber liquor. Fine, rich flavor.
A 760 —1 pound........ $ .50
A 762 —3 pounds....... 1.47
4 A 11437—5 pounds...... 2.42

Oolong
Very fragrant, light amber liquor.
A 730 —1 pound........ $ .50
A 732 —3 pounds....... 1.47
4 A 11436—5 pounds...... 2.42

Old Fashioned Tea
(Green)

Natural Leaf
One pound, 67c

Old fashioned Natural Leaf Japan Tea is of fine quality, giving a pale liquor that is delightfully fragrant. The flavor is very delicate.
A 736 —1 pound......... $ .67
A 737 —3 pounds....... 1.98
4 A 11427—5 pounds...... 3.28

See Page 30 for Freshly Baked Cakes and Crackers

Included in Five-Pound Cartons of Tea
We pack a 7-inch Japanese Hand Painted Plate in every 5-pound carton of Triangle Club Brand Tea. With each 5-pound carton of our Oriental and Arcadia Brand Teas we pack a beautiful Japanese Hand Painted Cup and Saucer. It doesn't take long to get a complete set of this handsome chinaware if you buy your teas in 5-pound cartons.

Japan Tea Siftings
Two 1-pound packages, 38c

Japan Tea Siftings is the small broken leaves sifted from the Early Spring Teas. Fluid is pale in color and very refreshing. First pickings of the early leaves.
1-Pound Packages.
A 74— 2 packages.................. $ .38
A 74— 5 packages.................. .92
A 74—10 packages.................. 1.77

Ward's Black Ceylon Tea

One pound 69c

We want you to try our own brand of Ceylon Tea. Fresh, new season's crop flavory Ceylon tea, packed by experts on the plantation in Ceylon in 1-pound lead packets. *Equal to advertised brands sold at much higher prices.*
A 77—One 1-lb. lead packet.. $ .69
A 77—Three 1-lb. lead packets 2.04
A 77—Five 1-lb. lead packets.. 3.30

Lipton's Ceylon Tea
Blend A (Yellow Label)
A 5591—1-pound can........ $ .79
A 5593—Five 1-pound cans .. 3.90

Triangle Club Preserves and Jellies are like the home made kind.

ILLUS. 10-10. June, 1922 Montgomery Ward and Co. *Pure Food and Groceries* catalog.

PLATE 77. Doll's Tea Party Cup and Saucer from Hahne & Co..

PLATE 78. Doll's Tea Party Cup from Emery, Birel, Thayer Co., Kansas City.

PLATE 79. Mint Dish, scenic, souvenir of Tuscarora Mountains, PA.

ILLUS. 10-11. Hand-colored postcard published by Leslie W. Seylar, printed by The Altertype Co., Brooklyn, New York, depicting "Doc" Seylar's Rest House, no date. Note word "souvenir" on window behind gasoline pumps.

ILLUS. 10-12. Hand-colored postcard published by Leslie W. Seylar, printed by The Altertype Co., Brooklyn, New York, depicting "Doc" Seylar's Rest House, no date.

PLATE 80. Plate, 6″, Chinese Coin, advertising Young's Hotel, York Beach, ME and Boone Island Lighthouse, York, ME.

PLATE 81. Souvenir Teapot, 3″, Geisha in Cards.

PLATE 82. Souvenir Teapot, reverse, Geisha in Cards.

PLATE 83. Stamped mark on Souvenir Teapot in Plates 81-82.

Marks

Marks are the name, signature or trademark found written, stenciled, stamped or printed on a paper label. Most are found on the base of an item, but they have been known to appear on or inside a lid or as a part of a pattern. Marks may represent the porcelain manufacturer, decorator, importer or retailer, or location of manufacture.

Raised circles, stars and rings are sometimes found on the base of a porcelain form and mistaken as marks. These were used to improve the firing stability of the porcelain and are not to be confused with identification marks. The intense heat of the kiln causes the porcelain to expand. By allowing the item to stand as free-floating as possible, uneven firing caused by physical constrictions is minimized. Kilns of antiquity often used spurs to accomplish this task. Circles and stars are a more modern, decorative means. They have been found on items bearing many different marks including Kutani, Japan and Made in Japan.

Dating

Collectors often use marks as a means of identifying both the origin and dating of a porcelain item. It is important to remember that the marks should be taken into consideration **along with** all other facets of an item's creation.

Prior to 1891, porcelain items imported into the U.S. were marked only if the manufacturer or artisan desired to do so. Thus, items from that period may or may not bear a mark of some sort.

In 1891, the U.S. Government declared that all items coming into the country were to be marked with the country of origin. Japan decided to use the romanization of her Japanese name, i.e., Nippon. Thus began what we now refer to as the Nippon period. It connotes a timeframe in addition to a place.

In 1921, the U.S. Government made a specific decision concerning the marking of import wares coming from Japan. It was declared that Nippon was a Japanese word and that, henceforth, all her wares should be marked with the English name for the country — Japan. Thus, "Nippon" ceased being used and "Japan" or "Made in Japan" became the new notation.

General rules-of-thumb are thus established. They are (1) items marked "Nippon" date between 1891 and 1921 and (2) items marked "Japan" or "Made in Japan" date post-1921. I emphasize rule-of-thumb because there are exceptions.

Some items which found their way to U.S. were originally exported to other countries with different trademark laws. In 1908, Noritake registered the Tree Crest mark (#8) in England. Note that it reads "Made in Japan". In 1911, the M-in-Wreath Nippon mark (#15a) was registered by Noritake in the U.S. By 1918, the mark was changed to read "Made in Japan" (#15b). Thus, here are two "Made in Japan" marks that actually date from the Nippon period onward.

Joan Van Patten has pointed out that there were certain loopholes to the trademark laws[1]. Group tagging was allowed. If the major item in a set was marked, the entire set was allowed to pass. The shipping crate could have been marked, but not its contents. The items might have had paper labels, which came off over the course of years. Thus, **it is a fallacy to state that unmarked items pre-date the Nippon period.** In fact, an unmarked item could have been made during the Nippon period or as recently as last year.

Likewise, a Japanese character marking does not automatically mean the wares are old. Japanese signatures have been found accompanying both the words Nippon and Japan, on the Czechoslovakian pieces, and in modern reproductions which have the name of the importing firm in Japanese characters.

Value

Rightfully or wrongly, the marketplace tends to value some marks more than others. Certain marks command higher prices because of the reputation of their manufacturer. Such examples are the Kutani (J#16) mark, denoting production from one of Japan's most famous kiln sites, and the Green-M-in-Wreath (#15) mark, readily associated with the popular Noritake firm. Nippon-period items command exceptional prices, while items marked Japan, or bearing no mark, are priced considerably lower.

This phenomenon is unfortunate because age and trademarks are not necessarily synonymous with quality. There are poorly executed Nippon-period pieces and exquisite examples of Japan-period items. There are poorly executed Kutani and Noritake items and magnificient items from other firms.

Another problem with placing importance on marks is the fact that certain decorators bought marked porcelain blanks from numerous kilns. The Geisha Girl Temple pattern A is a prime example of this. No less than seven different marks have been found on identically decorated pieces.

Nonetheless, the importance of marks as a market indicator must be reckoned with when buying or selling an item.

On the Origin of Marks

Japan considered her export wares a means of improving the economy. They were not looked upon as an artistic endeavor. Thus, few explicit records were kept of their production. Many of those that did exist were destroyed with the companies during World War II.

Today's collector of Japanese wares is not privy to as much company history as are collector's of English or American wares. Over 130 marks found on Geisha Girl Porcelain are cataloged in this volume in two sections, those depicted in Japanese characters and those originally portrayed in English. Wherever possible a translation and descriptive information is noted.

Japanese Marks

1. **Yachi**, craftman's name, red-orange, hand written.
2. **Yachi tsukuru**, "Made by Yachi", craftsman's name, red-orange, hand written.
3. **Yachiko**, related to the above, second ideograph indicates a "boy-name", a name held by a male child until the age of fifteen when he receives a second or adult name, red-orange, hand written.
4. **Jida tsukuru**, "Made by Jida", craftsman's name.
5. **Ushijima**, island or family name of painter, red-orange stencil.
6. a. **Tashiro**, possibly Tashiro Shoten, manufacture commenced 1879, hand written gold on red, red-orange stencil[1].
   b. **Dai Nihon Tashiro tsukuru**, "Made in Japan by Tashiro", red-orange stencil.
7. **Kinan Sei**, "Made by Kinan", red, hand written.
8. a-b. **Dai Nihon**, "Made in Japan", hand written red, red-orange stencil.
   c. green.
9. a. **Dai Nihon Sai Ryu sei**, "Made in Japan, Ryu studio", red-orange stencil.
   b. **Sai Ryu**, "Ryu studio", red-orange stencil.
10. a-b. **Shibata tsukuru**, "Made in/by Shibata", **Shibata** is both name of a town in Echigo and family name of painter, red, hand written.
11. **Shiba**, administrative division of Tokyo, gold, hand painted.
12. **Tamaru**, family name, gold on red, hand painted.
13. **Kichi**, "lucky", gold on red, hand painted.
14. a. **Yoshi tsukuru**, "Made by Yoshi", craftsman's mark, red on gold, hand painted.
    b. **Yoshi**, craftsman's mark, red on gold, hand written.
15. a. **Terasawa tsukuru**, "Made by Terasawa", family name, gold on red, hand written.
    b. **Terasawa tsukuru**, "Made by Terasawa", family name, underglaze blue.
    c-d. **Terasawa tsukuru**, "Made by Terasawa", family name, red-orange, hand written.
16. a-b. **Kutani**, production site, red-orange, hand written.
    c. **Kutani**, production site, gold on red, hand written.
    d. **Kutani tsukuru**, "Made in Kutani", production site, gold on red, hand written.
    e. **Dai Nihon Kutani tsukuru**, "Made in Kutani, Japan", production site, gold on red, hand written.
    f. **Nihon, Kutani**, "Kutani, Japan", production site, gold on red, hand written.
17. **Kushiya**, town.
18. **Kuromizu**, town, red-orange, hand written.
19. **Ozan**, town, gold on red, hand painted.
20. **Imai tsukuru**, "Made by Imai", family name of painter, red, hand written.
21. a-b. **Shimamura tsukuru**, "Made by Shimamura", family name of painter, gold on red, hand written.
22. **Yana**, administrative division of Mikawa province.
23. **Yana**, administrative division of Mikawa province, red-orange stencil.
24. **Suzuki**, family name, painter, red, hand written.
25. **Suzuki Harunobu ga**, "picture by Suzuki Harunobu", 18th century Ukiyo-e artist, black stencil; found on Bellflower pattern; used in remembrance of the Ukiyo-e artist or because the scene was taken from one of his original works of art.
26. **Yana Suzuki**, indicates that Suzuki was located in Yana, see 22-24 above, red-orange stamp.
27. **Dai Nihon Yana**, "Yana, Japan".
28. **Yana Giku**, factory name, red-orange, hand painted.
29. **Nagoya Mukomatsu sei**, "Made on Matsu street in Nagoya", certain areas of towns were often designated for the production and marketing of certain crafts, apparently this area in the city of Nagoya was devoted to ceramics, red stencil.
30. **Oyama**, town.
31. **Rokusan**, "63", craftsman's trademark, red on gold, hand written.
32. **Tsuchida**, family name of painter.
33. **Nihon Maya Nimei**, "Maya Nimei, Japan", individual and family name of craftsman, red-orange stamp.
34. **Ito**, family name of painter, gold on red, hand written.
35. **Taniguchi**, Taniguchi Bros. was family firm in Kaga province circa 1910, gold on red, hand written.
36. **Dai Nihon Kato zo**, "Made by Kato in Japan", painter, potter, red stencil.
37. **Sawaki**, family name, gold on red, hand written.
38. **Dai Nihon Nakajima Sei**, "Made in/by Nakajima, Japan", administrative division of Owari province, also family name of painter, red.
39. **Nihon Tokusei**, "Specially made, Japan", used by supplier WINCLER who exported to Europe, red-orange stamp[1].
40. **Hayu sei**, "Made by Hayu", craftsman's name, red stencil.
41. Indescipherable, red, hand written.
42. **?shichi hatachi?**, "? seven twenty ?", black stencil.
43. **Yoshi**, art name, gold on red, hand written.
44. **Kumo**, art name, red, hand written.
45. **Kuchi ?**, unknown, gold on red, hand written.
46. **Yasutera**, place name, gold on red, hand written.
47. **Do Ran Yen Sei**, "Made by mate of Ran Garden", "yen" as used here indicates a business rather than a literal garden, indicates that the piece was made by an employee of the Ran establishment, underglaze blue.
48. **Kimi**, "sovereign", indicative of a title bequeathed upon the maker, gold on red, hand written.
49. **Ichidai**, "great one", name awarded by political borough in which artist resided as form of official recognition.
50. **Naruhito**, craftsman's mark, red, hand written.
51. **Matsumaru, Kutani**, Name of maker located in Kutani.
52. **Sho tsukuru**, "Made by Sho", art name, red, hand written.

53. **Midzukagami sei**, "Made by Midzukagami", family name, red stencil.
54. **Iman**, family name.
55. **Kosuke sei**, "Made by Kosuke", craftsman's name.
56. **Shiya Boryu Ken**, "Made by House of Boryu, China", red-orange stencil.
57. Stylized mark of 1970's Oriental Shop, red-orange stencil.
58. Czechoslovakian pseudo-Oriental mark, red stamp.
59. Czechoslovakian pseudo-Oriental mark, red stamp.
60. **Dai Nihon Iyu tsukuru**, "Made in Japan by Iyu", craftsman's name, red stencil.
61. **Dai Nihon Moku**, "Made in Japan by Moku", family name, red stencil.
62. **Naka**, administrative province of Tango, modern day Sagami, gold, hand written.
63. **Showa Kinsei**, respectfully made by Showa, red stamp, reproduction mark.
64. Czechoslovakian pseudo-Oriental mark, red stamp.
65. Nippon in Cherry Blossom.
66. **Yamakuru** or **Yamamune tsukuru**, made by the artist, ideograph unclear.
67. **Shimidzu**, harbour, family painter.
68. Nippon, Stone Lantern.
69. **Ichiban**, "the best", used by A.A. Vantine & Co.
70. **Niban**, "second", used by A.A. Vantine & Co.
71. **Kyo**, art name.

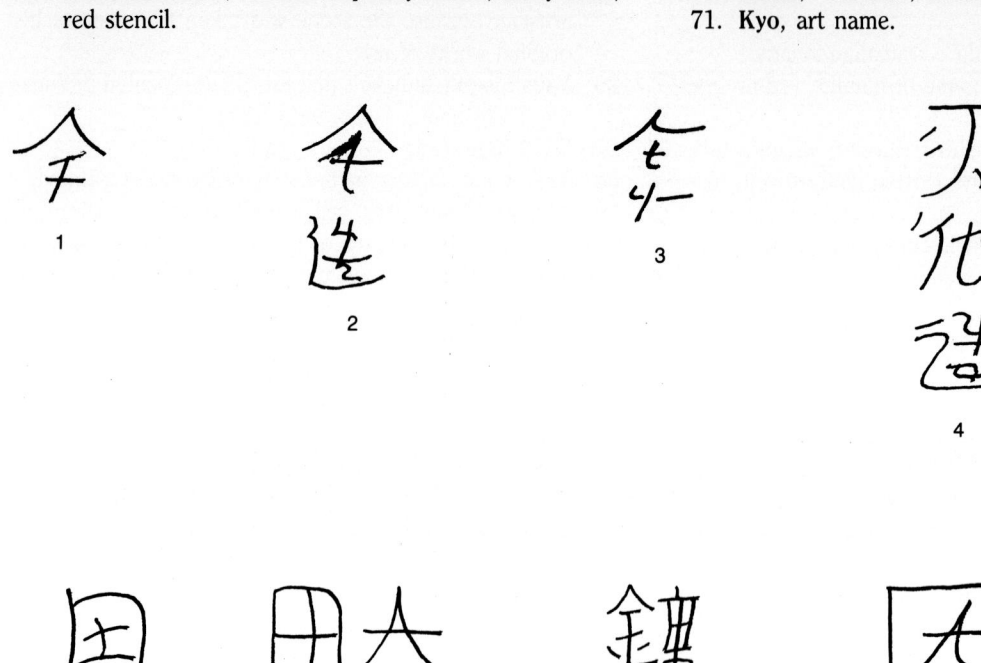
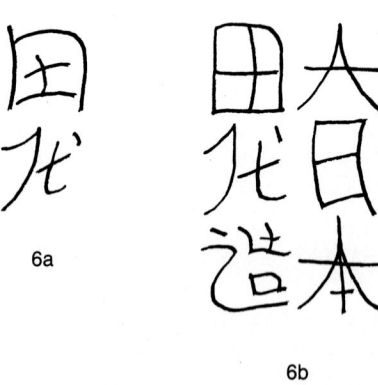
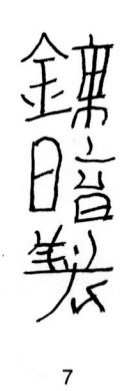
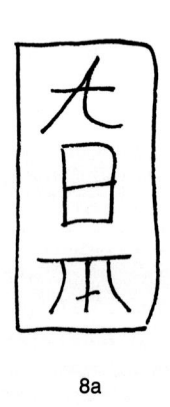

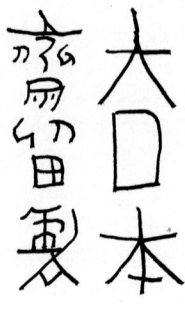
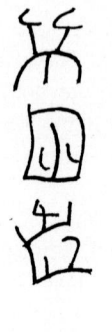
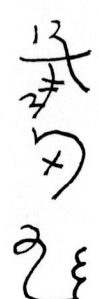

11 12 13 14a 14b

15a-d

16a-g

17 18 19 20

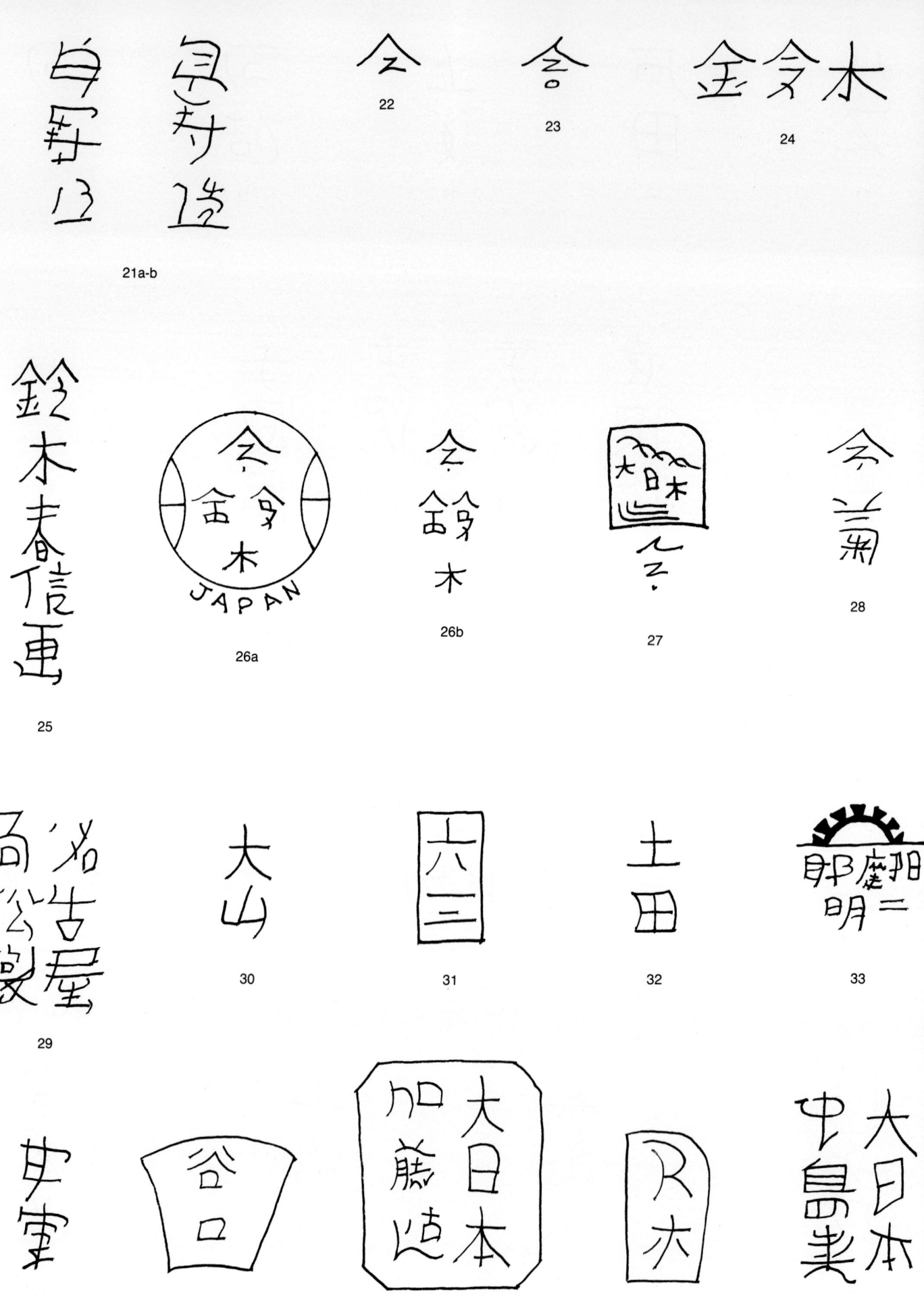

59

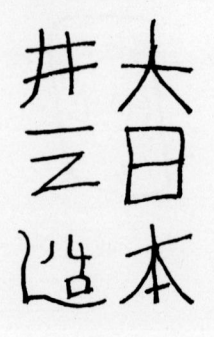
60

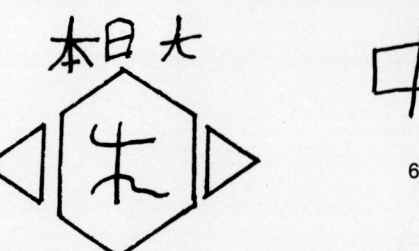
61

中
62

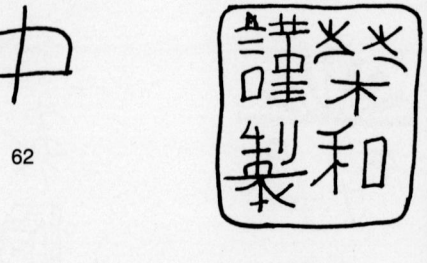
63

64

65

66

67

68

69

二番
70

71

English Language Marks

1. a-b. Torii, Made in Japan, various colors.
   c. Torii, Made in Japan, turquoise decal.
2. a. Torii, Nippon, blue-green decal.
   b. Torii, Nippon, various colors.
   c. Torii, Nippon, red stencil.
3. a-e. "t't", red, black or green stencil.
   f. Indecipherable kanji, red stencil.
4. T in Cherry Blossom, believed to belong to Tashiro Shoten, production commenced 1879, divided into a few factories, one existing as of 1973, red stencil[1].
5. T in Cherry Blossom, Made in Japan, as in (4) above, "made in Japan" in underglaze blue, remainder in red stencil.
6. T in Cherry Blossom, see (4), green decal or red stencil.
7. Jo or Shiro, surname, red stamp.
8. Noritake Tree Crest, mark registered in England in 1908, turquoise transfer.
9. Komoa Tee, name of a tea producer, red.
10. T&Z, name of New York importer, full name and history unknown, aqua decal.
11. Diaper, green.
12. Royal Kaga, Nippon, aqua transfer.
13. a. Double T in Diamond, one source indicates that it is mark of Takito, established in 1880 and gone during World War II; however, 13b is found on 1980 reproduction wares, green decal.
    b. Double T in Diamond, blue with "Made in Japan" in red.
14. Double T in Diamond, black stamp.
15. a. Green M-in-Wreath, Nippon, registered in U.S. by Noritake in 1911.
    b. Green M-in-Wreath, Made in Japan, registered in U.S. by Noritake in 1918.
16. SNB, Nippon, producer in city of Nagoya, green.
17. SNB, Nagoya, Nippon, aqua decal.
18. Made in Japan, red.
19. Japan, black, red, green or blue stencil or stamp.
20. a. Made in Japan, black, red or green stencil or stamp.
    b. Made in Japan, red.
21. Maple Leaf, Nippon, registered by Noritake in 1919, but used as early as 1891, green if first grade ware, blue if second grade ware.
22. SH, Nippon.
23. Pagoda, Nippon, aqua transfer.
24. Pagoda, Made in Japan, aqua transfer.
25. Ardalt, Made in Occupied Japan, with design or form number, red.
26. TE-OH China, Nippon, blue-green decal.
27. Nagoya, Shofu, Nippon, Shofu sector of Nagoya, Japan, green decal.
28. G.R.P., Shofu, Nippon, G.R.P. maker in Shofu, Nagoya, Nippon.
29. Soko China, manufacturer, gold.
30. Hakusan China, producing during 1950's.
31. Mikado, Japan, producer.
32. a. TN in Wreath, Japan, blue-green or black stencil.
    b. TN in Wreath, Nippon, blue-green stencil.
33. Pow Sei Cot Ure, WPSK, Nippon.
34. Plum Blossom, Japan, red stencil.
35. Plum Blossom, Made in Japan, red stencil.
36. Nikonica China, E-W, Occupied Japan, black.
37. Crown.
38. ME in Wreath, Japan, appears with gold on red Kutani (J#16).
39. ME in Wreath, MC, Japan.
40. KQK, kanji translates to "House of", second character indecipherable.
41. Vantine trademark, A.A. Vantine Co., New York, 1885 - c. 1951, red stencil.
42. Vantine stamp, A.A. Vantine Co., New York, 1885 - c. 1951, violet stencil with raised white enamel serrations.
43. Yamasan China, Made in Occupied Japan, brick red stencil.
44. Mikado, Japan, possibly same firm as in (31), green.
45. Nippon, Yamamasu, firm name, red stamp.
46. Made in Nippon.
47. Nippon, various colors, stamp.
48. MI, Nippon.
49. Sampan, kanji in sail translates to "yu", probably an indication of wares made for export, red.
50. Paulownia Blossom, Nippon, decal, stem and "hand painted" in rust, balance is green.
51. C.O.N., Nippon, mint green decal.
52. Chikaramachi crown, black stencil.
53. Action-Lobeco, reproduction mark.
54. TK, gold, sometimes on red triangle, hand written.
55. Noritake, Nippon, Kutani, Noritake began use of this mark in 1906 for items exported to the U.S. Whether the items were formed in Kutani and decorated by Noritake, or whether Noritake merely acted as the export agent is unknown.
56. Plum Blossom Branch, Japan, maroon decal.
57. Yamakyo, Cherry Blossom, Japan, center kanji reads Yamakyo, a maker in Tajimi prior to World War II[1], kanji above blossom is indecipherable.
58. Made in Nippon Crown, green decal.
59. E.R.H., reproduction mark, red stencil.
60. Plum Blossom, Nippon.
61. I.E., R?, in Wreath.
62. Kanji indecipherable, pattern number, Made in Japan, black stencil.
63. Double Cherry Blossom, Japan.
64. Porcelain Factory Victoria in Altrohlau, Czechoslovakia, red stamp.
65. Horsehead, pale yellow with partial red frame.
66. Paulownia, Made in Japan, green stamp.
67. JF?I, red stamp.
68. SGK China, Occupied Japan.
69. Y,F,n, red stencil.
70. Vantine's, Made in Japan.

[1] J. Oates, Phoenix Bird Chinaware Book I, 1984.

1a

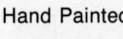

1b

Made in Japan

1c

Hand Painted

NIPPON
2a

2b

Torii

Nippon
2c

t"t"
Made in Japan
3a

3b

3c

3d

Hand Painted

t't'

3e

3f

4

5

6

HAND PAINTED

7

8

KOMOA
TEE

9

10

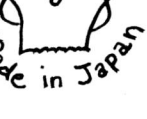

11

12

13a

13b

HAND PAINTED MADE IN JAPAN

14

15a

15b

16

17

18

JAPAN

19

MADE
IN
JAPAN

20

MADE
IN
JAPAN

20b

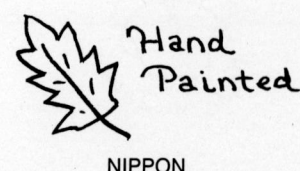
Hand Painted
NIPPON
21

22

Hand Painted
Nippon
23

Made in Japan
24

NO. 6076
ARDALT
MADE IN
OCCUPIED
JAPAN
25

Hand Painted
NIPPON
26

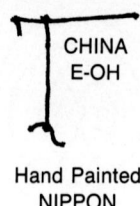
27

28

Hand-Painted
29

30

31

32a

32b

33

JAPAN
34

35

36

Hand Painted

Japan

37

38

39

K Q K
{←|U ᒊ}

40

41

42

43

JAPAN

MIKADO

44

45

MADE IN

NIPPON

46

NIPPON

47

48

49

50

69

NIPPON
51

MADE IN JAPAN
52

54

55

56

57

58

59

60

61

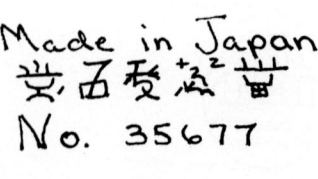
62

70

JAPAN

63

64

65

66

67

Occupied Japan

68

Y, F, n

69

Vanline's

MADE IN
JAPAN

70

Reproductions

Due to the ongoing popularity of Geisha Girl Porcelain, it is still being produced. One could, up until a couple of years ago, find a wide variety of items in many Oriental import stores. Reproduced items include teasets, plates, nut bowls, cocoa sets, vases, demitasse cups, ginger jars, sake sets, plates, dresser sets, toothpick holders, tumblers, toothbrush holders, children's demitasse cups and even tea caddies.

There are several distinguishing features which aid the collector in identifying modern Geisha wares. The porcelain of new items is very white and smooth when contrasted with the older clays. It is generally thinner and often more evenly shaped due to the improved methods of mold production in use today.

The reproduction porcelain form is simple — usually plain and round. Fluting and relief molding are unknown, as are any signs of hand shaping.

Enamel usage often helps to date an item. Background color washes to denote areas of grass, sky or water often are lacking on reproductions, imparting a rather stark appearance to the wares. Gold is rarely used. When it is found, it is quite bright. It does not display the tarnish or patina brought on by age.

Reproduction borders tend to be very thin, exceedingly straight lines around the porcelain edge. The majority of borders on reproduction wares are red-orange with a brown tinge, although a particular set of children's demitasse cups come in a multiplicity of colors including red, brown, black, bright blue, yellow and greenish-blue. Another item with multiple color schemes is a small three inch vase with a black underlying design of one or two geisha. These have either a red-orange, bright blue or yellow edge and neck. Sometimes they are marked "Handcrafted in Japan Action-Lobeco."

Another characteristic of reproduction Geisha Girl Porcelain requires some careful comparative studies. The noses of geishas on modern pieces are very pointy and often placed at an odd angle with respect to other facial features. It sounds queer, but is a fact to take into consideration.

Reproductions do find their way into flea markets and antique stores, so caution is the key word here.

Illus. 12-1 is an ad from a 1982 Swiss department store flyer. Note the plain border and bamboo handle which are typical of reproduction wares. This set is in the Meeting A pattern and cost was equivalent to $65.00 (American).

Illus. 12-2 is from the same Swiss store, but dates from 1984. Note the sterile appearance and the straight red-orange border. It is in the Fan A variant, a pattern which has been used since the Nippon era. It was priced around $55.00 (American).

The plate (Plate 84) is circa 1980, also in the Fan A pattern. It was purchased for $5.95 in San Francisco's Chinatown. Again note the reproduction characteristics — very white porcelain, even, unadorned border and sparseness of color and background washes. It bears a blue "Double T-in-Diamond" mark and a red stamp reading "Made in Japan."

Plate 85 depicts a modern reproduction teaset with lithophaned cups in the Child Reaching for Butterfly pattern. The child's sugar and creamer (Plate 86) are in the same pattern, but are actually decorated with decals of the pattern!

A modern dresser set (Plate 87) is comprised of a tray, hair receiver and powder jar. The latter are ribbed and all items bear an unadorned red-orange border. The author has seen numerous sets like these in the Porch pattern and the coloring is consistant. The geisha in the middle wears light green and leans over a fence. The geisha to the right is in red and the one to the left is in blue. The flower coloring is daubed on, and the overall background coloring is very sparse, especially on the jars. They are marked "Japan".

There are also modern productions of the Garden Bench, Parasol C (Plates 88-89) and a variation of Parasol E that is known to appear only on modern pieces, accompanied by the words "Made in Japan" in tiny green, capital letters (Plates 90-93). An interior border of alternating flowers and butterflies is characteristic of this Parasol Modern pattern.

It is wise to consider all facets of an item before deciding upon a purchase. While one may take a fancy to a modern item, it would not be desirable to pay a price deserved of a comparable older item.

ILLUS. 12-2. Reproduction Tea Set, Fan A pattern; 1984 Swiss department store catalog.

ILLUS. 12-1. Reproduction Tea Set, Meeting A pattern; 1982 Swiss department store catalog.

PLATE 84. 1980 Reproduction Plate, 7", Fan A, mark #13.

PLATE 85. Reproduction Tea Set, Child Reaching for Butterfly, with lithophanes.

PLATE 86. Reproduction Sugar and Creamer, Child Reaching for Butterfly, decaled, mark J#63.

PLATE 87. Modern Dresser Set, Porch.

PLATE 88. Modern Bowl, 11", Parasol C, mark #19.

PLATE 89. Bowl, 6", Parasol Modern.

PLATE 90. Pitcher, 2½", Parasol Modern.

PLATE 91. Dish, 7", Parasol Modern, mark #20.

PLATE 92. Cake Platter, Parasol Modern, mark #20.

PLATE 93. Stickpin Holder, Parasol Modern, mark #20.

Cataloging A Collection

Through years of collecting, having a quick reference catalog available at one's fingertips can save considerable time and energy during the identification and research process. Further, the procedure of cataloging trains a collector to become more attuned to the idiosyncracies of each item and how to compare and contrast them. This, in turn, leads to observations which help the collector learn more about the collection as a whole, become a more educated buyer, and perhaps develop a finer collection.

In addition, detailed descriptions and pictures are invaluable tools when dealing with the insurance company or police in recovering your collection or investment, should the need arise. Prints may be attached to the catalog pages or a separate slide library may be maintained. Keep one catalog handy for revisions and put a second copy either off the premises or in a fireproof box.

To that end, the author's catalog form is reproduced herein to be used as a reference point upon which the reader may create a catalog specific to his/her needs. Each part of the form has been assigned a number and its use described. Depending upon the collector's particular use for these forms, they may be alphanumerically ordered by Pattern Name, Catalog No., or Type of Piece.

For those who have access to a computer, much of this information may be put into a data base. There are many off the shelf inventory or record-keeping software packages that may be put to use to catalog a collection.

There are also several data base packages available to those who desire to do their own programming. Even a BASIC program will do the job. Creating a master file of numbers assigned to pattern, form, color, etc. will allow for quick input and detailed output, as required. Again, I do recommend keeping either a hard copy or back up disk in a safe place.

(1) PATTERN: Insert the appropriate pattern number and name, if desired, from the Catalog section of this book.

(2) CATALOG NO.: Assign each item a number as you record it. Place a small sticker bearing that number on the base or inside of the piece, or mark the number on the base with a porcelain marking pen.

There are many ways of assigning catalog numbers and several books[1] which describe such systems in depth. The simplest method is to assign numbers in ascending order. Variations include numbering by year, such that 84.1 is the first item purchased in 1984, 85.1 the first in 1985, etc. Items may also be numbered within patterns, i.e. 2.3 is the third item acquired in the Bamboo Tree pattern.

It is best to mark sets such that the assignation on one member makes it clear that there are other members. Items in a set may share the same master number, but each piece, including lids, should have a different suffix. For instance, if catalog no. 100 is a teaset, the pot may be marked 100P, the sugar 100SU, the creamer 100CR, the first set of cups and saucers 100C-1, 100S-1, etc.

Another method is to mark the members of a ten part set 100a through 100j.

(3) FORM: Is it a bowl, table plate, toy cup, etc.?

(4) CIRCA: Note your estimation of the age of the piece by a year or year range and the reasons you believe your dating to be accurate. When you can positively identify a date for one piece, its characteristics may be compared with other items and dates may be adjusted, if necessary.

(5) BORDER COLOR: Write in the color name or use a numeric code, such as the following:

1 = Black	11 = Gold	21 = Green-yellow
2 = Blue, cobalt	12 = Gray	22 = Green & red-orange
3 = Blue, light	13 = Green, apple, dk.	23 = Maroon
4 = Blue, pale cobalt	14 = Green, apple, light	24 = Nishikide
5 = Blue, teal dark	15 = Green, grass	25 = Orange
6 = Blue, turquoise	16 = Green, mint	26 = Red, regular
7 = Blue-green	17 = Green, olive, dark	27 = Red, brick
8 = Blue & red-orange	18 = Green, olive, light	28 = Red-orange
9 = Brown, dark	19 = Green, pine	29 = Tan
10 = Brown, golden	20 = Green, sea	30 = Yellow

(6) DESIGN QUALITY: Describe in words or use a rating scale, e.g. 1 = poor to 5 = excellent. Include in your determination the quality of the enameling and border application.

(7) UNDERLYING DESIGN COLOR: This refers to the color of the stenciled underlying design. The same scale may be used as in (5) above.

(8) UNDERLYING DESIGN QUALITY: For stenciled items only, use the same scale as in (6) above. Take into consideration the detail and application of the stencil.

(9) PURCHASE PRICE (ORIGINAL ASKING PRICE): Jot down the price paid for the item and the tag price, if it was discounted. This is a quick reference, but be sure to file your receipts for proof of purchase price. It may be needed when you resell the item or for insurance purposes.

(10) DATE/PLACE PURCHASED: This helps you to identify places you might want to revisit, either to ask questions about a purchased item or to look for other acquisitions. One often receives generic receipt forms, so it is wise to note the seller information on the receipt as well.

(11) SALE PRICE/DATE OF SALE: You might also want to include the name and address of the person to whom the item was sold. While this space doesn't get used too often, it is important when thinning out or upgrading one's collection.

(12) SIZE SPECS: List the width, depth, height and/or diameter of the cataloged item, as applicable.

(13) CONSTRUCTION SPECS: Note the structural characteristics of each item. Is it round, square, thinning toward the base? Is it pedestaled or flat bottomed? What shape are the finial, handles or spout? In short, note the particular characteristics that identify this item as distinct from your others.

(14) BORDER SPECS: Border color is noted in (5). This section should detail the form of the border, e.g. scalloped,

[1] D.B. Reibel, *Registration Methods for the Small Museum*, American Association for State and Local History, 1978; D. Dudley and I. Wilkinson, *Museum Registration Methods*, American Association of Museums, 1979.

wavy, etc. and any border enhancements, e.g. gold lacings, flowers, etc.

(15) PATTERN SPECS: Note any diversions from the standard pattern description, the color of reserve outlines, decoration in addition to the pattern, etc.

(16) CONDITION: Note any chips, cracks, enamel wear or missing parts.

(17) MARK: Copy down the mark or its number from the Mark section of this book. You might want to indicate whether it is signed, stenciled, decaled or stamped and the color of the mark.

(18) APPRAISED VALUE: This can be an actual appraised value, the value from the Price Guide of this book or your personal estimation. Going through this process upon cataloging an item and at least once annually for the entire catalog, will keep you aware of current market values and train you to better evaluate future purchases.

(19) DATE: Jot down the date your observations were made.

	1	Pattern

Catalog No.	3			
2		Border Color		5
Circa 4		Design Quality		6
Purchase Price (Asking Price)	9	Underlying Design Color		7
Date/Place Purchased	10	Underlying Design Quality		8

Date/Price Sale   11

Size Specs: 12

Construction Specs: 13

Border Specs: 14

Pattern Specs: 15

Condition: 16

Mark: 17

Appraised Value: 18   Date: 19

Photo Album

PLATE 94. Lemon Plate, Art Show.

PLATE 95. Plate 7¼", Bamboo Tree, #19.

PLATE 96. Teapot, Bamboo Tree, #19.

PLATE 97. Pair of Basket Vases, 8½", Bamboo Trellis.

PLATE 98. Bowl 7½", Bamboo Trellis.

PLATE 99. Plate 6½", Bamboo Trellis.

PLATE 100. Saucer, After-Dinner, Bamboo Trellis.

PLATE 101. Master Nut Bowl, Basket A.

PLATE 102. Cocoa Pot, 6½", Basket A.

PLATE 103. Cocoa Pot, 8", Basket A.

PLATE 104. Plate, 8½", Basket A.

PLATE 105. Sugar and Creamer, Basket A.

PLATE 106. After-Dinner Cup and Saucer, Basket B.

PLATE 107. After-Dinner Cup and Saucer, Basket B.

PLATE 108. Cocoa Cup and Saucer, Basket B.

PLATE 109. Sauce Dish, Basket of Mums A.

PLATE 110. Biscuit Jar, Basket of Mums B.

PLATE 111. Butter Pat, 3¼", Basket of Mums B.

PLATE 112. Cocoa Pot, 8", Battledore.

PLATE 113. Cocoa Pot, 9" Battledore.

PLATE 114. After-Dinner Cup and Saucer, Battledore.

PLATE 115. Tea Cup and Saucer, Battledore.

PLATE 116. Hair Receiver, Battledore.

PLATE 117. Jug, 5", Battledore.

PLATE 118. Sugar and Creamer, Battledore.

PLATE 119. Sugar Bowl, Battledore.

PLATE 120. Covered Urn, 8", Battledore.

PLATE 121. Lemonade Set, Bellflower, #19.

PLATE 122. Tea Cup, Bicycle Race.

PLATE 123. Salt Shaker, Blind Man's Bluff.

PLATE 124. Pin Tray, 5" x 3", Boat Dance.

PLATE 125. Cake Platter, 11", Boat Festival, #35.

PLATE 126. Celery Dish, 13", Boat Festival, #35.

PLATE 127. Bowl, 9½", Boy's Processional.

PLATE 128. After-Dinner Cup and Saucer, Boy's Processional, #2b.

PLATE 129. Jug, 5", Boy's Processional.

PLATE 130. Biscuit Jar, Carp A.

PLATE 131. Bud Vase, 4½", Carp A.

PLATE 132. Rice Bowl, Carp D.

PLATE 133. Bowl, 8¾", Cat, Garden Bench K and Parasol H in reserves, global view.

PLATE 134. Bowl, 8¾", Cat, Garden Bench K and Parasol H in reserves, close-up of Cat pattern.

PLATE 135. Bowl, 7½", Cherry Blossoms.

PLATE 136. Jug, 6⅓", Cherry Blossoms.

PLATE 137. Tea Cup and Saucer, Child Reaching for Butterfly, #20.

PLATE 138. Salt Shaker, Child Reaching for Butterfly.

PLATE 139. Berry Set, Chinese Coin motif with Mother and Son B, Garden Bench H, Meeting B, Futon, Pointing I, Battledore, Washday and Gardening patterns.

PLATE 140. Bowl, 7½", Chinese Coin motif with Battledore, Washday and Flower Gathering patterns.

PLATE 141. Bowl, 10", Chinese Coin motif.

PLATE 142. Cocoa Set, comes with six cups and saucers, Chinese Coin motif with Gardening, Pointing I, Meeting B, Garden Bench H, Futon, Washday and Battledore patterns.

PLATE 143. Close-up of Futon pattern from cocoa pot in Plate 142.

PLATE 144. Plate, 8½", Chinese Coin motif with Mother and Son B, Meeting B, Washday, Battledore and Futon patterns.

PLATE 145. Plate 8½", Chinese Coin motif, close-up of Washday pattern.

PLATE 146. Sugar and Creamer, Chinese Coin motif with Washday, Meeting B. Futon, Pointing D and Fan C patterns.

PLATE 147. Salt and Pepper Shakers 2¾", Chrysanthemum Garden.

PLATE 148. Stein, 7½", Chrysanthemum Garden.

PLATE 149. Tea Saucer, Circle Dance.

PLATE 150. Vase, 5½", Cloud A.

PLATE 151. Tete-a-Tete Set, Cloud B, J#6a.

PLATE 152. Dish, 5⅝", Court Lady.

PLATE 153. Chamberstick, Courtesan Processional.

PLATE 154. Relish Dish, 8", Courtesan Processional.

PLATE 155. Syrup Pitcher, Courtesan Processional.

PLATE 156. Vase, 3½", Cricket Cage.

PLATE 157. Bowl, 8⅝", Daikoku.

PLATE 158. After Dinner Cup and Saucer, Daikoku.

PLATE 159. Plate, 7½", Dragonboat.

PLATE 160. Plate, 8″, Dragonboat, J#16.

PLATE 161. Teapot, Dragonboat.

PLATE 162. Jug, 6″, Drum A in floral reserve.

PLATE 163. Same jug, Drum A in fan reserve.

PLATE 164. Same jug, Drum B.

PLATE 165. Same jug, Drum C.

PLATE 166. Bowl, 8", Drum D, J#16.

PLATE 167. Plate, 10", Duck Watching A, #20.

PLATE 168. Tea Cup and Saucer, Duck Watching B, #6.

PLATE 169. Bowl, 8¾", Fan A, Geisha Face and other figures in reserves.

PLATE 170. Teapot, Fan A reserve, J#16.

PLATE 171. Teapot, reverse, Fan Dance A and scenic reserves.

PLATE 172. Toothbrush Holder, Fan A.

PLATE 173. Toothpick Holder, Fan A.

PLATE 174. Toothpick Holder, Fan A reserve, J#2.

PLATE 175. Same Toothpick Holder, second side, Court Lady reserve.

PLATE 176. Same Toothpick Holder, third side, Garden Bench H reserve.

PLATE 177. Vase, 8″, Fan A reserve.

PLATE 178. Same Vase, reverse, Court Lady and Garden Bench H reserves.

PLATE 179. Vase, 7½" x 5½", Fan A, J#16.

PLATE 180. After-Dinner Cup and Saucer, Fan B.

PLATE 181. Cocoa Cup and Saucer, Fan D.

PLATE 182. Demitasse Pot, Fan Dance A.

PLATE 183. Sugar and Creamer, Fan Silhoutte of Hoo Bird, J#6a.

PLATE 184. Teaset, Fan Silhoutte of Hoo Bird, J#6b.

PLATE 185. Tea Tile, Feather Fan, #12.

PLATE 186. Plate, 6⅛", Flag.

PLATE 187. Saucer, Flower Gathering A.

PLATE 188. Biscuit Jar, 6½", Flower Gathering B.

PLATE 189. Butter Pat, 3¼", Flower Gathering B.

PLATE 190. Tea Cup and Saucer, Flower Gathering B.

PLATE 191. Sauce Dish, 4¾", Flower Gathering B.

PLATE 192. After-Dinner Cup and Saucer, Flower Gathering C.

PLATE 193. Napkin Ring, Flower Gathering C.

PLATE 194. After-Dinner Cup and Saucer, Flower Gathering D in bottom reserve, J#6b.

PLATE 195. Plate, 6", Flute and Koto.

PLATE 196. Cocoa Set, Footbridge A, includes six cups and saucers, front of Pot, 9½", #9.

PLATE 197. Close-up of Footbridge A pattern.

PLATE 198. Reverse of cocoa pot.

PLATE 199. Condiment Bowl with attached underplate, Footbridge B, J#36.

PLATE 200. Reverse of Condiment Bowl displaying figure in boat.

PLATE 201. Cocoa Cup and Saucer, Footbridge B.

PLATE 202. Celery Dish, Foreign Garden.

PLATE 203. Matchholder, Garden Bench A.

PLATE 204. Pitcher, 3½", Garden Bench A.

PLATE 205. Bon-bon dish, 6", Garden Bench B.

PLATE 206. Bon-bon dish, 6¼", Garden Bench B.

PLATE 207. Bowl, 7⅓", Garden Bench B, #69.

PLATE 208. Box, 6", Garden Bench B, #20.

PLATE 209. Cocoa Pot, 8", Garden Bench B.

PLATE 210. Creamer, 4", Garden Bench B.

PLATE 211. Tea Cup and Saucer, Garden Bench B.

PLATE 212. Drip Plate, 6¼", Garden Bench B.

PLATE 213. Sugar Bowl, Garden Bench B.

PLATE 214. Rose Bowl, 6" x 4", Garden Bench C reserve.

PLATE 215. Reverse of Rose Bowl with scenic reserve.

PLATE 216. Cocoa Pot, 6½", Garden Bench C.

PLATE 217. Tea Cup, Garden Bench C.

PLATE 218. Plate, 7", Garden Bench C.

PLATE 219. Plate, 8", Garden Bench C.

PLATE 220. Puff Box, Garden Bench C.

PLATE 221. Teapot, 4¾", Garden Bench C, #19.

PLATE 222. Dessert Bowl, Garden Bench D.

PLATE 223. Hatpin Holder, 4⅛", Garden Bench D.

PLATE 224. Refreshment Set, Garden Bench D.

PLATE 225. After-Dinner Saucer, Garden Bench D.

PLATE 226. Low Cracker Jar, Garden Bench E, J#16.

PLATE 227. Nappy, 4¾", Garden Bench F, J#16.

PLATE 228. Toothpick Holder, Garden Bench F, J#16.

PLATE 229. Creamer, 4", Garden Bench G, J#19.

PLATE 230. Vase, 5¼" x 6", Garden Bench G, smudged Japanese mark.

PLATE 231. Ewer, 5", Garden Bench H.

PLATE 232. Bowl, 6", Garden Bench I.

PLATE 233. Bouillon Cup with lid and drip plate, Garden Bench J, #32a.

PLATE 234. After-Dinner Cup, Garden Bench K.

PLATE 235. Pitcher, 5", Garden Bench K, #20.

PLATE 236. Salt Cellar, Garden Bench M, J#16, interior view.

PLATE 237. Salt Cellar, Garden Bench M, J#16, exterior view.

PLATE 238. Tea Cup and Saucer, Garden Bench N, #19.

PLATE 239. Plate 6⅛", Garden Bench O.

PLATE 240. Cocoa Cup and Saucer, Garden Bench P.

PLATE 241. Condiment Set, Garden Bench Q, #13.

PLATE 242. Jug, 4½", Garden Bench Q, #6.

PLATE 243. Ring Tree, Garden Bench Q, J#16.

PLATE 244. Bowl, 10½", Gardening.

PLATE 245. Condiment Bowl with attached underplate, Gardening.

PLATE 246. Tea Cup and Saucer, Gardening, J#36.

PLATE 247. Mint Dish, 6¾", Gardening.

PLATE 248. Footed Pin Tray, Gardening, interior view.

PLATE 249. Footed Pin Tray, Gardening, exterior view.

PLATE 250. Teapot, Gardening, #20.

PLATE 251. Tea Cup and Saucer, Geisha Band, #20.

PLATE 252. Plate, 6″, Geisha Dance.

PLATE 253a. Butter Pat, Geisha Face.

PLATE 253b. After-Dinner Cup and Saucer, Geisha Face.

PLATE 254. Tea Cup and Saucer, Geisha Face.

PLATE 255. Sake Cup, Geisha Face.

PLATE 256. Tea Cup and Saucer, Geisha in Sampan B.

PLATE 257. Hair Receiver, Geisha in Sampan B, #3d.

PLATE 258. Lemonade Mug, Geisha in Sampan B, #19.

PLATE 259. Plate, 6½", Geisha in Sampan B, #21.

PLATE 260. Tea Saucer, Geisha in Sampan B, #20.

PLATE 261. Bowl, 10½″, Geisha in Sampan D, #63.

PLATE 262. Bowl, 9½″, Geisha in Sampan E, #47.

PLATE 263. Vase, 3⅜″, Geisha on Parade.

PLATE 264. Plate, 8½″, Geisha Presentation.

PLATE 265. Plate, 9⅝″, Gift Processional.

PLATE 266. Sauce Dish, Her Master's Keeper.

PLATE 279. Biscuit Jar, Lady in Rickshaw B.

PLATE 280. Nut Cup, Lady in Rickshaw B, J#18.

PLATE 281. Cocoa Pot, 9½", Lantern B, #20.

PLATE 282. Tea Cup/Saucer, Lantern B.

PLATE 283. Matchholder, Lantern B, front.

PLATE 284. Matchholder, Lantern B, back.

PLATE 285. Matchholder, Lantern B, striker on side.

PLATE 286. Toothpick Holder, 3½″, Lantern B.

PLATE 287. Lantern Dance, Plate, 9½″, J#16.

PLATE 288. Tea Caddy, Leaving the Teahouse.

PLATE 289. Cake Platter, 10½″, Lesson and Parasol A.

PLATE 290. Cocoa Set, 8″ pot, includes five cups and saucers, Parasol A reserve, #19.

PLATE 291. Back of Cocoa Pot with Lesson reserve.

PLATE 292. Cocoa Set, 9½" pot, includes five cups and saucers, Lesson and Parasol A.

PLATE 293. Creamer, Lesson pattern on front.

PLATE 294. Creamer, Parasol A pattern on back.

PLATE 295. Tea Cup and Saucer, Lesson and Parasol A, J#1.

PLATE 296. Tea Strainer, Lesson and Parasol A.

PLATE 297. Tea Cup and Saucer, Long-Stemmed Peony.

PLATE 298. Hatpin Holder, Long-Stemmed Peony, #20.

PLATE 299. Mustard Jar, Long-Stemmed Peony.

PLATE 300. Nappy, Fan Dance A, Meditation, Mother and Daughter patterns in reserve.

PLATE 301. Same Nappy, close-up of Meditation pattern.

PLATE 302. Perfume Bottle, Meeting A.

PLATE 303. Cookie Jar, Meeting B.

PLATE 304. Cake Platter, 11″, Meeting C, #20.

PLATE 305. Condiment Tray, 7½″, Meeting C, #20.

PLATE 306. Ashtray, Miscellaneous.

PLATE 307. Tea Cup and Saucer, Miscellaneous, J#16.

PLATE 308. Tea Cup and Saucer, Miscellaneous, J#51.

PLATE 309. Hair Receiver, Miscellaneous.

PLATE 310. Matchholder, Miscellaneous, J#16.

PLATE 311. Tea Saucer, Miscellaneous.

PLATE 312. Creamer, 4", front, Mother and Daughter in reserve.

PLATE 313. Creamer, reverse, scenic in reserve.

PLATE 314. Jewel Chest, 4½" x 3½", Mother and Daughter, J#43.

PLATE 315. Double Eggcup, Mother and Son A, front.   PLATE 316. Double Eggcup, Mother and Son A, back.

PLATE 317. Roll Tray, 12½", Mother and Son B.

PLATE 318. Bowl, 10", Mother and Son C, J#66.

PLATE 319. Cake Platter, 10", Mother and Son C.   PLATE 320. Plate, 8", Mother and Son C, J#16.

114

PLATE 321. Left: Sauce Dish, 4¾", Mother and Son C, #19.
Right: Sauce Dish, 6", Mother and Son C, #19.

PLATE 322. Vase, 10½", Mother and Son C, #60.

PLATE 323. Individual Berry Bowl, Oni Dance A.

PLATE 324. Biscuit Jar, 7½", Oni Dance B.

PLATE 325. Cocoa Pot, 9½", Oni Dance B, #20.

PLATE 326. Handleless Teacup, front, Oxen Song.

PLATE 327. Handleless Teacup, reverse, Court Lady.

PLATE 328. Sauce Dish, 4¾", Parasol A, unusual in that it is not accompanied by Lesson pattern.

PLATE 329. Jug, 5½", Parasol B.

PLATE 330. Powder Jar, Parasol B.

PLATE 331. Salt Shaker, Parasol B.

PLATE 332. Right: Creamer, 4¾", Parasol C. Left: Jug, 5", Parasol C, #20.

116

PLATE 333. Manicure Jar, 2¼", Parasol C, #19.

PLATE 334. Muffineer, Parasol C, #20b.

PLATE 335. Vase, 6½", Parasol C.

PLATE 336. Bowl 8⅝", Parasol D, interior view.

PLATE 337. Same Bowl, exterior view.

PLATE 338. Dresser Tray, Parasol D.

PLATE 339. Gravy Boat, Parasol D, #19.

PLATE 340. Box 4½", Parasol E, #20.

PLATE 341. Mustard Jar, Parasol E, #56.

PLATE 342. Salt and Pepper Shakers, 3¼", Parasol E.

PLATE 343. Cocoa Saucer, Parasol E.

PLATE 344. Teapot, Parasol E, #3d.

PLATE 345. Teaset, Parasol E, #20, teapot, creamer and sugar.

PLATE 346. Teaset, Parasol E, #20, cup and saucer.

PLATE 347. Bowl, 6¼", Parasol F.

PLATE 348. Pin Tray, 4" x 3", Parasol F.

PLATE 349. Master Nut Bowl, Parasol G, J# 29.

PLATE 350. Close-up of Nut Bowl border showing Japanese seals from which the pattern's nickname derives.

PLATE 351. Spoon Tray, Parasol H, #15a.

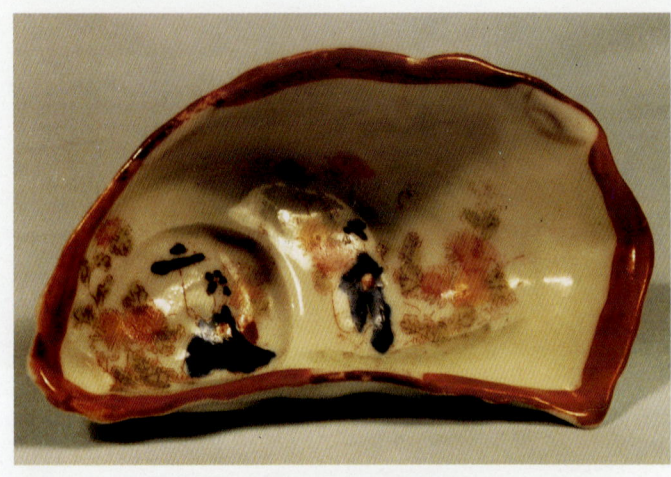

PLATE 352. Spoon Warmer, Parasol K, interior.

PLATE 353. Exterior of Spoon Warmer showing oyster-shape relief molding.

PLATE 354. After-Dinner Cup and Saucer, Parasol L, #1.

PLATE 355. Tea Cup and Saucer, Parasol L, #22.

PLATE 356. Talcum Shaker, Parasol L.

PLATE 357. Bowl, 7", Parasol L.

PLATE 358. Handleless Teacup, Peacock.

PLATE 359. Tea Cup and Saucer, Peacock on a Flowered Stone Roof.

PLATE 360. Bowl, 6", Picnic A, #3d.

PLATE 361. Dish, 5½" x 6½", Picnic A, J#39.

PLATE 362. Lunch Set, Picnic A, J#15.

PLATE 363. Sugar and Creamer, Picnic A, J#16.

PLATE 364. Relish Dish, Picnic B.

PLATE 365. Tea Cup and Saucer, Picnic C.

PLATE 366. Tea Cup and Saucer, Picnic D.

PLATE 367. After-Dinner Cup and Saucer, Plum Blossom Branch.

PLATE 368. Creamer, Pointing A.

PLATE 369. Tea Cup and Saucer, Pointing B.

PLATE 370. Bowl, 5¼", Pointing D.

PLATE 371. Bowl 7½", Pointing D, smudged Japanese mark.

PLATE 372. Celery Dish, Pointing D.

PLATE 373. Manicure Box, Pointing F.

PLATE 374. Nut Set, comes with five cups, Pointing F, J#16.

PLATE 375. Refreshment Set, Pointing G.

PLATE 376. Tea Cup and Saucer, Pointing J.

PLATE 377. Bowl, 8", Porcelain Bench, #19.

PLATE 378. After-Dinner Cup and Saucer, Porch, #2b.

PLATE 379. Tea Cup and Saucer, Porch, #3f.

PLATE 380. Dish, 7", Porch.

PLATE 381. Plate 7⅜″, Porch, #2c.

PLATE 382. Tea Cup and Saucer, Privileged Perambulator, J#16.

PLATE 383. Pitcher, 5″, Processional.

PLATE 384. Plate, 6″, Processional.

PLATE 385. Powder Jar, Processional, J#16.

PLATE 386. Vase, 7″, Processional, J#16.

PLATE 387. Powder Jar, Pug.

PLATE 388. Cocoa Pot, Recital on an Ikebana.

PLATE 389. Cocoa Pot, Recital on an Ikebana, pattern continuation.

PLATE 390. Condensed Milk Jar, Rendevous, J#21.

PLATE 391. Reverse of Condensed Milk Jar.

PLATE 392. Mustache Cup, Rendevous, J#16.

PLATE 393. Reverse of Mustache Cup, displaying scenery instead of usual figural reserve.

PLATE 394. Plate, 9", Rendevous, J#67.

PLATE 395. Tea Saucer, Rendevous.

PLATE 396. Berry Bowl, Rivers Edge.

PLATE 397. Cocoa Pot (sans lid), 11", Rivers Edge, #5b.

PLATE 398. Front of Cocoa Pot showing ornate decoration under spout.

PLATE 399. Napkin Ring, Rivers Edge, #6.

PLATE 400. Plate, 7¼", J#14b.

PLATE 401. Tea Saucer, Rivers Edge, #32a and J#16.

PLATE 402. Sweetmeat Set in lacquer box, Rivers Edge.

PLATE 403. Close-up of lacquer box.

PLATE 404. Teaset, Rivers Edge, #17.

PLATE 405. Teaset, Rivers Edge.

PLATE 406. Creamer, Rokkasen, main pattern.

PLATE 407. Same creamer, reverse side with J#40 imbedded in pattern.

PLATE 408. Same creamer, bottom showing unusual form.

PLATE 409. Tea Caddy, Rokkasen.

PLATE 410. Hair Receiver, front, Sake Time in reserve.

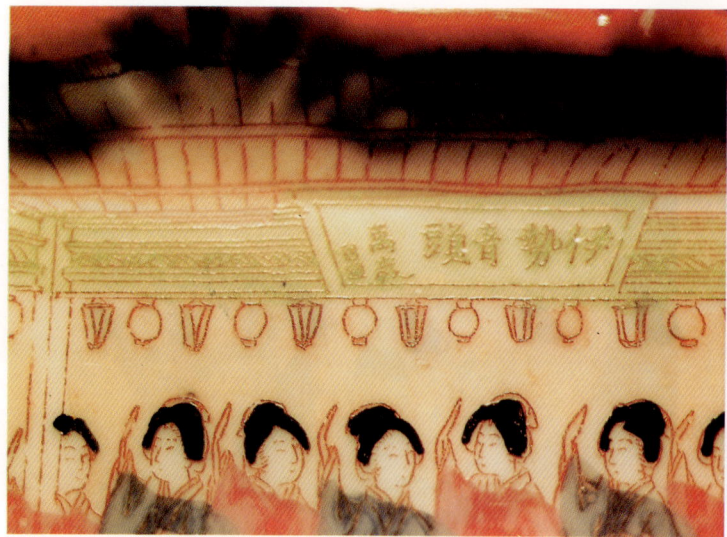

PLATE 423. Same tray, close-up of banner over stage.

PLATE 424. Same tray, close-up of scenic reserve showing entire temple complex.

PLATE 425. Sugar and Creamer, Small Sounds of Summer.

PLATE 426. Pancake Server, So Big, J#16.

PLATE 427. Cracker Jar (sans lid), front, Spider Puppet, J#17.

PLATE 428. Cracker Jar, back, scenic reserve.

PLATE 429. Hair Receiver, Spider Puppet.

PLATE 430. Bowl, 6¾", Stepping Stones.

PLATE 431. Eggcup, front, Takara Bune.

PLATE 432. Eggcup, reverse.

PLATE 433. Ashtray, Temple A, #15a.

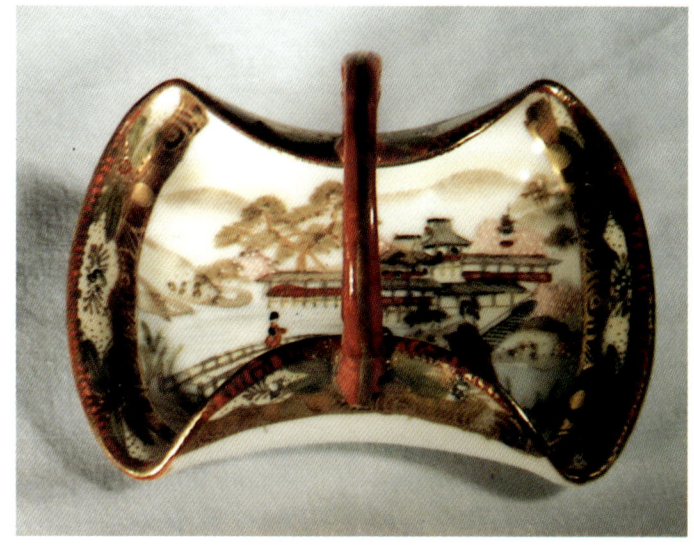

PLATE 434. Basket, Temple A, #15a.

PLATE 435. Biscuit Jar, Temple A, J#16.

PLATE 436. Cocoa Pot, 7", Temple A.

PLATE 437. After-Dinner Cup, Temple A, #47.

PLATE 438. Demitasse Set, includes six cups and saucers, Temple A, J#16.

PLATE 439. Manicure Box, Temple A, #15a.

PLATE 440. Mayonnaise ladle, Temple A, #12.

PLATE 441. Mayonnaise Set, Temple A, J#16.

PLATE 442. Nappy, Temple A.

PLATE 443. Nut Set, includes five individual cups, Temple A, #12.

PLATE 444. Salt Dish, Temple A, J#16.

PLATE 445. Salt Dish, Temple A, #8.

PLATE 446. Sugar Shaker, Temple A.

PLATE 447. Sugar Tray, Temple A, #12.

PLATE 448. Vase, 5", J#16.

PLATE 449. Tea Cup, Temple B.

PLATE 450. Tea Cup, interior, Temple B.

PLATE 451. Tea Cup, exterior, Temple B.

PLATE 452. Dish, Temple B, unrecognizable Japanese mark.

PLATE 453. Double Eggcup, Temple B.

PLATE 454. Pitcher, 8½″, Temple B.

PLATE 455. Plate, 7½″, Temple B, J#53.

PLATE 456. Ring Tree, Temple B, J#16.

PLATE 457. Sugar Shaker, Temple B.

PLATE 458. Plate, 6″, Temple Vase.

PLATE 459. Hair Receiver, Thousand Geisha.

PLATE 460. Plate, 6", To the Teahouse, #3c.

PLATE 461. Powder Jar, To the Teahouse, J#16.

PLATE 462. Salt Dish, To the Teahouse, J#16.

PLATE 463. After-Dinner Cup and Saucer, Torii.

PLATE 464. Individual Salt and Pepper Shakers, Visiting with Baby.

PLATE 465. Plate, 7¼", Visitor to the Court, #19.

PLATE 466. Teaset, Visitor to the Court, #19.

PLATE 467. Plate, 8¾", Wait for Me.

PLATE 468. Cocoa Pot, 9¾", Waterboy, #1b.

PLATE 469. Cocoa Pot, 9½", Writing A, #20.

PLATE 470. Cocoa Saucer, Writing A, #19.

PLATE 471. Plate 7⅜", Writing A, #19.

PLATE 472. Plate, 8½", Writing A, #19.

Glossary

Amado - Wooden sliding doors used as nighttime exterior walls of traditional Japanese dwelling.

Battledore - A game similar to badminton, played with a flat, oblong wooden paddle and a shuttlecock.

Beading - Small semispheres of enamel used for decoration of porcelain body, usually to enhance flat enameling.

Bento bako - Tiered containers used to store food for picnics, etc.

Biscuit - Porcelain body that has been fired once, but not glazed.

Decal - Screen printing of a design on specially treated paper; by saturating parts of fine mesh with special solutions, those parts are made impenetrable; special inks or enamels are then forced through the unprotected parts of the mesh, creating a design on specially treated paper laying below; enamels are chemically fixed onto this paper, the paper placed onto the ceramic body, then wetted and removed, leaving the enamels in place on the ceramic; telltale sign is area of color created by many dots.

Diaper pattern - Any design sequence repeated ad infinitum as a means of decoration.

E-boshi - Tall, black lacquered hat worn by Japanese court noble.

Enamel - Decorative coating of color baked on ceramic wares; may have a glossy (shiny) or matte (flat) finish.

Finial - Handle atop lid of sugar bowl, cocoa and tea pots, etc., may be spherical, teardrop, floral, etc.

Firing - Application of heat to harden glazes or pottery.

Fluting - Alternatively concave/convex form used as decorative shaping on rims of plates or vases.

Fuku - Japanese word for Good Luck.

Fususa - Rice paper stretched across framework of light wood used as sliding doors inside Japanese dwelling.

Futon - Sleeping mat or quilt.

Geisha - Literally "art person", female trained in social graces including speaking and writing the ancient language, singing, dancing, playing of musical instruments, serving of food and wine, etc.

Glaze - Coating of colored, opaque or transparent material applied to ceramics which renders the clay impervious to other elements which might discolor or otherwise cause wear or deterioration of the ceramic body or colors applied under the glaze.

Go - Japanese game employing black and white stones and a board marked with many intersecting lines.

Hakama - Akin to our culottes with slit on side, worn over kimono.

Haori - Loose jacket often worn with *hakama*.

Hashira-ye - Pillar prints, vertical prints measuring twenty-seven to twenty-eight inches in length and nine to twelve inches in diameter.

Hoo - Mythical bird often referred to as a phoenix.

Ikebana - Flower arrangement, the Japanese art of flower arranging.

Kabuki - Japanese public theatre in which majority of roles were traditionally played by men.

Kakemono - Hanging scroll with picture or calligraphy.

Kasa - Sedge hat, flat, circular, woven hat peaking at small point in center of head.

Kiln - Brick-lined oven where firing of ceramics takes place.

Kimono - Loose outer garment with short wide sleeves held closed by an *obi*, the traditional dress of Japan.

Koinobori - Cloth or paper carps strung from poles, symbolize man's struggle against the current of life, displayed on special holidays.

Koto - Thirteen, seventeen or nineteen-stringed oblong instrument, similar to the harpsichord.

Kuon - Japanese for Good Fortune.

Mark - The signature or trademark of an artisan or company, usually found on the base of an item, may be hand painted, decaled or stenciled.

Melon Ribbed - Bulbous body with vertical indentations, making its appearance akin to a melon or pumpkin.

Mold - The frame or model which is often used to give clay its shape or form.

Molded in Relief - Porcelain form which stands out from the porcelain body due to the manner in which the body was molded, can vary from a ⅛" raised design such as leaves or lacing to severe changes from the surface plane, sometimes erroneously called "blown out."

Mt. Fuji - Highest peak and extinct volcano, located southwest of Tokyo.

Nihon, Nippon - Japanese word and its romanization meaning Japan; also used to describe the period between March 1, 1891 and August, 1921.

Nishikide - Design of various diapers and colors completely covering a given area.

Obi - Sash or belt worn over kimono.

Origami - Japanese art of folding paper into forms of birds, flowers, etc.

Pagoda - Japanese architectural form of multi-tiered building.

Reserve - Area of decoration set off from the balance of the design by enclosure in an outline which may be floral, fan, geometric, circular or abstract in shape.

Sake - Japanese rice wine, generally served warm in a thin bottle with slender neck and drunk from very small cups.

Samisen - Three-stringed instrument with small square body and long neck.

Sampan - Small boat.

Samurai - Japanese warrior.

Screen of State - Wooden frame from which hang draperies or other textiles beyond which women concealed themselves, remaining audible to but not visible by guests.

Seam - Point at which two molded pieces are jointed.

Shinto - Religion or dogma indigenous to Japan based on the utmost respect for nature.

Shoji - Semi-transparent sliding doors used as daytime exterior walls of traditional Japanese dwelling.

Shuttlecock - The "birdie" used in battledore.

Slip - Liquid clay applied to leather-hard porcelain body to achieve raised decoration.

Stencil - When speaking of Japanese porcelains, applies to a design carved into a block of wood which is inked or enameled, specially treated paper applied thereto and removed with ink adhering to paper, paper is then placed upon the ceramic surface and wetted, leaving ink adhering to the ceramic body, enameled ceramic is then fired.

Swirl Fluted - Fluting of the body rim extends into the body and the indentations are curved rather than straight.

Takara Bune - Ship of Good Fortune, see pattern by same name.

Tatami mat - Straw mat used as floor covering in traditional Japanese dwelling.

Tokonama - Alcove in Japanese dwelling used for the few shelves, cabinets, wall or floral decorations employed in the traditional Japanese abode.

Torii - Large wooden or stone gateways consisting of two vertical posts topped by two horizontal ones with a short vertical in between them for support, all curved upward and outward; used to denote entrance to Shinto shrines.

Uchiwa - A round fan not capable of being folded.

Underglaze - Enamels applied before a glaze is placed on the ceramic surface.

Just For Fun

Collecting is more than a hobby, more than research, more than writing, more than an investment. More importantly, collecting is and should be **fun**. Part of that fun includes sharing laughs and experiences. Frank and I want to share our fun with you through a couple of poems we have written over the years[1]. Hope you enjoy them.

Collector's Dilemma

by Frank and Elyce Litts

There was a collector who lived in a shoe,
She had so many antiques she didn't know what to do,
So she packed up her boxes and moved to a sock.
No longer having laces, she kept them all locked.

The sock, it did stretch out too far,
So her next move was to a jar.
However, the situation looked very grim
Because before too long the jar was filled to the brim.

A tisket, a tasket, she moved to a basket
Which didn't last long for it wasn't elastic.
With all those antiques she couldn't go far
So she packed them all up and moved to a car.
And sooner than you could say "quick as a flash"
Antiques and collectibles were adorning the dash.

This worked out fine until she got stuck,
Then her next move was to a big truck.
The truck, it did seem, had plenty of room
But at the rate she was buying she'd have to move soon.

She then met a sailor who owned a large trailer
And kindly many a shelf he did nail for her.
One sunny day when he went off to sea,
"Ah ha", she said, "his trailer's all for me."

When he returned he told her to pack
So she moved with antiques strapped to her back.

She got tired of walking on the hard cement,
So her next move was to an apartment.
For months there were many spots to fill.
She lined up antiques on the window sill.

Then came along the day she did dread,
The wind blew a vase down on the landlady's head.
"I've had enough of this," the landlady said in dismay,
So. Ms. Collector moved to a house that very same day.

For years in the house her collection did grow,
She piled antiques up high and down low.
She spent so much time dusting and rearranging
That she began to find life not very engaging.

She finally gave in, sold her antiques to a museum
So everyone else could come there and see them.
Without all that fussing and dusting to do,
She sold her house and moved back to a shoe.

She settled in with her one little bag,
But somehow life just seemed such a drag.
So for amusement she went out with a friend,
And at a flea market their jaunt did end.

She saw an old "this" and and interesting "that"
And soon an old habit was newly begat!

The next one has a typical non-collector's perspective. Of course, it was written before that individual turned into a collector himself!

Living With A Collector

by Frank Litts

Living with a collector can be lots of fun,
But you better be prepared to be on the run.

A garage sale here, a flea market there,
Always looking for that piece that is rare.

Neither rain nor sleet nor even snow,
Will stop the collector from being on the go.

And just when you think the day of rest is near,
She finds another sale and says, "Just one more, Dear?"

That one leads into another and another
And, before you know it, you're back into summer.

Then one bright sunny day when you're out on the road
She finds that one piece that she really loves so.

The price is too high, she walks away with head shaking
But then she drags you back, just to find its been taken.

She promises herself that next time it won't get away.
Rather than not have it at all, she'll just have to pay.

And then - there it is - she can't pass this one up,
A beautiful Geisha Girl Porcelain cup.

The saucer is there and it's very rare
And she thinks that the price is really quite fair.

So you pay the dealer who says "Lots of luck,"
You're finally on your way home; can't wait to put your feet up.

But just when you think your chance to rest is near,
She finds another sale and says, "Just one more, Dear?"

[1]Reprinted with permission of *The Geisha Girl Porcelain Newsletter*.

Bibliography

Andacht, S. "East Meets West," *Antique Trader Weekly*, July 2, 1980.

Andacht, S. *Satsuma, An Illustrated Guide*. Iowa: Wallace-Homestead Books, Inc., 1978.

Antiques Research Publication. "China and Glassware," *1925 Butler Bros. Catalog*, reprint.

Antiques Research Publication. "China and Glassware," *1930 Butler Bros. Catalog*, reprint.

Baelz, T., Ed. *Awakening Japan: The Diary of a German Doctor, Erwin Baelz*. Bloomington, IN: Indiana University Press, 1974.

Belli, M. *Life and Law in Japan*. Bobbs-Merrill Co., Inc., 1960.

Belshaw, J. "China on our Tables," *Arts and Decoration*, January 1932, 34:58-59.

Bolger, L. *The Dictionary of World Pottery and Porcelain*. New York: Charles Scribner and Sons, 1971.

Chamberlain, B.H. *Japanese Things*. Vermont: Charles E. Tuttle Co., 1971.

Clarke, F. "China from the Modern Shops," *Arts and Decoration*, August 1925, 23:52.

Cooper, A. *History of Pottery*. St. Martins Press, 1972.

Dilts, M.M. *The Pageant of Japanese History*. New York: Longmans, Green and Co., 1946.

Dornberg, J. *Eastern Europe: A Communist Kaleidoscope*. New York: Dial Press, 1980.

Dudley, D. and I. Wilkinson. *Museum Registration Methods*. Washington, D.C.: American Association of Museums, 1979.

Encyclopedia of Collectibles: Inkwells to Lace. Virginia: Time-Life Books, 1979.

Fulton Democrat. Pennsylvania: Nov. 11, 1937.

Gorham, H. *Japanese and Oriental Ceramics*. Vermont: Charles E. Tuttle Co., Inc. 1971.

"Japanese Pottery Industry," *Review of Reviews*, April 1920, 61:441-442.

Jenyns, S. *Japanese Porcelain*. New York: Frederick A. Praeger, 1975.

Johnes, R. *Japanese Art*. London: Spring Books, 1961.

Kansas City Star, December 1892.

Kansas City Times, November 26, 1938.

Koop, A. and H. Inada. *Japanese Names and How to Read Them*. London: Routledge and Kegan Paul, 1972.

Korbel, J. *Twentieth Century Czechoslovakia*, New York: Columbia University Press, 1977.

Kosloff, A. *Ceramic Screen Printing*. Cincinatti: Sign of the Times, 1962.

Litts, E. *Geisha Girl Porcelain Newsletter*, January 1982 - November 1985.

Macy, R.H. and Co., *Fall/Winter Catalog, 1906-1907*. New York, 1906.

Mew, E. *Japanese Porcelain*. New York: Dodd and Mead, 1909.

Munsterberger, H. *The Arts of Japan*. Vermont: Charles E. Tuttle Co., 1957.

Nakagawa, S. *Kutani Ware*. Tokyo: Kodansha International Ltd., 1979.

"New Glass and China," *Harper's Bazaar*, February 1904, 38:198-200.

Noma, S. *The Arts of Japan*. New York: Kodansha International Ltd., 1978.

Oates, J. *Phoenix Bird Chinaware*. Michigan: privately published, 1984.

Ogrizek, D. *The World in Color: Japan*. London: McGraw Hill, 1957.

Our Drummer. St. Louis: Butler Brothers, 1906.

Our Drummer. St. Louis: Butler Brothers, 1907.

Our Drummer. St. Louis: Butler Brothers, 1908.

Our Drummer. St. Louis: Butler Brothers, 1909.

Our Drummer. St. Louis: Butler Brothers, 1910.

Our Drummer. St. Louis: Butler Brothers, 1911.

Our Drummer. St. Louis: Butler Brothers, 1913.

Our Drummer. St. Louis: Butler Brothers, 1914.

Our Drummer. St. Louis: Butler Brothers, 1915.

Our Drummer. St. Louis: Butler Brothers, 1916.

Our Drummer. St. Louis: Butler Brothers, 1919.

Poche, E. *Porcelain Marks of the World*. New York: Arco Publishing Co., 1974.

Pure Food Groceries. St. Paul, MN: Montgomery Ward and Co., 1908.

Pure Food Groceries. St. Paul, MN: Montgomery Ward and Co., 1920.

Pure Food Groceries. St. Paul, MN: Montgomery Ward and Co., May-June, 1921.

Pure Food Groceries. St. Paul, MN: Montgomery Ward and Co., July-Aug, 1921.

Pure Food Groceries. St. Paul, MN: Montgomery Ward and Co., May-June, 1922.

Pure Food Groceries. St. Paul, MN: Montgomery Ward and Co., Nov - Dec, 1923.

Reibel, D. *Registration Methods for the Small Museum*. Nashville, TN: American Association for State and Local History, 1978.

Rontgen, R. *Marks on German, Bohemian and Austrian Porcelain: 1710-Present*. PA: Schiffer Publishing Co., 1981.

Rose-Innes, A. *Beginners Dictionary of Chinese-Japanese Characters and Compounds*. Yokohama: Yoshikawa, 1944.

Sakade, D., Ed. *A Guide to Reading and Writing Japanese*. Vermont: Charles E. Tuttle Co., 1978.

Scidmore, E. "The Porcelain Artists of Japan," *Harper's Weekly*, January 22, 1898, 42:83-88.

Shalleck, J. *Tea*. New York: Viking Press, 1971.

Shugio, H. "Ceramic Artists," *International Studio*, October 1910, 41:286-293.

Smith, B. *Japan, A History in Art*. New York: Doubleday Co., Inc., 1964.

Stitt, I. *Japanese Ceramics of the Last 100 Years*. New York: Crown Publishers, 1974.

Tachau, H. "Modern China for the Table," *House Beautiful*, January 1918, 43:98-99.

The Oriental Store. New York: A.A. Vantine and Co., Inc., 1914.

Wiskemann, E. *Czechs and Germans: A Study of the Struggle in the Historic Provinces of Bohemia and Moravia*. New York: Oxford University Press, 1938.

Van Pattern, J. *The Collector's Encyclopedia of Nippon Porcelain*. Paducah, Kentucky: Collector Books, 1979.

Pattern Catalog and Price Guide

How To Use & Understand A Price Guide

This catalog contains descriptions of all patterns cataloged by the author through the third quarter, 1986. Datings referred to in pattern descriptions by the phrase "as early as" indicates the earliest year that the pattern has been found in advertising, catalogs, etc. The pattern may actually have been produced prior to that year.

The price guide contains listings for over 1,000 items, including those photographed. It is structured in alphabetical order by pattern name. Each listing includes, in the order noted, a Plate number, where applicable, the form, shape and size, border color, idiosyncratic detail, mark number and value guide.

In using the price guide, one must remember the meaning of the word "guide" — "an example or criterion of accuracy; to direct or advise." Simply stated, its purpose is to set the collector in the right direction, allowing a realistic degree of leeway.

Geisha Girl Porcelain was imported and sold most heavily in the eastern and western portions of the country. Because of the greater availability, prices tend to be more moderate in these areas than in the southwest, for example. When selling an item, one can expect only as much as the buyer's geographic location and personal interests permit.

When selling to a dealer, the amount received for an item will rarely reach more than 60% of the book value, if even that much. The price guide value is comparable to a retail listing. The dealer, however, is purchasing at wholesale.

Determining The Value Of An Item

The values listed in the price guide are for items in very good condition. They represent an averaging of prices throughout the country and take into consideration rarity of pattern and form. To determine whether your piece is of like value, the following factors should be taken into consideration.

Condition is of utmost importance. Chips, cracks, hairlines, missing parts and worn enamels all serve to lower value. The percentages noted below can be deducted from book value to determine a fair value for a damaged piece.

Hairline	10%
Worn gold	10%
Chip on base	10%
Lightly worn enamel	15%
Heavily worn enamel	50%
Missing part	50-70%
Major chip on body	60%
Crack	70%
Repaired defects	If a chip or enameling has been professionally repaired such that it is all but invisible to the naked eye, deduct 30% less for the defect. Repairs that are as visible as the original defect do not add to the value.

Is the design well applied? For example, is the stencil continuous or does it have an abrupt beginning and end which don't mesh? Consider, too, the amount of detail (use of gold, highlighting, definition) as well as the finesse with which the enamels were applied.

Reference earlier chapters to determine whether the border or stencil color is unusual, or the mark is highly desirable. It must be emphasized that it is the combination of all qualities that go into the marketplace determination of value.

Determining The Value Of An Unlisted Item

To determine the value of Geisha Girl Porcelain not specifically listed, note the value of similar forms in other patterns. Taking into consideration the border color, condition and rarity of the particular pattern involved, adjust the value accordingly.

---

1. **Art Show.** Ladies viewing a number of decorated screens.
   Plate 94, Lemon Plate, 5¾", red with gold .. 15.00
2. **Bamboo Tree.** Pattern adds pine green bamboo trees to a Processional type pattern; border is thin line of pine green, enhanced with white or yellow enameling; dates circa 1928.
   Cup/Saucer, Tea #1b 7.00
   Plate, 6" 5.00
   Plate, 7", chrysanthemum-shaped 12.00
   Plate 95, Plate 7¼", #19 .... 10.00
   Plate 96, Teapot, #19 .... 20.00
   Teaset, 16 pieces (covered pot, creamer, sugar, six cups/saucers, lemon plate), #19 ...... 100.00
3. **Bamboo Trellis.** Three ladies standing and kneeling at water's edge; behind them is large bamboo trellis overgrown with peonies, as early as 1906.
   Plate 97, Basket Vase, pair 8½", green handle circumference & rim where body meets footrim, brown footrim, both with gold 150.00
   Bon-bon Dish, red with gold 45.00
   Plate 98, Bowl, 7½", footed, light apple green with gold 35.00
   Cocoa Set, 13 pieces (pot, six cups/saucers), red-orange 75.00
   Cocoa Set, 13 pieces (pot, six cups/saucers), fluted, cobalt blue, lattice-work backdrop for pattern in reserves, J#51 & J#16 ... 225.00
   Cup/Saucer, After-Dinner, red-orange with gold buds 10.00
   Cup/Saucer, Tea, scalloped cobalt blue, gold line down handle 20.00
   Cup/Saucer, Tea, red with gold, floral spray inside, pattern on exterior 22.00
   Cup/Saucer, Tea, dark green, #20 .... 18.00

Hair Receiver, red-orange 20.00
Mint Dish, red-orange with gold buds 10.00
Mint Dish, scalloped, red-orange 6.00
Mug, 4" x 3", red with gold buds, #19 . . . . 18.00
Mustard Pot, scalloped blue 25.00
Plate 99, Plate, 6½", blue-green with gold
    buds, simple decor 8.00
Salad Set, 7 pieces (9" master, 5" six individu-
    al), red with gold 55.00
Sauce Dish, red-orange 8.00
Sauce Dish, eight-lobed, red with gold 10.00
Plate 100, Saucer, red-orange with gold buds . . 3.00
Serving Dish, oval, cut-out handles, red-orange 25.00
Sugar/Creamer, double "O" handles and finial,
    red-orange with yellow 20.00
Teapot, footed, red-orange with gold 35.00
Vases, pair, 4½", red-orange, #14 . . . . 25.00

4. **Basket A.** Four ladies gathering cockle shells from river and placing them in purple baskets; two of the ladies are standing in the water, a third is bending over with her hands in the water, fourth is on bank; lady second from left is pointing toward her counterparts and holding her own basket (compare with Basket B); bank is covered with red-orange chrysanthemums and reeds; overhead are pink and white enamel dotted cherry blossoms; other detailing includes stilted dwellings and Japanese flag.
Plate 101, Bowl, Nut, master, 6", nine-lobed,
    three feet, dark apple green 30.00
Plate 102, Cocoa Pot, 6½" tall, conical body,
    dark apple green with gold 45.00
Plate 103, Cocoa Pot, 8", conical with slight
    melon ribbing, dark apple green with gold 55.00
Creamer, bulbous, red-orange with gold buds 10.00
Cup/Saucer, cocoa, fluted, light apple green
    with gold 25.00
Plate 104, Plate, 8½", swirl fluted, scalloped
    edge, dark apple green 30.00
Salt Shaker, sea green 8.00
Plate 105, Sugar/Creamer, fluted with scal-
    loped edge, dark apple green with gold . . 32.00

5. **Basket B.** As above, except the lady second from left is not pointing, but helping another geisha hold a basket.
Plates 9-10, Creamer, footed, dark apple green 20.00
Plate 106, Cup/Saucer, After-Dinner, straight
    sided, dark apple green with gold, floral
    spray inside, pattern on exterior 15.00
Plate 107, Cup/Saucer, After-Dinner, curved
    sides, dark apple green, floral spray on ex-
    terior, pattern on interior 20.00
Plate 108, Cup/Saucer, Cocoa, fluted, dark apple
    green with gold, pattern on exterior, floral
    spray on interior 25.00
Cup/Saucer, tea, red with gold buds and violet
    chrysanthemums, pattern on interior, violet
    chrysanthemums and stenciled floral spray
    on exterior 20.00
Salt/Pepper Shakers, apple green 25.00

6. **Baskets of Mums A.** Lady going back and forth through garden carrying flat baskets of chrysanthemums; child holds one in her hand.

Plate 109, Sauce Dish, four-lobed, one with
    cut-out for handle, mint green with gold
    line below 8.00

7. **Baskets of Mums B.** Lady carrying basket of chrysanthemums; child holding square flat dish of them; bringing them toward two ladies on balcony, one of whom is pointing to flower bearers; other on balcony ornately dressed, apparently mistress of the house.
Plate 110, Biscuit Jar, three-footed, melon
    ribbed, red with gold 49.00
Plate 111, Butter Pat, 3¼", red-orange with
    gold buds and stripes, heavily enameled and
    gold highlighted 8.00

8. **Battledore.** Formerly called the Butterfly pattern, this features several ladies and children playing battledore — a game similar to badminton. The Japanese version is played with oblong paddles, flat on one side and beautifully decorated on the other. Colorful butterflies flit about overhead; cobalt blue and orange chrysanthemums underfoot; gold cranes fly beyond pink cherry blossoms. With rare exception, each piece has a single shuttlecock placed slightly off center just above ladies' heads; dates as early as 1906; green bordered items sport border enhancements of gold, pink, yellow and white chrysanthemums; pattern also found on Chinese Coin motif items.
Berry Set, 6 pieces (master, five individual),
    three-legged, red-orange 40.00
Plate 1, Bon-bon Dish, mum-shaped, olive green 22.00
Bowl, individual berry, six-lobed, apple green 12.00
Butter Pat, yellow green 10.00
Celery Dish, apple green with gold 38.00
Plate 112, Cocoa Pot, 8", conical body,
    yellow green 55.00
Plate 113, Cocoa Pot, 9", ewer-shaped,
    yellow green 85.00
Plate 8, Cocoa Pot, 9½", ribbed conical
    body, yellow green 75.00
Plate 114, Cup/Saucer, After-Dinner, straight
    stded, dark apple green 15.00
Plate 115, Cup/Saucer, Tea, yellow green,
    pattern on exterior, interior has 2" length
    of border with hanging cherry blossoms 20.00
Plate 116, Hair Receiver, dark apple green
    with gold 35.00
Hair Receiver, red-orange with gold 25.00
Humidor, scalloped blue with gold line,
    figures larger than usual 70.00
Plate 117, Jug, 4¼" wide at base, 5" tall to
    upwardly extended spout, fluted edge & base,
    ribbed body, yellow green with gold 35.00
Plate 6, Plate, 6", swirl fluted, scalloped edge,
    yellow green 14.00
Plate, 6¼", swirl fluted, scalloped edge,
    red-orange 10.00
Plate, 8½", swirl fluted rim, red with gold . 20.00
Plate, 9", red with gold, design segmented
    in pinwheel fashion, each sector showing
    geometrics, scenery or subject pattern, J#45 55.00
Saucer, Tea, yellow green 3.00

Plate 118, Sugar and Creamer, melon ribbed
squat bodies, yellow green................ 40.00
Plate 119, Sugar Bowl, bulbous slenderizing
towards top, bamboo style handles, apple green 15.00
Plate 44, Teapot, 6″, bulbous, footed dark
apple green........................ 50.00
Teapot, 7″, infuser, dark apple green..... 45.00
Plate 120, Urn, 8″, covered, inverted "U"
handles, olive green................. 135.00

9. **Bellflower.** Ladies picking bellflowers in the shade of large yellow tree; one holds two shallow reed baskets containing flowers; another adjusts her kasa; third picks flowers. To left of scene is mark J#25, translating to "picture by Suzuki Harunobu"; the scene is probably taken from one of his paintings. Minimal brown stenciling; overall design simply executed, suggestion being made via few strokes of paint rather than heavy detailing.
Plate 121, Lemonade Set, 6 pieces, (Pitcher,
five mugs), brown with green enhancements, #19........................ 125.00

10. **Bicycle Race.** Two ladies riding bicycles, each having a different flag waving from its perch in back of their obis; gold bicycle tires with yellow spokes.
Plate 122, Cup/Saucer, Tea, wavy red-orange
border, gold lacing below.............. 30.00

11. **Bird Cage.** Lady holding a bird cage and child are featured standing in garden.
Cup/Saucer, Tea, red-orange, interior floral
frame............................. 12.00
Plate 54, Plate, toy, pine green with white... 12.00
Plate, 6″, red-orange with gold............ 8.00
Plate 16, Roll Tray, red-orange with gold
lines and curves, J#28................ 35.00
Teaset, 5 pieces (pot, two cups/saucers), red-
orange, interior floral frame............ 38.00

12. **Blind Man's Bluff.** Blind Man's Bluff is a game wherein a blindfolded person tries to locate another individual by sound, smell, etc.; a blindfolded lady with arms outstretched is standing in a chrysanthemum garden; another by large group of flowers awaits discovery.
Plate 123, Salt Shaker, swirl fluted body,
light apple green..................... 10.00
Teapot, toy, red-orange with gold buds.... 35.00

13. **Blue Hoo.** Japanese mythology relates that the hoo, "Singing Bird of Heaven," was sent down to remind the Young Prince of his duties to the Heavenly gods who sent him to quell the unrest on the Luxuriant Reeds Plains (earth). However, he had fallen in love with an earthly being who convinced him to slay the bird who, he was lead to believe, sang of evil. He shot an arrow at the helpless creature, but the God of Deep Thoughts caught the bloodied arrow in Heaven. He flung it back to earth stating that if the Young Prince shot the arrow at evil dieties, it would not harm him but, if he used it for evil, he would perish — and so he did.

The hoo, sometimes referred to as a phoenix, has been a common decorative motif on Japanese wares. This pattern features a cobalt blue hoo perched upon a tree under which several ladies stroll; exterior border is red-orange; interior red stencil border of diapered diamonds; both bird and diamonds have cobalt blue enamel wash.
Cup/Saucer, Tea....................... 14.00
Cup/Saucer, Tea, toy................... 10.00
Plate, 4¼″, toy........................ 8.00
Plate, 7½″, J#39...................... 10.00
Sugar Bowl, toy, J#36................. 15.00

14. **Boat Dance.** Boat is docked near iris-lined shore; in lieu of a sail three lanterns hang from the mast; one lady plays a samisen, another a drum, third dances with an open fan in each hand.
Bread Tray, jagged edge, deep reddish brown
with gold, three butterfly-shaped reserves,
subject pattern in one, Garden Bench and
Parasol variants in others.............. 45.00
Hair Receiver, ribbed, grass green with gold 24.00
Plate 124, Pin Tray, 5″ x 3″, hand molded edges,
grass green with gold lacing........... 14.00
Powder Jar, ribbed, grass green with gold
lacing............................. 25.00

15. **Boat Festival.** The Japanese celebrate several lively festivals by taking to the rivers in elaborately decorated boats. In this pattern, one's bow is formed as a large dragon, the other like a rooster, wings outspread; all display interior frame of gold lacing.
Bowl, Berry, individual, pale cobalt blue, #35 10.00
Bowl, 8″, pale cobalt blue, #35.......... 25.00
Bowl, 9½″, pale cobalt blue............. 35.00
Plate 125, Cake Platter, 11″, pale cobalt blue, #35 30.00
Plate 126, Celery Dish, 13″ x 5⅝″, wavy red-
orange with interior gold lacing, #35.... 28.00
Compote, 6″ tall, pale cobalt blue, #4..... 45.00
Container, 6″ x 6″, two handles, narrowing
toward base, cobalt blue neck.......... 55.00
Dresser Box, 6″ diameter, red-orange, #19. 30.00
Plate, 7″, pale cobalt blue, #4........... 14.00
Sugar Bowl, pale cobalt blue............. 15.00
Sugar Shaker, pale cobalt blue, #4...... 45.00

16. **Bouncing Ball.** Two ladies kneeling and bouncing ball between them; kettle and pots in background.
Cup/Saucer, Tea, blue-green with gold buds 25.00
Salt/Pepper Shakers, blue-green.......... 22.00
Teapot, blue-green with gold buds........ 55.00

17. **Boy With Doll.** Mother is attending to little boy who is holding on to doll; little girl is taking box off low cabinet.
Plates 49-50, Cup, toy, 2″ tall, red, diaper of
variety of forms, two reserves of subject
pattern and scenery................... 10.00

18. **Boy With Scythe.** Young boy with scythe cutting through shrubbery to allow passage of two ladies.
Creamer, #20, cobalt blue with gold....... 15.00
Cup/Saucer, Tea, cobalt blue with gold.... 14.00
Cup/Saucer, Tea, red with gold.......... 12.00
Plate, 6″, cobalt blue with gold.......... 10.00
Sugar, #20, cobalt blue with gold........ 18.00
Teapot, #20, cobalt blue with gold....... 30.00

19. **Boy's Processional.** Ladies with small boys walk off into distance from iris garden in foreground; effect accomplished by diminishing sizes.

Plate 127, Bowl, 9½″, red-orange with yellow 40.00
Plate 128, Cup/Saucer, After-Dinner, red-
   orange with gold, #2b 15.00
Mug, 5″, red with yellow lacing 25.00
Plate 129, Jug, 5″, red with yellow lacing 28.00
Plate, 6¼″, swirl fluted, scalloped edge, red-
   orange with gold 9.00
Ramekin, no saucer, red with gold 14.00
Toothpick, tri-corner, red-orange with yellow 17.00

20. **Butterfly.** See **Battledore.**
21. **Butterfly Dancers.** Two ladies taking part in festival honoring the Spring are dressed in multi-color winged costumes; dancer to left is kneeling, one to right standing; both beating **kakka** hung on cords around their waists.
   Cup/Saucer, After-Dinner, red with gold 25.00
   Plate 13, Plate, 7″, red with gold 25.00
22. **Carp A: Watching The Carp.** In the midst of a stream swims a school of carp; on one side of the bank stands a lady, flowers in hand, and child; on other side two ladies watch from balcony overhanging the stream; magnificent floor lantern adorns balcony; dates as early as 1906.
   Plate 130, Biscuit Jar, footed, red-orange with gold 45.00
   Cocoa Pot, ribbed conical body, red-orange
      with yellow dots 35.00
   Cocoa Set, 11 pieces (covered pot, five cups/
      saucers), red with gold, undecipherable
      kanji mark 110.00
   Hair Receiver, ribbed through center of
      double height bottom, scalloped cobalt blue
      with gold, #2b 30.00
   Powder Jar, deep brownish red with gold .. 26.00
   Sake Bottle, red with gold, J#47 .... 65.00
   Salt Shaker, cobalt blue neck, red top 8.00
   Plate 131, Vase bud, 4½″, red-orange
      neck and shoulders with gold lacing 18.00
23. **Carp B: Feeding The Carp.** Two ladies tossing rice to carp.
   Plate, 7″, red with gold 15.00
24. **Carp C: Feeding The Carp.** Two ladies and young girl holding string of rice cakes; feeding carp from their vantage point on bridge; mother with infant stands on opposing bank.
   Bowl, 6″, red with gold 18.00
   Creamer, 4″, ribbed hour-glass shape, red
      with gold 17.00
   Sugar, 4½″, ribbed, red with gold 25.00
25. **Carp D: Fish Bowl.** The Japanese use large pottery bowls, much like jardineires, as an outdoor fish bowl to enhance their gardens. Subject pattern depicts one fed by pumped water with carp seemingly jumping in and out.
   Plate 132, Bowl, Rice, red 12.00
26. **Cat.** Kneeling lady is playing with cat while another lady looks on.
   Plates 133-134, Bowl, 8¾″ x 2¾″, raised footrim, nine-lobed, mint green with gold, background diaper of butterflies and peonies, three reserves with subject pattern, Garden Bench
   K and Parasol H, red and gold leaves
      on exterior 75.00
27. **Cat and Crab.** Three ladies on a balcony watching a cat play with a crab; moon is seen overhead; to right is fancy shoji and ikebana; to forefront a box, waterjar and cup.
   Cup/Saucer, Tea, red with gold buds 30.00
28. **Checkerboard.** Bust of lady holding folding fan and two butterflies encased in rows of reserves which alternate with rows of cherry blossoms.
   Cookie Jar, three footed, cobalt blue 85.00
   Plate, 6½″, swirl fluted, scalloped edge,
      cobalt blue 12.00
   Plates 72-73, Sachet Jar, Vantine's, cobalt blue
      and gold neck and border, store name, location and logo included in overall decoration
      of jar, #41 .... 75.00
   Sugar & Creamers, pedestaled, blue with gold 95.00
29. **Cherry Blossoms.** The Japanese cherry blossom tree is cultivated in Japan for its blossom; it bears no fruit. At the turn of the century, the blossoms were often preserved in salt and made into a fragrant, but very bitter, tea.
   Pattern is a grouping of two reserves. In one, lady holds an open parasol and a branch of cherry blossoms; accompanied by two other ladies, one holding an open fan. In second, central figure holds a single cherry blossom; lady with fan is not depicted. Scattered cherry blossoms form the backdrop.
   Plate 135, Bowl, 7½″, red-orange edge 35.00
   Plate 136, Jug, 6⅓″, red-orange edge 35.00
30. **Cherry Blossom Ikebana.** The word **ikebana** means flower arranging which is classified as an art in Japan. This pattern features an artisan arranging cherry blossoms in a pot perched upon a short stool; tradesman is approaching; commonly found on eggcups.
   Eggcup, cobalt blue 10.00
   Plate 43, Eggcup, green 15.00
   Eggcup, red, #20 .... 7.00
   Salt/Pepper Shakers, red 15.00
31. **Child Reaching For Butterfly.** Two ladies talking in garden while child attempts to catch butterfly alighted on chrysanthemum blossom; green fence juts in at angle from the right; three other ladies converse on porch; dates as early as 1911, but found on modern productions, too.
   Cocoa Pot, fluted, red-orange with black
      stencil, #20 .... 45.00
   Compote, 3½″ x 7½″, punch bowl shaped,
      two curled handles, red-orange, #20 ..... 30.00
   Cup/Saucer, Tea, red-orange band, modern, #20 5.00
   Cup/Saucer, Tea, red-orange 10.00
   Plate 137, Cup/Saucer, Tea, red-orange with
      gold buds, #20 .... 12.00
   Eggcup, single, red with gold 7.00
   Eggcup, double, red with gold 15.00
   Mustard Jar, red 15.00
   Plate, 7¼″, swirl fluted edge, red 10.00
   Salt and Pepper Shakers, red 10.00
   Plate 138, Salt Shaker, red border, blue top .. 7.00

Plate 86, Sugar and Creamer, toy, red, decaled,
    modern, J#63 .... 10.00
Sugar and Creamer, pine green 26.00
Tea and Coffee Set, 12 pieces (teapot, coffee
    pot, four cups/saucers, creamer, sugar), red 85.00
Teaset, 15 pieces (pot, creamer, sugar,
    six cups/saucers), red, modern 55.00
Plate 85, Teaset, 15 pieces (pot, creamer,
    sugar, six cups/saucers), red, geisha litho-
    phanes in cups, modern 65.00
Teaset, 21 pieces toy (pot, creamer, sugar,
    six cups/saucers, 6 cake plates), red, #19 . 65.00
Toothpick Holder, red 10.00

32. **Child Wearing E-Boshi.** An e-boshi is a tall hat worn by a man of the court; this pattern in the diminutive styling features a mother standing between two sons, one of whom wears this hat.

Cup/Saucer, Cocoa, cobalt blue-gray wash
    with pink flowers over radiating red
    stenciled lines, #2b 15.00

33. **Children In Boat.** Three children are sailing across stream in small boat; their mothers keep watchful stance from nearby bridge; dates as early as 1911.

Plate, 8½", swirl fluted, scalloped edge, cobalt
    blue with gold lacing 30.00

34. **Child's Play.** Lady in garden with children; girl holds flower baskets and boy holds long stick with circular object at end; background includes hand-painted pink roses.

Cocoa Set, 13 pieces (pot, six cups/saucers),
    red with gold 55.00
Cup/Saucer, Cocoa, cobalt blue with gold buds 14.00
Plate, 6½", cobalt blue with gold buds, #19 10.00

35. **Chinese Coin.** Motif is so named because surface, aside from Geisha Girl reserves, is covered with stylized Chinese coins of pink or green circles with gold on a red-orange enamel backdrop.

Plate 139, Berry Set, 6 pieces (master, five
    individual), 12 reserves: Mother and Son B,
    Garden Bench H, Meeting B, Futon, Pointing
    I, Battledore, Washday, Gardening and 4
    scenic 150.00
Bowl, individual berry, Washday, Battledore
    and scenic reserves 15.00
Plate 140, Bowl, 7½", Battledore, Washday,
    Flower Gathering scenic reserves, maple
    leaves and stylized wind on exterior, J#15 65.00
Bowl, 8½", Meeting, scenic reserves, maple
    leaves and stylized wind on exterior, J#15 75.00
Bowl, 10", ruffled, pierced handle, Battle-
    dore and others, J#15 .... 85.00
Plates 142-143, Cocoa Set, 13 pieces
    (pot, six cups/saucers), Pot, 13 reserves: Garden-
    ing, Pointing I, Meeting B, Garden Bench H,
    Futon, Washday, Battledore and five scenic;
    Cups: Futon, Washday and scenic; Saucers:
    Meeting B, Washday and scenic 225.00
Creamer, Battledore and scenic reserves ... 25.00
Cup/Saucer, Tea, molded-in-relief decor, il-
    legible signature 30.00
Plate, 6", Meeting, Futon and scenic reserves 15.00
Plate 80, Plate, 6", three reserves: Young's Hotel,
    York Beach, ME, Boone Island Lighthouse,
    York, ME and several geisha 30.00
Plates 144-145, Plate, 8½", 8 reserves: Mother
    and Son B, Meeting B, Washday, Battledore,
    Futon and 3 scenic 25.00
Plate 146, Sugar/Creamer, melon ribbed, Sugar
    Lid: Washday, Sugar Body: Washday,
    Meeting B, Futon and 2 scenic, Creamer:
    Washday, Pointing D, Fan C and scenic ... 45.00

36. **Chrysanthemum Garden.** The chrysanthemum is the National Flower of Japan. It generally was not found growing wildly, but in the gardens and greenhouses of expert florists where late 19th century visitors noted as many as 465 blossoms on a single stem or 1,320 blossoms on a single plant!

In this scene, several ladies are strolling through a chrysanthemum garden; same as Paper Carp except that carp banners are not displayed; red bordered examples are decorated with sets of three triangularly placed yellow dots over the border and an interior frame of gold lacing.

Cocoa Set, 9 pieces (fluted pot, four cups/-
    saucers), cobalt blue with gold, #19 ..... 75.00
Creamer, toy, red 10.00
Cup/Saucer, After-Dinner, red, J#16 .... 25.00
Cup/Saucer, After-Dinner, floriate shaped,
    red with yellow dots & gold lacing beneath 20.00
Cup/Saucer, After-Dinner, fluted, red, #20 ... 14.00
Pitcher, toy, red, #6 .... 15.00
Plate, 6", swirl fluted, scalloped, red, #20 ... 5.00
Powder Jar, melon ribbed, wavy red with
    gold lacing beneath, pattern on lid & body 32.00
Plate 147, Salt and Pepper Shakers, painted
    top with gold stripes, red border and neck . 20.00
Plate 148, Stein, 7½", red-orange with gold buds 100.00
Vase, 9", brown order, background of cobalt
    blue and maroon flowers on cream ground,
    two reserves of subject pattern & Butterfly 75.00

37. **Circle Dance.** Ladies with fans and samisens dance in a circle, sometimes on diapered background of cherry blossoms; dates as early as 1906.

Plate, 6¼", swirl fluted, scalloped, red-
    orange with yellow sashes 12.00
Plate 149, Saucer, Tea, scalloped cobalt blue
    with gold lacing, interior floral frame, back-
    drop of stylized flowers 7.00
Toothpick, cylindrical, red 12.00

38. **Cloud A.** Stylized clouds comprised of many small dots swirl over body of each example as backdrop for ladies and children with fans, parasols, mandolins, balls, stick horse and wagons; occasionally accompanied by **Takara Bune** treasures.

Eggcup, red 20.00
Marmalade Jarm 5", melon ribbed, red-
    orange with yellow, J#6a 28.00
Salt Dish, red-orange with flowers 14.00
Plate 150, Vase, 5½", cobalt blue with gold
    dripping down neck and around rim, co-
    balt blue scallops around base 30.00

39. **Cloud B.** As above, but ladies are playing variety of instruments.

   Cup/Saucer, Tea, red-orange with yellow ... 10.00

   Plates 68-69, Jar, Vantine's Geisha Toilet Cream, crossed flags trademark and company name on lid, red with gold lacing, pattern in two square green scalloped reserves, hand-painted lavender, pink and red mums with green and yellow leaves and green wash as backdrop 65.00

   Salt and Pepper Shakers, square body with round tops, green decal of pattern around body, cherry blossoms on top 12.00

   Teapot, melon ribbed, red-orange with yellow 30.00

   Plate 151, Teaset, 13 pieces (pot, creamer, sugar, five cups/saucers), melon ribbed, red-orange with yellow, J#6a 95.00

40. **Court Lady.** Lady with floral headdress and kimono of many folds is kneeling on a **tatami** mat, eyes demurely cast downward, fan open before her; above is a lantern decorated with crane and waves; to the side is a fancy box on a low lacquered table.

   Biscuit Jar, cobalt blue, backdrop of dots, phoenix, water and chrysanthemums, five black outlined reserves: one large and three small pinched corner rectangles with subject pattern, four-lobed with Garden Bench H, stylized fan with Fan A, J#1 .... 55.00

   Bowl, Dessert, cobalt blue, backdrop of dots, phoenix, water and chrysanthemums, three black outlined reserves: one with subject pattern, four-lobed with Garden Bench H, stylized fan with Fan A 7.00

   Bowl, Salad, red with yellow stripes, backdrop of dots, phoenix, water and chrysanthemums, five black outlined reserves: one with subject pattern, four-lobed with Garden Bench H, stylized fan with Fan A 30.00

   Demitasse Pot, miniature 1½", hand-painted geisha in reserve on floral backdrop 15.00

   Plate 152, Dish, 5⅜", scalloped and lobed, one lobe smaller as handle, cobalt blue with gold, pattern in one reserve, large gold peacock in another, crosshatch background 12.00

   Plate, 7", backdrop of dots, phoenix, water and chrysanthemums, five black outlined reserves: one large and three small pinched corner rectangles with subject pattern, four-lobed with Garden Bench H, stylized fan with Fan A, J#36 .... 18.00

   Plates 327-328. Teacup, 2¾" x 3¼", handleless Japanese style, red with gold, subject pattern and Oxen Song in unusually shaped reserves 50.00

   Plates 174-176, Toothpick Holder, five-sided, melon ribbed, footed, backdrop of dots, phoenix, water and chrysanthemums, three black outlined reserves: one pinched corner rectangle with subject pattern, one four-lobed with Garden Bench H, one stylized fan with Fan A, dripping with gold, coralene beading and slip J#2 .... 38.00

   Plates 177-178, Vase, 8", wide footed bottom narrowing to neck and widening to fluted rim, two handles, cobalt blue top, handles and feet, backdrop of dots, phoenix, water and chrysanthemums, five black outlined reserves: one large and three small pinched corner rectangles with subject pattern, four-lobed with Garden Bench H, stylized fan with Fan A 135.00

41. **Courtesan Processional.** Group of courtesans attired in red-orange and lilac cross a bridge accompanied by young ladies-in-waiting attired in green and red-orange and a manservant holding an open parasol over her finely coiffed head; disproportionately large maple leaves in green, yellow and red-orange are scattered about; common to cobalt blue bordered items with gold lacing.

   Plate 153, Chamberstick 60.00

   Cocoa Pot, J#16 .... 75.00

   Plate, 6½", swirl fluted, scalloped edge 15.00

   Plate 154, Relish Dish, 8" x 5" 28.00

   Plate 155, Syrup, no drip plate 35.00

42. **Cricket Cage.** Two ladies kneel among peonies, one holds a cricket cage. Crickets were kept as pets in small pierced cases. The owners enjoyed listening to their "music.".

   Eggcup, red-orange 12.00

   Plate 156, Vase, 3½", deep red-orange 10.00

43. **Daikoku.** Ladies performing a ceremonial dance around **Daikoku**, one of the Seven Gods of Good Fortune, who holds a magic hammer which, when struck, is supposed to produce anything wished for. Some pieces show only the dancing ladies and not **Daikoku**.

   Plate 157, Bowl, 8⅝", cobalt blue with gold extends inward to form alternating clover and scallops pattern over the lobes, pattern circles around side of bowl, center has chrysanthemum shape reserve of hand-painted scenery 75.00

   Plate 158, Cup/Saucer, After-Dinner, ribbed, red and green floral border 28.00

   Mustard Jar, red with gold lacing 25.00

   Teaset, 3 pieces (pot, creamer, sugar), scalloped red with gold 45.00

44. **Doll's Tea Party.** Distributed to stores all over the country, these wares feature tiny ladies and trees above a stenciled diaper pattern along with the words "Doll's Tea Party"; The stores often had their names and logos added to the motif; common to light apple green borders.

   Plate 78, Cup, Emery, Birel, Thayer, dated 1916 10.00

   Plate 79, Cup/Saucer, cup has motif and bottomstamp #47, saucer bears Hahne's name and logo 25.00

45. **Dragonboat.** Man and woman, son and daughter in elaborate dress are in a sampan whose bow is elaborate dragon head. The dragon is another favored motif which takes its place in Japanese lore as a symbol of spiritual aspiration.

   Berry Set, 6 pieces (master, five individual), cobalt blue with gold 85.00

   Bowl, 7", six-lobed, blue with gold 25.00

Plate 306, Ashtray, red-orange, female child .. 10.00
Berry Set, 5 pieces (master, four individual), cobalt blue with gold slashes, three reserves: scenic, geisha & child, men & torii 125.00
Box, elongated manicure, red bottom rim and cobalt blue top rim, three reserves: men and **torii**, two geisha, child 25.00
Cup/Saucer, Cocoa, cobalt blue border, two geisha in reserve, J#16 .... 10.00
Cup/Saucer, After-Dinner, floriate-shaped, pale cobalt blue border with gold slashes, red handle diaper pattern of cobalt blue octagons encompassing stylized flowers, circular reserve with geisha, rectangular reserve of geisha picking wisteria, J#6a 18.00
Cup/Saucer, After-Dinner, toy, modern set of four with orange, cobalt blue, red and green borders 10.00
Plate 27, Cup/Saucer, Tea, orange lustre, single geisha, J#68 .... 12.00
Cup/Saucer, Tea, red and green with gold, two geisha in reserve, hand painted, J#6 ..... 20.00
Plate 307, Cup/Saucer, Tea, pedestaled, gold rim, backdrop of beige with gold stars and red and gold coins and maple leaves, fan reserve with two geisha, chrysanthemum reserve with man, geisha and child, oval scenic reserve, hand painted, J#16 .... 30.00
Plate 308, Cup/Saucer, Tea, wavy cobalt blue border outlined in gold, handle blue on exterior, red on interior, inside double band of gold and red, two abstractly-shaped reserves with geisha and scenery on deep green ground overlaid with swatches of red and pink with gold, J#51 .... 26.00
Dish, oval, red band, two geisha, #35 ..... 12.00
Dresser Jar, cobalt blue with gold buds and slashes, three reserves: men and **torii**, man and boy, geisha on stage before geisha and child 36.00
Plate 309, Hair Receiver, melon ribbed, grass green 20.00
Hair Receiver, large footed, figures, scenery and dragon in three reserves with butterflies on a beige ground, J#16 .... 38.00
Plate 310, Matchholder, cobalt blue with gold border, turquoise blue backdrop, single geisha in plum blossom reserve, J#16 .... 32.00
Mint Dish, 5" x 3⅞", gold rim, "Tuscarora Summit" in black over scenery, #66 ..... 35.00
Nut Cup, cobalt blue with gold scallops, red between scallops, five alternating geisha and scenic reserves with light green outline, #1c 10.00
Nut Cup, red with gold, one scenic reserve, two with diapers, another with many geisha, #67 .... 10.00
Powder Jar, molded-in-relief, two diminutive geisha on backdrop of oversized pink and white cherry blossoms 60.00

Plate 311, Saucer, cobalt blue with gold buds and slashes, three reserves: men and **torii**, man and boy, geisha on stage before geisha and child; cobalt blue waves around saucer depression 10.00
Teapot, squat, melon ribbed, red border, black cranes as backdrop for two reserves: man and geisha, geisha and children, J#16 ... 45.00

135. **Mother and Daughter.** Mother and small girl standing in garden by shore; dates as early as 1914.
Plate 28, Box, 5" x 4" x 2", gold rim, beige ground with raised gold plum blossom branches, subject pattern and Samisen Recital in reserves, decaled, #68 .... 32.00
Cocoa Set, 11 pieces (10" pot, five cups/saucers), scalloped red 135.00
Plates 312-313, Creamer, red with gold lacing, subject pattern and scenery in reserves on yellow ground with hand-painted pink and lavender chrysanthemums 35.00
Plate 314, Jewel Chest, 4½" x 3½", gold rim, red-orange pomegranate finial, overall background decor of green and red-orange ground, pink and yellow cherry blossoms, violet roses, swirls of coralene and gold, pattern in reserve, J#43 .... 125.00
Plates 300-301, Nappy, lobed, linear design molded in relief near inner rim, red with gold lacing, backdrop of turquoise cobalt blue with gold crosshatching, fan-shaped reserves with Fan Dance A and Meeting B patterns, four-lobed reserve with Meditation and plum blossom reserve with subject pattern........................... 65.00
Sugar Bowl, red with gold, paulownia flower backdrop, two reserves, one with subject pattern, one with geisha, boy and girl 10.00

136. **Mother and Son A.** Mother kneeling among peonies to the right of son who stands with arms outstretched either facing or with his back to the mother.
Plate 52, Cup, toy, blue-green border & neck, pattern in reserve on red diapered ground... 8.00
Plates 315-316, Eggcup, double, blue-green, backdrop of plum blossoms, water lilies and birds, three reserves: boy facing mother, boy looking away from mother, geisha with fan . 16.00

137. **Mother and Son B.** Mother with closed fan is holding son's hand; long stilted building with many lanterns is to rear.
Creamer, unusually shallow, melon ribbed, wavy red with gold lacing, J#36 .... 20.00
Plate 317, Roll Tray, 12½", scalloped edge, dark apple green with gold netting and raised gold beads forming flowers 38.00
Saucer, red with gold lacing beneath, subject pattern in chrysanthemum-shaped reserve, geisha in kakemono reserve and scenic plum blossom reserve on scenic background 5.00
Sugar and Creamer, red-orange with gold, J#36 30.00

138. **Mother and Son C.** Simply executed, hand-painted ver-

sion of Mother and Son B, dates as early as 1908.
 Ashtray, oval, red with gold, J#8c 16.00
 Berry Set, 6 pieces (master, five individual), cobalt blue with gold, master marked #4, individuals J#16 .... 60.00
 Bowl, 6", chrysanthemum-edged, red-orange with gold, J#44 .... 18.00
 Plate 318, Bowl, 10", scalloped, gold rim, waved cobalt blue and gold border, partitioned into three sections of scenery, butterflies and subject pattern, J#66 .... 55.00
 Plate 319, Cake Platter, 10", scalloped edges with cut-out teardrop between each scallop, red with gold rim, blue-green with gold lace border interrupted by red and gold chrysanthemums and yellow green leaves, backdrop of beige with flowers as in border and blue-green tassels, square reserve with subject pattern, cherry blossom reserve with scenery 50.00
 Cocoa Set, 13 pieces (pot, six cups/saucers), red with gold, #19 .... 115.00
 Cup/Saucer, Child's, red, J#6 .... 12.00
 Cup/Saucer, Cocoa, red-orange with gold ... 16.00
 Nut Set, 6 pieces (footed master, five individual), red with gold 50.00
 Olive Dish, 7" oval, red-orange with gold, J#16 25.00
 Plate 320, Plate, 8", gold and brown with red-orange slashes, floral backdrop for subject pattern and scenery in reserve, J#16 ...... 25.00
 Plate 321, Sauce Dish, inverted lip, 4¾" molded-in-relief leaf decor, red with gold, #19 ..... 12.00
 Plate, 321, Sauce Dish, inverted lip, 6", molded-in-relief leaf decor, red with gold, #19 ... 16.00
 Sugar Bowl, red with gold, J#16 .... 22.00
 Teapot, floral finial, gold, J#16 .... 75.00
 Tete-A-Tete, 7 pieces (pot, sugar, creamer, two cups/saucers), red-orange with gold, J#50 . 45.00
 Tete-A-Tete, 7 pieces (pot, sugar, creamer, two cups/saucers), maroon with gold, J#16 ... 65.00
 Plate 322, Vase, 10½", red with gold handles, neck and footband, #60 .... 135.00

139. **Oni Dance A.** An **oni** is a mythical devilish creature with long fur and horns; dancer holds a **oni** mask on a staff; to her left is drummer; lady to her right carries lantern; dates as early as 1906.
 Plate 323, Bowl, individual berry, nine-lobed, scalloped edge, red-orange with gold, mark too worn to decipher 12.00
 Plate, 7¼", swirl fluted, scalloped, red with gold lacing 18.00

140. **Oni Dance B.** As above, except dancer is on cobblestone patio; to her left kneels lady with lantern while another watches them perform from distant porch; dates as early as 1908.
 Plate 324, Bisquit Jar, footed, 7½", scalloped red-orange with gold chrysanthemums 85.00
 Bowl, 10½", chrysanthemum-lobed, red with gold lacing, flower groupings on exterior . 95.00
 Plate 325, Cocoa Pot, 9½", fluted, cobalt blue with gold, #20 .... 65.00

 Cocoa Pot, 9½", fluted, red-orange with gold chrysanthemums 65.00
 Cocoa Pot, 9½", fluted, red-orange 50.00
 Dish, Bon-bon, 5½", fluted, scalloped red-orange with gold 15.00

141. **Origami.** Three ladies are folding origami papers while a gentleman sits watching; next to him is bonsai tree on small table; rolls of paper and gift boxes scattered about; fourth geisha bringing in more.
 Cocoa Pot, fluted, red-orange with gold buds, #20 .... 45.00
 Cup/Saucer, Tea, cobalt blue with gold, #19 14.00

142. **Oxen Song.** Young child playing flute riding side-saddle on back of an oxen; basket of crops is strapped to child's back.
 Plates 326-327, Teacup, Japanese handleless, 2¾" x 3¼", subject pattern and Court Lady in unusually shaped reserves, red-orange with gold 50.00

143. **Paper Carp.** May 5 of each year is known to the Japanese as **Tango no Sekku**, the Boy's Festival. Towns are decorated with large paper carps called **koinobori**. Legend has it that as the carp swim upstream against the current, so will the strong boy meet and overcome all obstacles as he makes his way through life.
 Pattern features **koinobori** hanging from the trees in a garden being readied for the festival by several ladies and children.
 Bowl, Berry, individual 7.00
 Creamer, 2¾", red-orange with yellow dots forming plum blossoms, gold lacing beneath, J#16 .... 15.00
 Cup/Saucer, After-Dinner, red-orange, #35 . 10.00
 Plate, 6¼", swirl fluted, scalloped, red-orange with yellow 7.00
 Relish Dish, fluted edge, cut-out handles, red 9.00
 Plate 46, Teapot, toy, 3", orange border with yellow enamel dots & interior gold frame, J#16 30.00

The **Parasol** series is one of the most common of the Geisha Girl patterns, featuring one or more geisha carrying parasols.

144. **Parasol A: Lesson Pattern Cousin.** Lady is about to pass through a gate, taking leave of the kneeling woman to her left; both are holding open parasols; found in reserve usually accompanied by the Lesson pattern.
 Plate 328, Sauce Dish, 4¾", inverted lip, molded-in-relief leaf decor, backdrop of pink chrysanthemums, Parasol A in reserve, unusual in that there is no accompanying Lesson pattern 16.00
 See Lesson pattern for remainder of listing.

145. **Parasol B: Torii and Parasol.** Two ladies, one kneeling with open fan and one standing with open parasol, are looking over their shoulders to the right; behind them is large **torii** and **pagoda**; dates as early as 1906.
 Bowl, Nut, master, red-orange with interior floral frame 10.00
 Cocoa Pot, cobalt blue with gold, #16 ..... 55.00
 Cup/Saucer, After-Dinner, red-orange with gold buds, celadon ground, #19 .... 25.00

Hair Receiver, lid has scalloped edge with relief molded vines, center rises up mimicking
shape of Mt. Fuji, red, #19 .... 29.00
Plate 329, Jug, 5½″, melon ribbed, red-orange
with apple green and gold circles 45.00
Plate 56, Pitcher, toy, 3⅝″, x 1¾″, cylindrical slenderizing towards top, almost indistin-
guishable pouring lip, #19 .... 15.00
Plate 330, Powder Jar, red-orange with apple
green and gold circles 28.00
Salad Set, 6 pieces (master, five individual),
wavy red 65.00
Salt Cellar, red band, #20 .... 10.00
Plate 331, Salt/Pepper Shakers, red-orange .. 10.00
Sugar Shaker, handled, pleated body, red-
orange with apple green and gold circles . 60.00
Teaset, 9 pieces (pot, four cups/saucers), co-
balt blue with gold, #19 .... 50.00

146. **Parasol C: Parasol.** By far the most common of the
series, it depicts two ladies facing each other, one of
whom holds an open parasol, the other a closed one;
dates as early as 1906 but also found on modern wares.
Basket, 5″ x 3″ x 5″ tall, handled, red-orange
border and handle, pattern on exterior,
flowers on interior 25.00
Berry Set, 5 pieces (master, four individual),
red with gold 32.00
Berry Set, 7 pieces (master, six individual),
cobalt blue with gold 50.00
Bowl, Berry, master, cobalt blue with gold . 35.00
Bowl, Berry, master, red with gold 25.00
Bowl, Dessert, red band, #20 .... 8.00
Plate 88, Bowl, 11″, red, #19 .... 15.00
Cocoa Pot, red 35.00
Cocoa Set, 13 pieces (pot, six cups/saucers),
cobalt blue with gold 125.00
Plate 332, Creamer, 4¾″, plain cobalt blue border 14.00
Cup/Saucer, After-Dinner, scalloped cobalt
blue, #2b 15.00
Cup/Saucer, Tea, red, #6 .... 8.00
Cup/Saucer, Tea, scalloped cobalt blue with
gold 12.00
Demitasse Set, toy, 15 pieces (pot, creamer,
sugar, six cups/saucers), #19 .... 65.00
Dish, small, eleven-lobed, red, #19 .... 11.00
Eggcup, red, modern 7.00
Hair Receiver, red-orange, #20 .... 14.00
Humidor, red with gold wavy line beneath .. 65.00
Plate 332, Jug, 5″ x 4¾″, wavy cobalt blue, #20 25.00
Plate 333, Manicure Jar, 2¼″, red, #19 ..... 20.00
Matchholder, cylindrical, red, #19 .... 14.00
Plate 334, Muffineer, fluted base, bulbous
body, wavy red, #20b 35.00
Mustard Jar, red with yellow 12.00
Nut Cup, individual, red-orange 4.00
Plate, 7½″, red-orange with gold buds, #11 10.00
Salt/Pepper Shakers, red with gold, #47 ... 20.00
Plate 14, Sauce Dish, scalloped edge extends
to pouring lip, red 14.00
Sauce Dish, chrysanthemum shape, scalloped
red, #20 .... 15.00
Sugar Bowl, red-orange, hand painted with
light cobalt blue & lavender ground, #15b 10.00
Plate 48, Sugar and Creamer, toy, red, #20 .. 15.00
Toothpick Holder, fluted, cobalt blue, #20 . 20.00
Toothpick Holder, octagonal, red with yellow 11.00
Toothpick Holder, octagonal, red, modern .. 7.00
Vase, 3″, red neck, modern, paper label
reading JAPAN 5.00
Plate 335, Vase, 6½″, milk bottle shape, two-
handled, deep red 10.00

147. **Parasol D: Processional Parasol.** Six women strolling
through garden looking left to the one remaining at the
dwelling; ladies at far right and left are carrying wooden
buckets of flowers; center figures are sharing a parasol;
those with a multi-color border are highly ornate and
well executed — this border is red-orange and pine green
with gold complimented by red-orange edges, beige with
gold floral insets and a green zig-zag.
Plates 336-337, Bowl, 8⅝″, chrysanthemum-
shaped, multi-color 55.00
Plate 338, Dresser Tray, rectangular, multi-color 65.00
Plate 339, Gravy Boat, ruffled edge, multi-
color, #19 .... 16.00
Hatpin Holder, multi-color, #19 .... 45.00
Plate 17, Nut Set, 5 pieces (footed master,
four individual), tan with gold, #19 .... 35.00

148. **Parasol E.** Same as D above, except ladies are carrying
parasols instead of baskets.
Plate 340, Box, egg shape, 4½″ x 3¾″ x 3½″,
red-orange, #20 .... 28.00
Cake Platter, 11¼″, pale cobalt blue, #20 . 30.00
Cup/Saucer, Tea, red-orange 11.00
Cup/Saucer, After-Dinner, pale cobalt blue .. 7.00
Dresser Tray, diamond-shaped, red 29.00
Dresser Tray, rectangular, scalloped pine
green border, with white zig-zags, yellow
and purple leaves 38.00
Hatpin Holder, brown, #19 .... 35.00
Plate 341, Mustard Jar, angled handles, pale
yellow with gold, red and gold linear interior
border, #56 .... 35.00
Pitcher, toy, red, #20 .... 10.00
Plate, 6½″, scalloped, blue-green with gold
below, #1b 7.00
Plate, 8½″, swirl fluted, scalloped edge, co-
balt blue with gold buds, #19 .... 20.00
Plate 342, Salt and Pepper Shakers, 3¼″, scal-
loped blue 12.00
Plate 74, Salt and Pepper Shakers, advertising
"Tiddy's Home Furnishings", red 35.00
Plate 42, Saucer, Tea, red-orange border, sub-
ject pattern and Mother and Son variant in
reserves on Phoenix backdrop, J#26b 6.00
Plate 343, Saucer, Cocoa, scalloped cobalt blue 3.00
Plate 344, Teapot, red-orange with gold buds, #3d 22.00
Plates 345-346, Teaset, 10 pieces (pot, creamer,
sugar, four cups/saucers), light green, #20 75.00
Teaset, 11 pieces (pot, creamer, sugar, three cups,
five saucers), pale cobalt blue border and

stencil, #19 .... 55.00
Teaset, 14 pieces (pot, creamer, six cups/-
saucers), red, #20 .... 45.00
Tea Strainer, red with yellow 28.00

149. **Parasol F.** Several ladies in an iris garden; one leans on closed parasol, another holds hers open; to the right sits a third with fan looking away from the others; dates as early as 1906.
Plate 347, Bowl, 6¼", eight-lobed, one smaller to serve as handle, cobalt blue with gold . 18.00
Calling Card Tray, 8" x 6", free form, cobalt blue with gold 35.00
Cocoa Set, 13 pieces (fluted pot, six cups/- saucers), cups fluted with top wider than bottom, ribbed, #19 .... 125.00
Plate 348, Pin Tray, 4" x 3", scalloped cobalt blue with gold 15.00
Salt/Pepper Shakers, three footed, red-orange 20.00
Trivet, cherry blossom shape with ½" edge, pine green, black stencil, #19 .... 25.00

150. **Parasol G: Good Luck, Good Fortune Parasol.** Several ladies, one holding parasol and child, scene by water, red with gold edge, red-orange and gold diapered border incorporating seals reading **fuku** and **kuon**, good luck and good fortune.
Cocoa Pot 85.00
Plates 349-350, Nut Set, 2 pieces (pleated, lobed, footed master, one individual cup), pattern on exterior, chrysanthemums on interior, stenciled, J#29 .... 35.00

151. **Parasol H.** Hand-painted version has child to left of lady seated by water; stenciled version has lady to right of child on bridge.
Plates 133-134, Bowl, 8¾" x 2¾", raised footrim, nine-lobed, mint green with gold, background diaper of butterflies and peonies, three reserves with subject pattern, Garden Bench K and Cat, red and gold leaves on exterior, stenciled .. 75.00
Plate 351, Spoon Tray, floriate-edged, red with gold stripes interrupted by stylized pink & gold chrysanthemums and green and gold leaves, gold handles, hand painted, #15a ... 55.00

152. **Parasol I: Black Parasol.** Two ladies share a black parasol.
Salt/Pepper Shakers, red-orange 10.00
Teaset, 9 pieces (pot, four cups/saucers), red, #20 .... 45.00

153. **Parasol J: Ribbon Parasol.** Two ladies stroll through the garden carrying multi-color floral parasols; hanging upside down from a tree overhead is a parasol from which ribbons are dangling.
Bowl, Nut, master, red-orange with gold ... 20.00
Sugar/Creamer, red-orange with gold 28.00

154. **Parasol K: Parasol and Basket.** Lady kneeling holding open parasol; another holding long-handled round basket.
Plate, 7", swirl fluted, scalloped cobalt blue with gold, three reserves with Parasol A, Lesson and subject pattern, J#53 .... 18.00
Plates 352-353, Spoon Warmer, oyster-shaped exterior, small well inside, red-orange with gold buds 25.00

155. **Parasol L: Miscellaneous.** Miscellaneous items wherein lady with parasol is focal point of scene.
Plate 354, Cup/Saucer, After-Dinner, cobalt blue with gold, #1 .... 15.00
Plate 355, Cup/Saucer, Tea, cobalt blue with gold, #22 .... 15.00
Plate 75, Mustard Jar, red, "Hoover Furniture Co., Harrisburg, PA" 28.00
Plate 76, Mustard Jar, red with gold buds, "Horner's Good Furniture, Hagerstown, MD" 28.00
Plate 356, Talcum Shaker, red-orange with yellow lacing, ladies all carrying open parasols . 28.00

156. **Parasol Modern: Processional Parasol.** Ladies are in the same format as Parasol D, only there are fewer of them, coloring is sparse, borders generally thin, plain brownish red accompanied by an interior frame of peonies and butterflies. Many examples bear a small green #20 mark.
Plate 89, Bowl, 6", sides curled in and scalloped, red 15.00
Bowl, Berry, individual, pale cobalt blue, #20 5.00
Cake Platter, red 18.00
Plate 92, Cake Platter, blue, #20 .... 22.00
Cocoa Set, 13 pieces (conical pot, six cups/- saucers), pale cobalt blue 50.00
Condiment Set, salt/pepper shakers, mustard jar spooner, red 25.00
Creamer, red, #20 .... 8.00
Plate 91, Dish, 7" oblong, red, #20 ...... 12.00
Eggcup, pale cobalt blue 7.00
Mustard, red, #20 .... 10.00
Plate 90, Pitcher, toy, 2½", red, modern 7.00
Plate, 6", pale cobalt blue 7.00
Plate, 6", red, #24 .... 5.00
Spooner, red, #20 .... 10.00
Plate, 93, Stickpin, red, #20 .... 15.00
Tea Caddy, red with gold, #59 .... 19.00

157. **Party.** Four ladies enjoying the outdoors. One plays a samisen, another sits surrounded by a tray with food-filled dishes, covered rice dish and sauce dishes.
Plate 357, Bowl, shallow, 7", ten-lobed, red-orange interrupted by gold buds, probably modern 20.00

158. **Peacock.** Ornately attired ladies watching brightly colored peacocks.
Berry Set, 6 pieces (master, five individual), red-orange with gold buds and slashes ... 40.00
Plate 358, Cup, Tea, Japanese style handleless, red-orange with gold buds, wavy gold line below 15.00

159. **Peacock On A Flowered Stone Roof.** A large bird, half peacock, half phoenix, perches upon a floral covered stone lantern watching over the figures in the garden.
Plate 359, Cup/Saucer, Tea, scalloped cobalt blue with gold lacing, red rim, handle 22.00

160. **Picnic A.** Blanket is spread on grass where two ladies are picnicking with a young boy; hand painted; dates as early as 1908.
Plate 360, Bowl, 6", four feet, sides scalloped and curved inward, relief molded vines on

bottom, red rim, blue with waved border, alternating turquoise and red-orange with gold circles between waves, pattern on interior encompassed by double circle of gold beading, #3d 48.00
Cup/Saucer, After-Dinner, melon ribbed, wavy red-orange with gold lacing 20.00
Plate 361, Dish, candy, 5½" x 6½", bamboo handle, gold, J#39 .... 25.00
Plate 362, Lunch Set, 3 pieces (lunch plate, cup/saucer), floriate shape with molded in relief swirls along edge, red with gold, J#15 ... 35.00
Plate, 8", red with gold, J#16 .... 28.00
Plate 363, Sugar and Creamer, unusual twisted "s" handles, ornately gilded red border, pattern and flowers in reserve on beige ground with gold speckles, flowers and coins, J#16 . 45.00

161. **Picnic B.** Two ladies seated on blanket with **bento bako**, other ladies in the garden, stenciled version.
Demitasse Pot, red with gold, #6 .... 30.00
Cup/Saucer, Tea, red-orange 10.00
Powder Jar, red, pattern in reserve surrounded by hand-painted birds among the clouds, J#16 .... 35.00
Plate, 364, Relish Dish, floriate-edged, red-orange with gold, chrysanthemum and butterfly backdrop for subject pattern and parasol variants in reserves 25.00
Sugar/Creamer, red with gold, floral and butterfly backdrop for reserves featuring subject and Parasol 30.00

162. **Picnic C.** Two ladies and a child kneel by a cloth upon which lies an open **bento** and a small bowl.
Plate 365, Cup/Saucer, Tea, blue-green with gold, diapered backdrop of vines and gold encircled, multi-color chrysanthemums, two cobalt blue green and gold reserves with Drum and subject patterns 28.00
Saucer, cobalt blue 7.00
Salt/Pepper Shakers, cobalt blue with a gold, red neck 22.00

163. **Picnic D.** Four women kneel on ornate textile laid with low table and four-tiered **bento bako**; one holds water-jar, another a goblet; dates as early as 1914.
Plate 366, Cup/Saucer, Tea, red-orange split at top and bottom by three circles of gold, red-orange and blue-green, overall gold embellishment 25.00
Teaset, 3 pieces (pot, creamer, sugar), melon ribbed, red-orange split at top and bottom by three circles of gold, red-orange and blue-green, overall gold embellishment ... 65.00

164. **Pillar Print.** Pillar prints **(hashira-ye)** were popular forms of household decoration made to fit the many narrow pillars comprising the skeleton of the Japanese home. Pattern features three ladies drawing **hashira-ye** of a superbly robed courtesan sitting elevated before them.
Cocoa Pot, cylindrical, deep red-brown with gold 75.00

165. **Playing Catch.** Hand-painted pattern is comprised of two reserves; one is a mother throwing a ball to a child, other depicts ball lying on ground between the two.
Plates 39-40, Compote, apple green with gold, Satsuma-style diapering, #56 .... 35.00
Plate 41, Cup/Saucer, After-Dinner, 1⅝" tall octagonal cup, cup and saucer finely fluted, red with gold, J#52 .... 30.00
Puff Box, red and green, #56 .... 25.00
Salt/Pepper Shakers, green 25.00

166. **Plum Blossom Branch.** Lady is carrying large branch of plum blossoms over her shoulder, accompanied by other women and young boy.
Bowl, Berry, individual, red-orange with gold 12.00
Plate 367, Cup/Saucer, After-Dinner, scalloped cup, floriate saucer, red-orange with gold lacing, interior floral frame 20.00
Salt/Pepper Shakers, red-orange with gold .. 18.00

167. **Pointing A.** Three women are looking to left and pointing accordingly with their fans.
Plate 368, Creamer, heart-shaped body with rim curled in, blue-green with interior gold frame 35.00
Creamer, 2½", red, #20 .... 14.00
Dresser Jar, red, #19 .... 40.00
Plate 61, Jar, toy, 2¼", red with yellow enamel dots 18.00
Plate 63, Pitcher and Waste Bowl Set, toy, pitcher 2⅞" tall, bowl 3⅝" x 1⅝", red with yellow lacing 25.00

168. **Pointing B.** Two ladies holding **uchiwa** fans standing on bridge; one points to left with her finger, the other with her fan; dates as early as 1906.
Condensed Milk Jar, drip plate, red 45.00
Plate 369, Cup/Saucer, Tea, scalloped apple green with gold 15.00
Salad Set, 6 pieces (master, five individual), red 50.00

169. **Pointing C.** Ladies and child are pointing the way for another lady.
Cup/Saucer, Tea, red-orange, #57 .... 9.00
Plate, 7¼", red-orange, #20 .... 12.00
Teapot, squat, melon ribbed, four feet, cobalt blue scalloped border, handle, cobalt blue ringed spout, #20 .... 28.00
Teapot, red, #20 .... 22.00

170. **Pointing D.** Similar to B, but lady is giving directions to another who is sometimes with a child; elaborate temple building generally adorns this version which dates as early as 1906.
Plate 370, Bowl, 5¼", red-orange with gold buds 7.00
Plate 371, Bowl, 7½", ten-lobed, red with gold, smudged Japanese mark 15.00
Plate 372, Celery Dish, fluted sides and middle, red-orange with gold lacing, rich maroon coloring 40.00
Creamer, toy, elongated upper spout, cobalt blue with gold 10.00
Cup/Saucer, After-Dinner, red 10.00
Cup/Saucer, Tea, cobalt blue with gold 15.00
Cup/Saucer, Tea, red, J#16 .... 18.00
Teapot, squat, red, J#16 .... 22.00

171. **Pointing E.** Four ladies strolling through garden; central two are pointing to others seated on nearby porch.

Bowl, Berry, individual, cobalt blue with gold 9.00
Mustard Jar, cobalt blue 24.00

172. **Pointing F.** Mother and child are pointing to the right, showing lady carrying basket where others are located.
Bowl, Berry, individual, apple green 11.00
Plate 373, Manicure Box, swirl ribbed body, apple green with gold 25.00
Plate 374, Nut Set, 6 pieces (10″ master, five footed individual cups), ornate multi-color border, J#16 75.00

173. **Pointing G.** Two ladies with fans pointing to approaching figures; garden resplendent with all commonly portrayed flora.
Plate 375, Refreshment (snack) Set, wavy red-orange with interior frame of gold lacing . 35.00
Teaset, 3 pieces (pot, sugar, creamer), red border, multi-color floral diaper outlined in red 45.00

174. **Pointing H.** One woman points to right; second with parasol in hand.
Plate 47, Teapot, toy, 3¾″, red with yellow lacing 15.00

175. **Pointing I.** Mother, son and daughter are pointing out something in lawn to another woman.
See Chinese Coin

176. **Pointing J.** Mother directing son's attention across a stream.
Plate 376, Cup/Saucer, Tea, scalloped blue with gold line, pattern in off-center reserve on stenciled peonies backdrop 25.00

177. **Porcelain Bench.** Lady is seated upon large, ornate porcelain garden seat, surrounded by other figures; contrast this to Garden Bench patterns which depict woman seated on wooden benches.
Plate 377, Bowl, 8″, lobed and lightly ribbed, wavy red-orange with gold buds, #19 . . . . 28.00
Matchholder, small hanging, cobalt blue dripping down somewhat obscuring pattern . . 18.00

178. **Porch.** Japanese dwellings were traditionally situated on stilts with walls of sliding doors called **shoji** which, when open during the day, created a porch overlooking the gardens; a number of women are sitting on the porches and walking through the gardens; dates from the Nippon era but also found on modern wares.
Berry Set, 6 pieces (master, five individual), scalloped edge, red with gold 35.00
Bowl, Berry, master, cobalt blue with gold . 20.00
Bowl, Berry, master, pierced, with underplate, red with gold buds, #20 . . . . 28.00
Bowl, Berry, individual, cobalt blue with gold, #2b 9.00
Bowl, Nut, master, cobalt blue, #2b 25.00
Bowl, Rose, melon ribbed, red-orange 20.00
Celery Set, 6 pieces (small rectangular master, five slats), red-orange with gold, #2c 35.00
Chocolate Set, 9 pieces (pot, four cups/saucers), red-orange, #19 . . . . 85.00
Creamer, red-orange, modern, #9 . . . . 5.00
Creamer, cobalt blue with gold, #2c 20.00
Cup/Saucer, After-Dinner, dark green, #20 . 10.00
Plate 378, Cup/Saucer, After-Dinner, cobalt blue with gold stripes, #2b 15.00

Cup/Saucer, Tea, cobalt blue with gold, #2b 12.00
Cup/Saucer, Tea, red-orange, modern 8.00
Plate 379, Cup/Saucer, tea, scalloped cobalt blue with two streams of gold lacing, gold stripe down handle, #3f 14.00
Plate 380, Dish, 7″, chrysanthemum shape, wavy red-orange with gold buds 12.00
Plate 87, Dresser Set, 3 pieces (rectangular tray, ribbed powder jar and hair receiver), red, modern 25.00
Plate 381, Plate, 7⅜″, swirl fluted, scalloped edge, cobalt blue with gold, #2c 14.00
Teapot, cobalt blue with gold, #2c 45.00

179. **Prayer Ribbon.** Ribbons of paper or cloth with sacred symbols or prayers are often hung on the cherry blossom trees at festival time or upon making a pilgrimage to a Shinto shrine. Three ladies stroll through gardens, at least one holds a prayer ribbon dangling from a string.
Cup/Saucer, Cocoa, blue border, bottom of handle red 18.00
Dish, footed, apple green with gold 32.00
Hatpin Holder, swirl fluted, red 45.00
Perfume Bottle, bulbous body with round stopper, red-orange stopper and neck decorated with intertwined gold circles 65.00
Tea Caddy, red, poor execution 27.00
Teaset, 6 pieces (Chinese-style pot with bamboo handle, five handleless cups), green border and stencil, probably modern, J#24 35.00
Trivet, red, #63 . . . . 15.00

180. **Privileged Perambulator.** B. Holmes[2], an author who wrote of his extensive travels in Japan during the 1890's, noted ". . . all day long the infants dangle from the shoulders of brother, sister, mother or aunt, the father's back alone being exempt . . . One happy infant did we see who had escaped thus far the torture of his suspended contemporaries, for he rested in a perambulator, a thing most rare in (Japanese) babyland." Such a privileged infant is portrayed in this pattern.
Plate 382, Cup/Saucer, Tea, scalloped cobalt blue with gold, half floral red and gold interior frame, J#16 . . . . 35.00

181. **Processional.** Many figures are strolling over a bridge and through a garden, not in rigid military formation, but one lagging behind the other; see also Bamboo Tree and Parasol series.
Bowl, 6″, six-sided, cobalt blue with gold, violet and magenta roses are backdrop for off-center subject pattern 10.00
Nut Bowl, footed master, brown, #2b 12.00
Nut Set, 5 pieces (master, four individual), multi-color border 48.00
Plate 383, Pitcher, multi-color geometric, red and gold handle and base border 22.00
Plate 384, Plate, 6″, gold border 8.00
Plate 385, Powder Jar, floriate pine green, red, beige and gold border, J#16 . . . . 34.00
Teaset, 3 pieces (pot, creamer, sugar), wavy red 35.00
Teaset, Miniature, 6 pieces (creamer, sugar, two cups/saucers), red 50.00

[2]B. Holmes, *The Travelogues.* Chicago: The Travelogue Bureau, 1918.

Tray, 5″ x 5″, heart-shaped, oversized irises,
thin red 14.00
Plate 386, Vase, 7″ x 3¾″, **nishikide** border,
gold handles and rim, J#16 . . . . 55.00

182. **Pug.** At the turn of the century, B. Chamberlain[3] wrote that pugs were highly revered animals in Japan, forming "charming ornaments to a ladies' boudoir." The dog is the size of a small cat with "goggle" eyes. "If at birth, the nose is not considered sufficiently snub, it is pressed in with the finger. Doubtless this process . . . induces the habit of constant sneezing with which many of the animals are afflicted." In this pattern, three women are walking a pug through the garden.
    Plate 387, Powder Jar, 4¼″, brick red 25.00

183. **Recital On An Ikebana A.** Geisha is reciting while another holds an **ikebana** before a court lady; accompanied by large stylized butterflies.
    Eggcup, apple green 17.00

184. **Recital On An Ikebana B.** Geisha is reading to another, a third kneels holding aloft an **ikebana**; other geisha in garden.
    Plates 388-389, Cocoa Pot, 7″, swirl ribbed,
    apple green 50.00

185. **Rendevous.** Hand-painted pattern is depicted in two reserves; one features geisha with young girl, other a court noble, sometimes with young boy; the children generally point to their counterparts in the opposite reserve.
    Bowl, 9″, deep lobed, multi-color border,
    beige ground with pastel decorations, scenic
    reserve in addition to subject pattern, heavy
    gold highlights, #61 . . . . 100.00
    Plates 390-391, Condensed Milk Jar with drip
    plate, geometric border of red, cobalt
    blue, pink, green and gold, gold speckled
    drip plate, J#21 . . . . 55.00
    Hair Receiver, footed, bright blue and red,
    flying cranes as backdrop, J#16 . . . . 35.00
    Hatpin Holder, vine and leaf backdrop for reserves, J#16 . . . . 38.00
    Plates 392-393, Mustache Cup, green pepper
    shape, red with gold netting, floral background, male reserve & scenic reserve, J#16 55.00
    Mustard Jar, pointed lid of turquoise cobalt
    blue, green, red-orange stripes above black
    & gold fan on one side, scenic reserve on
    other; body has border of yellow, turquoise,
    cobalt blue, red-orange & yellow-green
    with gold spirals, stars, vines and semicircles, J#16g 38.00
    Mustard Jar, apple green with gold 30.00
    Nut Cup, multi-color, J#16 . . . . 5.00
    Plate, 7″, cobalt blue with gold, J#16 . . . . . 20.00
    Plate 394, Plate, 9″, floriate edge, multi-color
    geometric serves as border and winding
    ribbon through plate, subject pattern in two
    reserves, flowers in two reserves, J#67 . . . 55.00
    Sake Server, three-legged, male and scenic
    reserves 150.00
    Plate 395, Saucer, Tea, hand-carved niches
    around edge, cobalt blue with gold, backdrop of maple leaves, tassels and **Takara Bune** symbols, heavy gold highlighting 15.00
    Plate 35, Sugar/Creamer, geometric border of
    red, cobalt blue, pink, green and gold,
    beige with gold background, J#21 . . . . 35.00
    Sugar Shaker, 6″, gourd-shaped, cobalt blue
    with gold 125.00

186. **Ribbon and Fan Dance.** Four dancers: one to left has folding fan and **kasa**, central figure has **uchiwa** fan and ribbon; third dances with both fan and ribbon.
    Sugar/Creamer, melon ribbed, red-orange
    with gold 25.00

187. **Rice Harvesters A.** Laborer and boy carrying bales of rice across a bridge, hand painted.
    Cup/Saucer, After-Dinner, black with gold, #20 17.00
    Gravy Boat and drip plate, leaf shape, mint
    green, deep green & red with gold border 24.00

188. **Rice Harvesters B.** Laborers sit and rest among bales of rice.
    Bowl, 6″, interior of bowl has blue, red &
    gold border, exterior has blue with gold
    and red stars, #6a 15.00

189. **Rivers Edge.** Numerous women, men and children are gathered along a river bank, conversing and looking out at the water; often found on hand-painted Kutani or Kutani-style wares, occasionally stenciled; marks and border designs vary widely.
    Plate 396, Bowl, Berry, master with holes,
    three curved feet, pine green with two redorange triangles and two red-orange semicircles with gold lines & buds 22.00
    Bowl, Berry, individual, green, orange & gold 20.00
    Cake Set, 7 pieces (master, six individual),
    mint green & red with gold, #51 . . . . 75.00
    Cocoa Pot, red with gold, large Torii in decoration, J#16 . . . . 65.00
    Cocoa Pot, cobalt blue waves with gold, interior of handle red, J#3 . . . . 45.00
    Plates 397-398, Cocoa Pot, 11″, narrow at
    base, widening in middle, narrowing toward
    lip, ornate cobalt blue, red, turquoise, pink
    & gold border, #56 . . . . 125.00
    Cocoa Set, 5 pieces (pot, two cups/saucers),
    red & cobalt blue, #23 . . . . 75.00
    Cocoa Set, 13 pieces (pot, six cups/saucers),
    scalloped blue border with red at base of
    spout & handles, #23 . . . . 125.00
    Creamer, toy, red-orange with yellow 12.00
    Creamer, red-orange, stenciled, #24 . . . . 10.00
    Cup, opening bud shape, cobalt blue with
    gold, #28 . . . . 15.00
    Cup/Saucer, After-Dinner, black with gold, #25 25.00
    Cup/Saucer, After-Dinner, black & red with
    gold, J#1c 10.00
    Cup/Saucer, After-Dinner, thin cobalt blue,
    stenciled 15.00
    Cup/Saucer, Tea, thin pine green, brown
    stencil, #52 . . . . 10.00
    Humidor, fluted bottom, gold zig-zag over

[3] B. Chamberlain. *Japanese Things*. Vermont: Charles E. Tuttle Co., 1971.

red with black outline, red with gold stripe
around base, #21 .... 65.00
Plate 399, Napkin Ring, semi-circular with flat
bottom, deep green, gold, red, #6 ...... 40.00
Napkin Ring, triangular shape, red 35.00
Plate, 6″, red with gold, #27 .... 10.00
Plate, 7″, red with gold, #24 .... 9.00
Plate, 7¼″, scallop and gold with pale yellow peaking through, J#14b 15.00
Plate 400, Plate, 7¼″, red-orange with gold, sub-
ject pattern and scenic in three reserves on
beige ground decorated with red and gold
bands, circles and leaves 22.00
Plate 19, Plate, 7½″, gold with scallop geo-
metric design of red, black and gold at
top and bottom, J#11 .... 15.00
Plate, 8″, floriate edge, gold border, large
gray Mt. Fuji, gold flowers, buildings 35.00
Powder Jar, small, red and green with gold,
#24 & indecipherable Japanese signature . 15.00
Relish Dish, fluted edge, multi-color border,
J#16 .... 35.00
Plate 401, Saucer, Tea, six-petaled, alternating
pine green, red-orange with extensive
gold embellishment, #32a and J#16 ..... 10.00
Saucer, Tea, gold & brown, large brown &
gold parasol extended inward from border 18.00
Sugar Bowl, melon ribbed, pine green with
white, red ground with gold roses, pattern in
reserve, J#6....................... 52.00
Sugar Shaker, bulbous, geometric red & mint
green shoulder, red & gold neck and fluted
base, J#16....................... 75.00
Sugar and Creamer, cobalt blue with gold, J#16 50.00
Plates 402-403, Sweetmeat Set, 9 pieces in lacquer box 75.00
Teaset, 3 pieces (pot, creamer, sugar), brown
with gold, gold floral finials, #23 .... 130.00
Plate 404, Teaset, 9 pieces (pot, creamer,
sugar, three cups/saucers), triple band border of green sandwiched between gold, #17 80.00
Teaset, 11 pieces (pot, creamer, sugar, four
cups/saucers), multi-color border with
heavy gold overlay, J#16 & #20 .... 135.00
Teaset, 13 pieces (pot & sugar with floral
finials, creamer, five cups/saucers), multi-
colored border, gold flowered spout, J#16 150.00
Teaset, 15 pieces (pot, creamer, sugar, six
cups/saucers) 138.00
Plate 405, Teaset, 20 pieces (pot, creamer,
sugar, six cake plates, six cups/saucers),
gold rim, multi-color border 155.00
Teaset, cobalt blue with gold 125.00

190. **Rokkasen.** The Six Poets, **rokkasen**, in their usual pose — sitting together writing poetry; of the six, one is usually a woman.
Plates 406-408, Creamer, leaf-shaped, bottom
shows relief molded swirls, red-orange, J#40
is part of a decorated screen which serves
as the pattern's background 30.00
Hair Receiver, swirl fluted body, cobalt blue
with gold 30.00
Manicure (trinket) Box, red-orange 22.00
Pitcher, 3″, red with yellow 12.00
Plate 409, Tea Caddy, cobalt blue with gold . 45.00

191. **Sake Time.** Two geisha are serving sake to a young man while a third brings in a tray of food.
Plates 410-411, Hair Receiver, ruffled edges,
subject pattern & Fan Dance A in reserves on
chrysanthemum backdrop, #45 .... 35.00

192. **Samisen Practice.** Two musicians on balcony practic-
ing samisen.
Plate 28, Box, 5″ x 4″ x 2″, gold rim, beige
ground with raised gold plum blossom branches, subject pattern and Samisen Recital in
reserves, decaled, #68 .... 32.00

193. **Samurai and Geisha.** Three geisha are waiting upon two samurai seated in the garden; in the distance two samurai can be seen gazing into the garden; border is blue-green with gold interrupted by four purple and yellow flowers; usually found with J#3.
Plate 412, Creamer, bulbous, J#23 .... 12.00
Cup, After-Dinner...................... 5.00
Hair Receiver, muddied enamels 13.00
Plate 413, Plate, 6″, swirl fluted, scalloped
edge, turquoise green with four gold dot-
ted mums, middle frame of gold lacing, in-
terior split frame of cherry blossom groupings 10.00
Plate, 7½″, swirl fluted, scalloped edge, J#23 20.00
Salt & Pepper Shakers, turquoise green with
gold 18.00
Plate 415, Sauce Dish, lobed, J#23 .... 12.00

194. **Samurai Dance.** Kabuki scene; Geisha holding drum is walking over footbridge while looking over her shoulder to watch a samurai figure dance; accompanied by **samisen** player; behind musician is decorative screen, half a colorful abstract, half birds in flight.
Bowl, Berry, footed individual, red-orange
with gold 18.00
Bowl, Rice, red-orange with gold 18.00
Bowl, Serving, 7″, shallow, cut-out handle,
red-orange with gold buds 25.00
Plate 416, Cracker Jar, low, red-orange with gold 65.00
Cup/Saucer, After-Dinner, red with gold.... 15.00
Plate, 6½″, scalloped, red-orange with gold 10.00

195. **Seamstress.** Lady carrying bolt of fabric pauses to talk to another woman.
Plate 417, Mint Dish, 5½″ x 4″, floral shape
with two pierced handles, maroon edge, background pink & amber washes, #19 .... 14.00

196. **Servant With Sacks.** Maidservant is bent over under the weight of two full sacks slung over her shoulder; she is waiting while her mistress and child chat with others; pattern dates as early as 1906.
Plate 418, Bowl, 7½″, red-orange with interior
frame of gold lacing 23.00
Bowl, 10″, red-orange with gold.......... 55.00
Cocoa Pot, cylindrical, red-orange with gold
buds........................... 35.00
Cup/Saucer, Tea, red, pattern on exterior,
floral spray on interior 8.00
Cup/Saucer, Tea, red with gold buds 12.00

  Eggcup, red 10.00
  Lunch Set, 34 pieces (teapot, creamer, sugar,
   six lunch & bread plates, six butter pats,
   six cups/saucers, serving bowl), red-orange
   with gold 250.00
  Plate 419, Plate, 6", swirl fluted, scalloped
   edge, red-orange, interior gold lacing 9.00
  Teapot, square, red 45.00

197. **Shell Game.** A popular game of the court nobility, the shell game involved matching decorated halves of clam shells. To the forefront of this pattern is a low table which sits atop a deep storage box filled with game shells; several ladies, large rug, waterjar and pot complete scene.
  Nut Dish, individual, footed, red with gold
   & geometrics of tan, red, aquamarine &
   cerulian with gold, J#46 . . . . 7.00

198. **Shishi.** The **shishi** is a mythical half-dog, half-lion whose legendary duty is to guard the temple. It is a popular art figure, and in this scene is unusually depicted acting like a real dog smelling the flowers.
  Plates 2-3, Cup/Saucer, After-Dinner, red &
   apple green circles with gold, backdrop of
   actual & stylized chrysanthemums, three reserves: subject pattern, Meeting B & scenic J#6 25.00

199. **Slowpoke.** Two ladies and son are waiting for little girl to catch up with them.
  Plate 420, Dish, 8", footed, red with gold, pat-
   tern in reserve on background of butterflies,
   chrysanthemums & gold 55.00

200. **Small Sounds Of Summer.** The Small Sounds of Summer is the name of this recital, claims the banner hung over the stage. A chorus of singers is gathered around a centered stage where others perform on samisen and flute for an audience of two ladies and a child.
  Candy Jar, red with gold, J#16 . . . . 75.00
  Cocoa Pot, red with gold 85.00
  Cup/Saucer, Cocoa, red 12.00
  Plates 421-424, Dresser Tray, 8" x 11¾", sub-
   ject pattern & scenery including entire tem-
   ple complex in overlapping reserves on red,
   gold & floral backdrop, J#16 . . . . 80.00
  Dresser Tray, brown with gold 28.00
  Ginger Jar, 5", red with gold, J#16 . . . . 65.00
  Plate 425, Sugar & Creamer, red-orange with
   gold, subject pattern & scenery in reserves on
   floral backdrop 26.00

201. **So Big.** Ladies, men and children milling on bridge and in garden looking at boy motioning with typical childlike movement indicating that something was "so big".
  Plate 426, Pancake Server, 9½" x 3½", floriate-
   edged dish with upward reaching rim, dome
   has squared handle & six steam holes, banded
   border — red with gold lacing, beige with
   gold chrysanthemums; tan with gold circles &
   netting, red with gold scalloped line & semi-
   circles, red & gold handle, J#16 . . . . 150.00

202. **Spider Puppet.** Mother is amusing her infant son with a spider puppet dangling by a cord from a bamboo pole; behind her a little girl peeks out from behind a **fusuma**; dwelling is open to the garden featuring ornate bamboo trellis; finely hand painted.
  Plates 427-428, Cracker Jar, footed & lobed,
   cobalt blue with gold border, feet & neck,
   pattern & scenery in reserves on backdrop
   of violet & magenta roses, J#7 . . . . 65.00
  Plate 429, Hair Receiver, ruffled edges, cobalt
   blue with gold, subject pattern on lid, hand-
   painted roses around base 40.00

203. **Stepping Stones.** Ladies walking through garden on path comprised of flat stones.
  Plate 430, Bowl, 6¾", wavy red with gold
   buds, #19 . . . . 20.00

204. **Takara Bune.** According to Japanese legend, **Takara Bune** is the Ship of Good Fortune which sails into port on New Year's Eve with the Seven Gods of Good Luck as passengers bearing treasures including the hat of invisibility, bag of gold, rolls of silk, jar with coral, mallet and angel feather robe. In this pattern, the bags of gold serve as a reserve containing two ladies.
  Plates 431-432, Eggcup, red-orange 25.00

205. **Tea Time.** Three women are kneeling around a low table while a fourth carries a large tray with teapot, cups and accessories.
  Bowl, 7½", lobed, red with gold 23.00

206. **Temple A.** Temple complex in background; bridge connects this area to foreground where several ladies are in the garden; often a third is depicted walking over bridge; diminutive styling; items noted as multi-color have minimal black stenciling and borders which are red and beige (lines sandwiching beige) ground decorated with gold leaves, red flowers, enamel beading and heavy gold highlights.
  Plate 433, Ashtray, spade-shaped, multi-color,
   #15a 25.00
  Ashtray, heart-shaped, red with gold, #2 . . . 25.00
  Plate 434, Basket, multi-color, #15a 45.00
  Plate 435, Biscuit Jar, hexagonal base widen-
   ing to bulbous form, multi-color, J#16 . . 110.00
  Bowl, Berry, master, multi-color 25.00
  Bowl, Nut, individual, multi-color, #2 . . . . . . 8.00
  Celery Set, 5 pieces (master, four salts), #12 75.00
  Plate 436, Cocoa Pot, 7", ribbed, cobalt blue
   with gold 45.00
  Cocoa Set, 13 pieces (9½" pot, six cups/
   saucers), #12 . . . . 250.00
  Creamer, toy, multi-color, #12 . . . . 25.00
  Cup/Saucer, After-Dinner, multi-color, #15a 20.00
  Cup/Saucer, After-Dinner, toy, multi-color, J#16 25.00
  Plate 437, Cup/Saucer, After-Dinner, red, #47 15.00
  Cup/Saucer, After-Dinner, multi-color, #55 . 25.00
  Demitasse Pot, multi-color, #15a 75.00
  Plate 438, Demitasse Set, 15 pieces (pot, cream-
   er, sugar, six cups/saucers), multi-color, J#16 185.00
  Gravy with drip plate, multi-color, #12 . . . . 72.00
  Hatpin Holder, multi-color, #15a 45.00
  Plate 439, Manicure (trinket) Box, multi-color,
   #15a 35.00
  Manicure Tray, 12" x 6", multi-color, #15a 95.00
  Mayonnaise Bowl with underplate, hexa-
   gonal, multi-color, #15a 38.00

Mayonnaise Ladle, multi-color, #12 .... 12.00
Plate 441, Mayonnaise Set, round footed bowl, ladle & underplate, multi-color, J#16 .... 38.00
Nappy, single handled, triangular, #15a 38.00
Plate 442, Nappy, single handled, hand-fluted edge, sea green border & underlying design 45.00
Nappy, double handled, fluted edge, circular, multi-color 30.00
Plate 443, Nut Set, 6 pieces (master, five individual round footed cups), #12 ...... 65.00
Plate, 6½", multi-color, #6............. 15.00
Plate, 7", multi-color, #12 .... 35.00
Relish Dish, cut-out handles, multi-color, #17 32.00
Relish Dish, basket shape, fluted sides with inverted "U" handles, red with gold, pattern on interior, maple leaves on exterior, J#16...................... 26.00
Plate 444, Salt Dish, bowl shape, red with gold, J#16....................... 8.00
Plate 445, Salt Dish, pedestaled, multi-color but with turquoise background instead of red, #8 .... 25.00
Salt Dish, pedestaled, red, #15a 15.00
Salt/Pepper Shakers, bulbous with long neck, multi-color, J#16.................. 15.00
Salt/Pepper Shakers, bulbous with squat neck, multi-color, #15a 40.00
Salt/Pepper Shakers, flat based, red 13.00
Sugar/Creamer, multi-color, #15a 90.00
Plate 446, Sugar Shaker, fluted, single handle, multi-color 85.00
Plate 447, Sugar Tray, oblong, 4½", multi-color, set of six, #12 .... 32.00
Plate 448, Vase, 5", cylindrical, multi-color, J#16 55.00

207. **Temple B.** Similar to A, but in the non-diminutive style, a lady and child stand out in the foreground.
Bowl, Berry, master, scalloped, cobalt blue with gold, internal amber frame, hand-painted violet & magenta roses pattern in off-center reserve 75.00
Bowl, Berry, individual, apple green with gold 15.00
Bowl, Dessert, 5", wavy red with gold lacing below, #20b 12.00
Cocoa Set, 13 pieces (pot, six cups/saucers), red-orange with gold, #20 .... 85.00
Cup/Saucer, After-Dinner, curved, red with yellow 9.00
Plate 449, Cup/Saucer, Tea, scalloped cobalt blue with gold lacing 13.00
Plates 450-451, Cup/Saucer, Tea, red with gold lacing, pattern & border inside cup, red with gold lacing & two oversize flower groupings on exterior 18.00
Plate 452, Dish, eight-lobed, red-orange with gold lacing, unrecognizable Japanese mark . 14.00
Plate 453, Eggcup, double, red with gold lacing 26.00
Gravy Boat, cobalt blue with gold, hand-painted violet & magenta roses around pattern ... 26.00
Gravy Boat, red with gold 20.00
Hatpin Holder, swirl fluted, red with gold, J#16 23.00
Nappy, 6", scalloped, red with yellow, J#16 & impressed "002R" on base 17.00
Nappy, 7½", eight-lobed with one lobe smaller for handle, red with gold 14.00
Nut Set, 7 pieces (master, six individual), red with yellow 30.00
Pitcher, 3¾" x 3⅜", slenderizing towards top, fluted edge, relief molded scallops around base, pattern in black rectangle on ground of hand-painted magenta & violet roses with green leaves, red-orange with gold 32.00
Plate 454, Pitcher, 8½", red-orange with gold lacing below, hexagonal, narrowing toward base 65.00
Plate, 6⅛", gold border, #19 .... 10.00
Plate, 7", red with gold buds, #21c 12.00
Plate 455, Plate, 7½", wavy red with gold lacing, J#53 .... 15.00
Plate 6, Plate, 8¼", cobalt blue with gold, internal amber frame, hand-painted violet & magenta roses pattern in off-center reserve .. 45.00
Plate, 8½", floriate shape edge with relief ribbing, red with gold lacing, impressed "176KG" on base 45.00
Plate 456, Ring Tree, stem with five curved hooks, red-orange with interior gold lacing, red rings around stem, J#16 .... 30.00
Plate 457, Sugar Shaker, thimble shape, turquoise 35.00
Sugar Shaker, gourd shape, red neck band, modern 25.00
Sugar/Creamer, footed, cobalt blue with gold, internal amber frame, hand-painted violet & magenta roses, pattern in off-center reserve 40.00

208. **Temple Vase.** Ladies stand on balcony beside a huge ikebana in vase. To left another figure stands in a boat.
Cocoa Pot, double band of cobalt blue & red with gold, undecipherable Japanese signature 100.00
Cookie Jar, cobalt blue with gold & red, J#45 75.00
Plate 458, Plate, 6", wavy red-orange with yellow lacing, second border of wavy pink diaper of stylized clouds, waves and flowers, internal border of cobalt blue, red & violet with yellow cherry blossoms 15.00

209. **Thousand Geisha.** The entire surface is covered with female faces; no scenery or other background is used except for gold which fills the spaces between the pattern and the edge of the porcelain body.
Bouillon cup & lid, cobalt blue with gold, J#42 30.00
Bowl, Berry, master, cobalt blue with gold, J#16 35.00
Bowl, Berry, individual, cobalt blue with gold, J#16........................ 22.00
Cup/Saucer, Tea, cobalt blue with gold 26.00
Plate 459, Hair Receiver, heart-shaped, scalloped cobalt blue with gold buds, J#6a 40.00

210. **To The Teahouse.** One lady crosses a bridge towards an island boasting a stone lantern and teahouse; occasionally other figures are depicted; hand-painted and stenciled versions.
Chocolate pot, yellow beading on gold rim, dull yellow border, #2a 65.00

Pin Tray, pedestaled, red-orange, beige & gold
floral & band border, hand painted 18.00
Plate 460, Plate, 6", swirl fluted, scalloped edge,
cobalt blue with gold, #3c 10.00
Plate 461, Powder Jar, base molded-in-relief
scallop & stripes extending to feet, scalloped
brown with gold, green leaves, red buds &
gold, hand painted, J#16 .... 28.00
Plate 462, Salt Dish, fluted sides, inverted "U"
handles, red with gold stripes, J#16 ..... 20.00
Salt/Pepper Shakers, red with gold, J#16... 28.00
Teapot, red with gold, multi-color frame, J#16 55.00
Teaset, 13 pieces, (pot, creamer, sugar, five
cups/saucers), multi-color border,
hand painted 135.00
Teaset, 13 pieces (pot, creamer, sugar, five
cups/saucers), red-orange with gold 95.00

211. **Torii.** Leftmost is a large **torii**, entranceway to the Shinto shrine; lady and child are walking through temple garden of pines and cherry blossoms; wash of cobalt blue water and grey Mt. Fuji and birds; pagoda dominates skyline; diminutive styling.
    Cocoa Set, 13 pieces (pot, six cups/saucers),
    gold, #52 .... 95.00
    Plate 51, Cup/Saucer, After-Dinner, toy, gold, #20 15.00
    Plate 463, Cup/Saucer, After-Dinner, golden
    brown with red buds, green leaves & gold 23.00
    Cup/Saucer, Tea, golden brown with red
    buds, green leaves & gold 25.00
    Plate, 6", golden brown with red buds,
    green leaves & gold 13.00
    Plate, 7", thin gold 9.00
    Plate, 7¼", thin grass green 12.00
    Plate, 7¼", golden brown with red buds,
    green leaves & gold, J#16 .... 35.00
    Plate, 7¼", golden brown with red buds,
    green leaves & gold, J#32a 38.00
    Plate, 8", thin gold 14.00
    Sugar/Creamer, squarish bodies, pine green,
    #2a 28.00
    Teaset, 3 pieces (pot, creamer, sugar), gold #19 40.00
    Teaset, 15 pieces (pot, creamer, sugar, six
    cups/saucers), green & red, #32a 180.00

212. **Vantine's Blue.** Powder blue border drips into curls around each pastel green lobe of the porcelain body with amber wedges in between, all outlined with gold beads; figures in lobes may alternate between a combination of men, women and children plus scenery; Vantine mark #42.
    Plate 65, Celery Dish, floriate edged, six-lobed,
    #42 .... 34.00
    Plate 66, Spooner, upright, scalloped edge, #42 40.00

213. **Visiting With Baby.** Two ladies stand by a lantern-topped fence. One holds a "rattle" of strung stones or shells to amuse the infant held by its mother on the other side of the fence.
    Plate 464, Salt & Pepper Shakers, individual,
    cobalt blue neck, gold stars over holes 20.00

214. **Visitor To The Court.** Lady stands in doorway of dwelling adorned with floor lamp and shoji featuring flying cranes; outside two others kneel on woven mat near which stands another decorative screen; at bamboo garden gate, a male visitor is greeted by a servant.
    Plate 465, Plate, 7¼", scalloped blue with
    gold lines, #19 .... 15.00
    Plate, 8½", swirl fluted, scalloped edge, co-
    balt blue with gold 24.00
    Plate 466, Teaset, 3 pieces (pot, sugar,
    creamer), scalloped blue border & spout tip,
    gold laced spout, #19 .... 45.00

215. **Wait For Me.** Lady carrying water bucket leaving other parasol-carrying ladies in garden; dog races behind her to catch up.
    Plate 467, Plate, 8¾", floriate shape, red-
    orange with gold buds 26.00

216. **Washday.** Several geisha are washing clothes on rocks at water's edge.
    See Chinese Coin

217. **Waterboy.** Boy is walking ashore with baskets hanging from a pole slung over his shoulder; geisha observe him from shore; diminutive styling.
    Cocoa Pot, 9¾", fluted, pine green 30.00
    Plate 468, Cocoa Pot, 9¾", fluted, pine
    green, #1b 35.00
    Cup/Saucer, Cocoa, pine green 10.00
    Cup/Saucer, Tea, pine green, #3 .... 12.00
    Pitcher, 4", cobalt blue with gold 15.00
    Plate, 7", pine green, #20 .... 18.00
    Sugar/Creamer, cobalt blue with gold, #3a . 20.00
    Sugar/Creamer, pine green, #3 .... 15.00
    Teapot, cobalt blue with gold, #2a 30.00
    Teaset, 11 pieces (pot, creamer, sugar, four
    cups/saucers), pine green, #3 .... 50.00

218. **Writing A.** Lady sitting on porch holding brush and long thin paper; before her on table rests a writing box and books, behind her a floor lamp and in the room beyond a large peony **ikebana**; three women in garden beyond, dates as early as 1908.
    Cocoa Pot, deep red-orange with gold buds as
    border & on spout 55.00
    Plate 469, Cocoa Pot, scalloped cobalt blue
    with gold lacing, #20 .... 68.00
    Cracker Jar, melon ribbed, footed, cobalt
    blue with gold 100.00
    Plate 470, Cup/Saucer, Cocoa, fluted, cobalt
    blue with gold, #19 .... 20.00
    Plate 471, Plate, 7⅜", scalloped cobalt blue
    with gold, #19 .... 15.00
    Plate 472, Plate, 8½", scalloped cobalt blue
    with gold, #19 .... 19.00
    Teapot with infuser, 6", scalloped cobalt
    blue with gold, #19 .... 35.00

219. **Writing B.** Several ladies-in-waiting surround their mistress who hands out writing paper and implements.
    Cocoa Pot, 9½", fluted, red with gold 65.00
    Cup/Saucer, Tea, blue with gold, #2b 15.00

Index

Advertising	12, 19, 41-47, 49-54, 73
Art Show	77, 146
Bamboo Tree	8, 77, 146
Bamboo Trellis	41, 77, 78, 146, 147
Basket	78, 79, 147
Baskets of Mums	79-81, 147
Battledore	9, 14, 27, 80, 81, 84, 85, 147, 148
Bedroom Furnishings	29
Bellflower	81, 148
Bicycle Race	81, 148
Bird Cage	13, 15, 39, 148
Blind Man's Bluff	81, 148
Blue Hoo	148
Boat Dance	82, 148
Boat Festival	82, 148
Borders	11, 16, 20, 72, 75
Bouncing Ball	148
Boy with Doll	38, 148
Boy with Scythe	148
Boy's Processional	82, 148, 149
Butler Bros.	16, 41
Butterfly	8, 149
Butterfly Dancers	13, 15, 149
Carp	8, 83, 149
Cat	83, 149
Cat and Crab	149
Cataloging a Collection	75, 76
Form	76
Checkerboard	50, 149
Cherry Blossoms	83, 84, 149
Cherry Blossom Ikebana	27, 149
Child Reaching for Butterfly	8, 11, 73, 84, 149, 150
Child Wearing E-boshi	150
Children	37-40
Children in Boat	150
Child's Play	150
Chinese Coin	43, 57, 84, 85, 150
Chrysanthemum Garden	85, 86, 150
Circle Dance	8, 149, 150
Clays	20, 23, 26
Cloud	49, 86, 150, 151
Court Lady	40, 86, 90, 91, 116, 151
Courtesan Processional	86, 87, 151
Cricket Cage	87, 151
Czechoslovakia	20, 21
Daikoku	87, 151
Decalcomania	20-22, 72, 73
Decorating Centers	10, 11, 23
Diminutive Styling	13, 14
Dining, After Dinner	29
Afternoon Tea	11, 28, 37
Breakfast	28
Dinner	28
Japanese Accents	29
Lunch	28
Doll's Tea Party	8, 42, 55, 151
Dragonboat	87, 88, 151
Dressing	152
Drum	88, 89, 152
Duck Watching	89, 152
Emery, Birel and Thayer Co.	42, 55
Evaluating Geisha Girl Porcelain	26, 146
Fan	11, 39, 50, 72, 73, 85, 89, 90, 152, 153
Fan Dance	13, 23, 24, 39, 111, 130, 153
Fan Silhouette of Hoo Bird	91, 92, 153, 154
Feather Fan	92, 154
Field Laborers	154
Fishing	37, 154
Flag Day	92, 154
Flower Gathering	8, 40, 41, 49, 92, 93, 154
Flute	154
Flute and Koto	8, 93, 154
Footbridge	94, 154, 155
Foreign Garden	95, 155
Futon	84, 85, 155
Garden Bench	11, 13, 24, 41, 83-85, 90, 95-101, 155-157
Gardening	84, 85, 102, 103, 157, 158
Geisha	8
Geisha Band	103, 158
Geisha Dance	103, 158
Geisha Face	89, 103, 104, 158
Geisha Girl Porcelain Newsletter	6
Geisha in Cards	57, 158
Geisha in Sampan	14, 39, 104, 105, 158, 159
Geisha on Parade	105, 159
Geisha Presentation	105, 159
Gift Processional	105, 159
Gold:	
Firing	16
Use Of	16, 23, 72
Grape Arbor	159
Greeting Grandma	159
Hahne and Co.	42, 55
Her Master's Keeper	105, 106, 159
Hoover Furniture Co.	42, 50
Horner's Good Furniture	42, 50
Ikebana in Rickshaw	106, 159
Ikebana Party	159
In A Hurry	107, 159
In Flight	107, 159
Inside the Teahouse	9, 159
International Day	107, 159
Japan, Architecture	8
Art	8, 10, 16, 23
Culture	8, 10, 11, 13
History	8, 10, 11, 20, 58
Language	8, 16, 58
Trade	10, 11
Western Interest In	10, 11
Kakemono	9, 159

Kenny, C.D.	42
Kilns	11, 58
Kite	107, 159, 160
Koto	107, 160
Kutani	11, 16, 19, 23-25, 58
Lady in Rickshaw	13, 15, 108, 160
Lantern	23, 108, 109, 160
Lantern Dance	109, 160
Lantern Gateway	160
Lantern Processional	160
Leaving the Teahouse	109, 160
Lesson	13, 14, 109, 110, 160, 161
Lithophanes	26, 73
Long-Stemmed Peony	39, 111, 161
Lustre Ware	17, 19
Macy, R.H. and Co.	41
Marks, Czechoslovakian	20, 21
English	41, 58, 65-71, 72
History of	20, 21, 58
Japanese	23, 41, 58, 59-64
Meditation	111, 161
Meeting	39, 72, 84, 85, 111, 112, 161
Methods of Design	16-19
Montgomery Ward and Co.	42, 51-54
Moriage	17
Mother and Daughter	111, 113, 162
Mother and Son	16, 24, 25, 38, 84, 85, 114, 115, 162, 163
Nippon	6, 41, 42, 58, 72
Oni Dance	115, 163
Origami	163
Oxen Song	115, 163
Paper Carp	27, 163
Parasol	8, 11, 13-17, 25, 38, 39, 41, 42, 50, 74, 83, 109, 110, 116-121, 163-165
Party	165
Patterns (see also individual pattern listings):	
Names	8, 13
Placement	13, 14
Variations in	13
Peacock	121, 165
Peacock on a Flowered Stone Roof	121, 165
Phoenix Bird China	6, 11, 23, 25
Picnic	121, 122, 165, 166
Pillar Print	166
Playing Catch	23-25, 166
Plum Blossom Branch	122, 166
Poems	143
Pointing	27, 40, 84, 85, 122-124, 166, 167
Porcelain	167
Porcelain Bench	124, 167
Porch	72, 73, 124, 125, 167
Prayer Ribbon	167
Privileged Perambulator	125, 167
Processional	40, 125, 167, 168
Pug	126, 168
Recital on an Ikebana	126, 168
Rendevous	23, 126, 127, 168
Reserves	13
Ribbon and Fan Dance	168
Rice Harvesters	168
Rivers Edge	11, 12, 16, 17, 19, 127-129, 168, 169
Rokkasen	129, 169
Sake Time	129, 169
Samisen Practice	169
Samurai and Geisha	130, 169
Samurai Dance	130, 169
Satsuma Wares	11, 23, 24
Seamstress	131, 169
Servant with Sacks	131, 169, 170
Sets	41
Seylar, "Doc" Leslie Wallace	42, 43, 56
Shell Game	170
Shishi	9, 170
Slowpoke	131, 170
Small Sounds of Summer	131, 132, 170
So Big	132, 170
Spider Puppet	16, 132, 133, 170
Stenciling	10, 11, 16, 17, 20, 23, 24
Stepping Stones	133, 170
Takara Bune	133, 170
Tea Time	170
Temple	9, 11, 58, 133-137, 170, 171
Temple Vase	137, 171
Thousand Geisha	138, 171
Tiddy's Home Furnishing Co.	41, 42, 50
To the Teahouse	138, 171, 172
Torii	38, 172
Tuscarora Summit	42, 55
Underlying Design	7, 16
Valuing Geisha Girl Porcelain	15, 41, 58, 76, 146
Vantine, A.A. and Co.	11, 12, 17, 19, 41, 48-50
Vantine's Blue	41, 49, 172
Visiting with Baby	138, 172
Visitor to the Court	139, 172
Wait for Me	140, 172
Washday	84, 85, 172
Waterboy	140, 172
Writing	140, 172

GEISHA GIRL PORCELAIN

NEWSLETTER

Enjoy . . .

Item of the Month   Pattern of the Month
Mailbag   History
Patterns   Marks
Special Collections   Prices
Geisha Exchange   Unusual Finds

Published Six Times Yearly
Annual Subscription $12.00   Single Issue $2.00

Geisha Girl P⟋ ⟍elain Newsletter
P.O. Box 394   ᴾlains, NJ 07950

☐ Please ent⟋   ⟋ion. Enclosed is $12.
☐ Please ⟋   ⟋py. Enclosed is $2.

—DISCONTINUED—

Name _____   _____

Address _____   _____

City _____   _____

State _____   _____ Zip _____

Schroeder's Antiques Price Guide

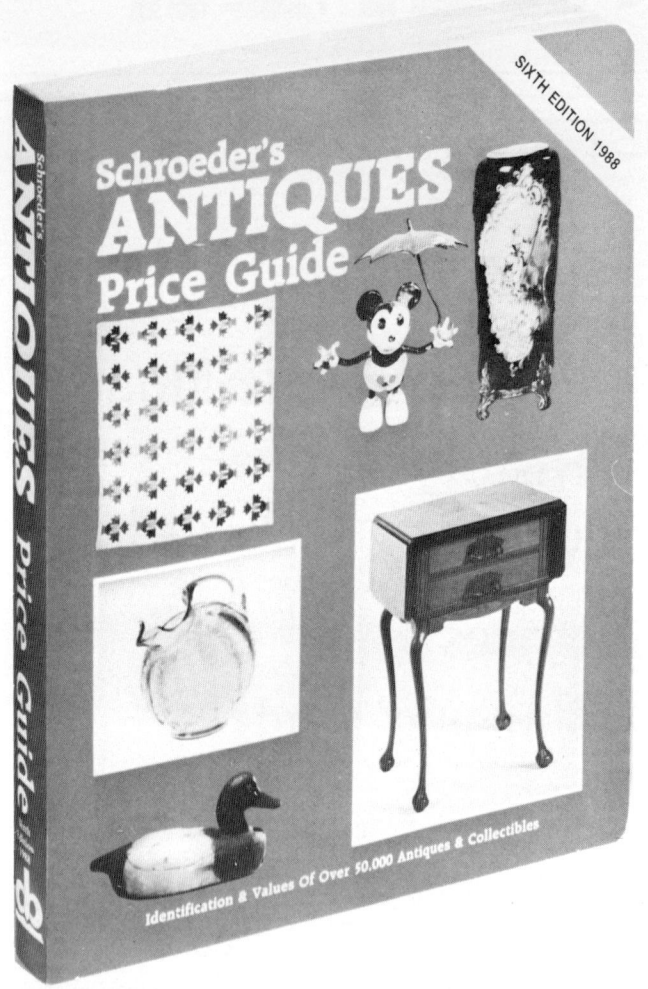

Schroeder's Antiques Price Guide has climbed its way to the top in a field already supplied with several well-established publications! The word is out, *Schroeder's Price Guide* is the best buy at any price. Over 500 categories are covered, with more than 50,000 listings. But it's not volume alone that makes Schroeder's the unique guide it is recognized to be. From ABC Plates to Zsolnay, if it merits the interest of today's collector, you'll find it in Schroeder's. Each subject is represented with histories and background information. In addition, hundreds of sharp original photos are used each year to illustrate not only the rare and the unusual, but the everyday "fun-type" collectibles as well -- not postage stamp pictures, but large close-up shots that show important details clearly.

Each edition is completely re-typeset from all new sources. We have not and will not simply change prices in each new edition. All new copy and all new illustrations make Schroeder's THE price guide on antiques and collectibles.

The writing and researching team behind this giant is proportionately large. It is backed by a staff of more than seventy of Collector Books' finest authors, as well as a board of advisors made up of well-known antique authorities and the country's top dealers, all specialists in their fields. Accurancy is their primary aim. Prices are gathered over the entire year previous to publication, from ads and personal contacts. Then each category is thoroughly checked to spot inconsistencies, listings that may not be entirely reflective of actual market dealings, and lines too vague to be of merit. Only the best of the lot remains for publication. You'll find *Schroeder's Antiques Price Guide* the one to buy for factual information and quality.

No dealer, collector or investor can afford not to own this book. It is available from your favorite bookseller or antiques dealer at the low price of $11.95. If you are unable to find this price guide in your area, it's available from Collector Books, P. O. Box 3009, Paducah, KY 42001 at $11.95 plus $1.00 for postage and handling.

8½ x 11, 608 Pages $11.95

COLLECTOR BOOKS
A Division of Schroeder Publishing Co., Inc.